Published by Cru ... d,

Co ...
Proo. ... administration by Caroljan.

First published in June 1994.
ISBN 1 - 898967 - 00 - 8

About the Authors

Paul Gaynor is editor of Vege-Tables, a directory of vegetarian restaurants in London compiled by members of London Vegans. He organises regular group visits to restaurants specialising in vegetarian food. He is a member of the Vegan Society and has lived in London for most of the last 20 years. As much as he loves and respects animals he is allergic to cats and scared of dogs. At present he works for a football club in south London.

Alex Bourke is a director of the Vegan Society and editor of the Vegans International Newsletter. He has previously written The Vegan Guide to Paris, The Hippy Cookbook, How to Write a Vegan Book, and regularly contributes to Vegetarian Living magazine, The Vegan, Vegetarian Quarterly and Holiday Vegetarian. He is currently working on The Vegan Activist's Handbook. To avoid having all his avocados in one basket, he also works as a computer software consultant.

THE CRUELTY-FREE GUIDE TO LONDON

by Alex Bourke and Paul Gaynor

Contributors:

British Tourist Authority
Meg Clarke
Caroljan
Antony Coles
Peter Despard
Paul & Lesley Dove
Zanne Gaynor
Frank Hutson
Lianne Kerry
Orna Klement
London Vegans
Oxford Vegetarians
Caryne Pearce
Lindsey Russell
Paul Russell
Maxine Simmons
Paulette Storey
David Walker
Louise Wallis
Jennifer Wharton

Special thanks to Caroljan for all your help.
We'll miss you when you're gone.

Remember to say you saw it in the Cruelty-Free Guide

CONTENTS

Remember to say you saw it in the Cruelty-Free Guide

CRUELTY-FREE LIVING

THE VEGETARIAN REVOLUTION

Cruelty-free living is growing explosively. 25% of butchers have closed in 10 years. 2,000 Britons become vegetarians every week. 24 million have reduced their meat consumption. Every school in Britain has introduced vegetarian food. One in four women under 25 do not eat meat, sowing the seeds for future generations to choose a more caring lifestyle. This is a major social revolution, and it's only just begun.

The first step on the path to a cruelty-free lifestyle is to stop eating animals. London is absolutely teeming with over 100 vegetarian restaurants and many more with extensive vegetarian menus. Vegans are now better catered for than ever, with a number of establishments serving an almost entirely vegan menu.

Adopting a cruelty-free lifestyle is not just about food so the guide tells you where to find cruelty-free cosmetics and toiletries, non-leather clothes and heaps of social activities. There are dozens of organisations where you can meet people who live happy, fun lives without hurting animals through their choices of food and clothing.

WHAT IS CRUELTY-FREE ?

This guide's not cruelty-free it's got egg in it!

What is cruelty-free to a vegetarian is not cruelty-free to a vegan is not cruelty-free to a fruitarian. All right—there aren't many around yet but then there weren't many vegans around 50 years ago and now there are 180,000 in Britain alone, not to mention over three million vegetarians.

As vegans we, the authors, are committed to a lifestyle that excludes the exploitation of animals for food, clothing, medical research or any other purpose. This means that we do not eat meat, fish, poultry, eggs, dairy products, honey or any food that is derived from an animal. We do not wear leather, wool, silk or any other fabric made from the outside of an animal. We don't eat the inside and we won't wear the outside.

Our primary motivation for doing this is that we believe that animals have rights like humans, that they experience fear like us and that they feel pain like us. We believe that in a supposedly animal loving and caring society, our treatment of our fellow creatures is unacceptable. Cruelty-free means finding alternatives to foods, drinks, goods and services that involve exploitation, cruelty or suffering to animals and other living creatures for taste, fashion, research or anything else.

LIVING WITHOUT CRUELTY
means dispensing with dairy products

Plamil

is established 'to promote and carry on the business of producing vegan foods'

Its soya milk is the most nutritious one in health stores being fortified with vegan calcium combined with vitamin D2 to absorb the calcium plus essential vitamins B2 & B12.

Its innovatory products include soya based

RICE PUDDINGS
CHOCOLATE & CAROB CONFECTIONS
VARIOUS SPREADS

EGG FREE MAYONNAISE

**For literature send SAE to
PLAMIL FOODS LTD. Bowles Well Gardens, Folkestone, Kent**

Remember to say you saw it in the Cruelty-Free Guide

v

We believe that millions of people from meat eaters to fruitarians share our concerns in different ways and to different degrees. We are not out to condemn everyone for having milk in their tea or eating what they choose. After all we didn't become vegans overnight. Making lifestyle changes can take considerable time and effort. How many of us have put off making those changes because we could not find any alternatives? Armed with The Cruelty-Free Guide to London, you will always be able to find them. If you've been waiting to make the jump to being vegetarian or vegan then this book will help you. If you just want a good animal free meal in London, then look no further.

We hope the book will encourage people to move towards a more compassionate way of living and show that there is an alternative. It's better for us, better for other animals, better for the planet and kinder on the wallet. There's no better place than London to find it. Guide in hand, you'll have no problem eating healthily, smelling sweet, looking good and meeting new friends.

This book is definitely not just for vegetarians and vegans — the more carnivores who get their teeth into it the better!

Remember to say you saw it in the Cruelty-Free Guide

HOW THIS GUIDE IS ARRANGED

INTRODUCING LONDON

The first few chapters are for everyone, whether you're a tourist, a new resident, or a Londoner who wants to explore beyond your local area. We list vegetarian and self-catering accommodation, explain the vast public transport system, and tell you about our favourite shopping and window shopping zones. You can also read about London's ethnic communities and their delicious cuisine.

CENTRAL LONDON

At the core of the guide are four chapters on Central London: EC (East Central), WC (West Central), W1 (West One), and the SW (Inner) (postcodes north of the river between Hyde Park, Fulham and Westminster). This is the business, shopping and entertainment heart of the capital, where you're likely to enjoy a day or night out.

LOCAL LONDON

These eight chapters will appeal to Londoners living outside the centre, and anyone wanting to explore London's many fascinating 'villages'. There's a chapter on each of East London, North, Northwest, Southeast, Southwest (outer), West London, and the closest parts of Middlesex and Surrey. Within each postcode area you will find attractions, vegetarian restaurants, non-vegetarian restaurants and shops. If we have been unable to find anything, we have omitted the postcode or heading.

ATTRACTIONS

You'll find all the famous tourist attractions with prices and opening times, and others that are healthy, fascinating or free.

VEGETARIAN RESTAURANTS

This guide includes over 100 vegetarian and vegan restaurants, cafes and takeaways, with times, prices, sample dishes and what's on the menu for vegans.

OTHER RESTAURANTS

We list non-vegetarian restaurants and cafes that either have a separate vegetarian menu or we know cater well for vegetarians and vegans. There are many ethnic restaurants including Indian, Mediterranean and Chinese.

Remember to say you saw it in the Cruelty-Free Guide

SHOPS

The shops in this guide are mainly healthfood and wholefood shops.
We have listed the specialities that the shops are known for or less
common products such as organic beers and wines, and whether they
have takeaway meals or snacks. Don't forget that Holland & Barrett
healthfood shops give 10% discount to members of the Vegetarian or
the Vegan Society. We've also included our favourite bookshops, 'green'
shops, and some famous stores in central London.

DAYS OUT

When you've been hanging out in the vegetarian paradise of London,
you might be apprehensive about foraging further afield. We've
checked out vegetarian weekends in the chapters on Bath, Brighton,
Bristol, Cambridge, Oxford, Stratford-upon-Avon and Windsor. We tell
you how to get there, where to stay, what to see, and most importantly,
where the grub is.

ACTION

At the end of the guide are ideas for learning more about cruelty-
free living, getting active in the movement, or meeting friends who
share your values. We've listed books, magazines, local and national
organisations.

THE SMALL PRINT

The restaurant sections are based on a database compiled by
London Vegans over a period of three years. It has been completely
revised in 1994 by the authors and members of London Vegans. The
other sections were researched and written by the authors and checked
by them and members of London Vegans. Whilst every effort has been
made to ensure accuracy, we do not accept any liability for errors or
omissions. We will be delighted to receive your comments, brickbats,
and suggestions for new entries.

BON APPETIT !

The only other thing that remains to be done is to wish you as much
fun eating, shopping and sightseeing your way around London as we
have had in compiling the guide.

Some people feel more fulfilled
knowing nothing they buy
has been Tortured, or killed.
besides eating Animal products
can cause Heart Disease ❤,
CANCER, Salmonella,...
even fleas ! ?
vegetable source foods are
ECOLOGICALLY SOUND
It's ethical, affordable
and there's more of it around

You can be a Gourmet,
you can be WELL-FED
with absolutley no need to eat anything
DEAD.

TOURIST ACCOMMODATION

Although accommodation in London is expensive, there are some cheap options, and there are places to get help finding accommodation sympathetic to vegetarians and vegans.

As a visitor your first step might be the London Tourist Information Centre (LTIC), Victoria Station Forecourt, SW1. Tel: 071 730 3488. Open till 19.00. Written enquiries six weeks in advance to 26 Grosvenor Gardens, SW1W 0DU. Other centres are at Heathrow (terminals 1, 2 & 3) and Gatwick Airports. Accommodation bookings, information, books and maps are all available.

LTIC has a list of hotels, self-catering apartments, bed and breakfast establishments and hostels. They charge £5.00 for making a booking and you have to pay a 15% refundable deposit. Hostel bookings are £1.50 with a £5.00 deposit which is refunded by the hostel when you settle your bill.

Information about accommodation throughout the United Kingdom, as well as entertainment bookings, car travel, books and maps can be obtained from the British Travel Centre, 12 Regent Street, Piccadilly Circus, SW1Y 4PQ. Tel: 081-846 9000 BTA Infoline. Open: Mon-Fri 9.00-18.30, Sat-Sun 10.00-16.00.

DIRECTORIES

A nationwide guide to vegetarian home stays, guesthouses and hotels is free through British Tourist Authority offices or £1.00 or US $5.00 airmail from Aunties (Great Britain) Ltd, 56 Coleshill Terrace, Llanelli, Dyfed SA15 3DA. Tel: 0554-770077. Those listed can cater for all diets. Bookings can be made by phone. There are 12 entries that cover the whole of London. From £15.00 per night.

A guide to hotels, guest houses, apartments and bed and breakfast establishments called 'Where To Stay in London' is £2.95 from The London Tourist Board, 25 Grosvenor Gardens, Victoria, SW1W 0DU. Tel: 071-730 3450. Fax: 071-730 9367. Overseas distribution is handled by the British Tourist Authority.

The British Tourist Authority produce a free guide 'City Apartments' that lists apartments in 12 of the UK's major cities. Prices range from under £250 to over £600 per week for a one bed apartment. Not a budget traveller's first choice but then not all veggies are budget travellers.

BED AND BREAKFAST

The cheapest ones are usually around Paddington, Victoria, Pimlico and King's Cross and advertised in the Evening Standard newspaper and at the Tourist Information Centre.

YOUTH HOSTELS

Get very crowded in summer and booking is advised. Rates vary from £11.75-£18.90 for adults, £7.85-£15.90 children. All have dormitory or multi-bed rooms and a cafeteria. The six hostels in London are:

Holland House,

Holland Park, Holland Walk, W8. Tel: 071-937 0748. Tube: South Kensington. Open: 07.00-23.30. Excellent setting and location. Adult £16.90, under 18 £14.90.

City of London

36 Carter Lane, EC4. Tel: 071-236 4965. Tube: Blackfriars, St Pauls. Open: 07.00-23.30. Adult £18.90, child £15.90.

Earls Court

38 Bolton Gardens, SW5. Tel: 071-373 7083. Tube: Earls Court. Open: 07.00-24.00. Adult £16.90, child £14.90.

Highgate

84 Highgate West Hill, N6. Tel: 081-340 1831. Tube: Highgate. Open: 08.45-10.00 & 13.00-23.30. Adult £11.75, child £7.85.

Hampstead

4 Wellgarth Road, NW11. Tel: 081-458 9054. Tube: Golders Green. Open: 07.00-23.30. Adult £13.90, child £11.80.

Oxford Street

14-18 Noel Street, W1. Tel: 071-734 1618. Tube: Oxford Circus. Adult £16.50, child £13.50.

Rotherhithe

Island Yard, Salter Road, SE16. Tel: 071-232 2114. Tube: Rotherhithe. Open: 07.00-23.30. New hostel in Docklands. Adult £16.50, child £13.50.

CAMPING

Tent City

Old Oak Common Lane, W3. Tel: 081-743 5708. Tube: East Acton. Open: 24 hours May-Oct. £4.00 adult, £2.00 child. Bunk beds in large mixed dormitory tents, or bring your own. Showers, toilets, snack bar.

Crystal Palace Campsite

Crystal Palace Parade, SE19. Tel: 081-778 7155. Train: Crystal Palace BR. Open all year. No shop.

Hackney Camping

Millfields Road E5. Tel: 081-985 7656. £2.50 per person. On bus route 38. No tent hire.

Lee Valley Park

Picketts Lock Centre, Pickets Lock Lane, N9. Tel: 081-803 4756. Train: Ponder's End, Lower Edmonton BR. £3.60 per person. Sports centre close by.

UNIVERSITY HALLS

These are more expensive than hostels and only available outside term times. Contact the British Universities Accommodation Consortium, University Park, Nottingham, NG7 2RD. Tel: 0602-504571, Fax: 0602-422505. They compile a list of facilities available. This includes a form for booking direct with a university. Price per night £15.45-£19.50. Some are in excellent locations and offer access to university amenities such as bars and sports facilities.

SLEEPING OUT

We wouldn't advise even the lowest budget travellers to do it. Street life in London, like any major city, can be very rough. If you must sleep out it's probably better to choose Hampstead Heath or one of the large parks. Tubes and railway stations are too regularly patrolled and get locked up at night. Avoid the Strand, Waterloo Bridge and the South Bank complex. These areas are extensively used by London's homeless.

ARRIVAL AND TRAVELLING AROUND

VISAS

No visa is required if you're from Australia, Canada, South Africa, Japan, Switzerland, Austria, Finland, Sweden , Switzerland, Iceland, Mexico, USA, or a Commonwealth citizen. Unless of course you have a Nigerian, Ghanaian, Indian, Pakistani or Sri Lankan passport. As a tourist you can stay for six months but it's a good idea to look respectable when passing through immigration.

EEC nationals don't need work permits. Commonwealth citizens aged 17-27 can get a working holiday permit for two years. Full-time USA students over 18 can get a six month work permit before leaving from the International Education Exchange, 205 East 42nd Street New York 10017. Tel: 212-661-1414.

CHANGING MONEY

Selling rates for £1.00 sterling in March 1994 were:

Australia	2.03
Canada	1.97
France	8.31
Germany	2.45
India	46.00
Italy	2.43
Netherlands	2.76
New Zealand	2.55
Spain	200.00
USA	1.45

Change money at a bank, open Mon-Fri 09.30-15.30, or a Bureau de Change open 24 hours. Avoid the 9% "let's sucker new arrivals" commission around Victoria Station, or change just enough to get you to a bank.

MAPS

The excellent British Tourist Authority colour map of central London shows tourist attractions, theatres, cinemas, markets, shopping streets, the underground and Docklands. Get it at the British Travel Centre, 12 Lower Regent Street (Piccadilly Circus tube) for £1.00, or free from overseas BTA offices.

If you plan to travel outside central London or stay for any length of time, a street map is essential, either the Geographers A-Z or Nicholson's Streetfinder, both in several sizes.

You can get free transport maps from newsagents selling Travelcards, in some underground stations, including Euston, Heathrow (Terminals 1,2 & 3), Kings Cross, Oxford Circus, Piccadilly and Victoria, or by calling 071-222 1234. There is a pocket tube map, a giant All-London bus map, night bus map, and 37 local bus maps.

PUBLIC TRANSPORT

Visitors from the provinces will tell you that public transport in London is very good. People who live in London and have to rely on it daily will tell you that everything is relative. London Regional Transport (LRT) operates London's underground system, the bus network and the Docklands Light Railway (DLR). 24-hour information 071-222 1234. Voice activated 'travelcheck' service on 071-222 1200.

OPEN TOP BUSES

If you're new to London you could try a sightseeing tour on an open top London bus. There are pick up points at Baker Street, Marble Arch, Haymarket and Victoria Railway Station. A 'Hop on Hop Off' ticket is £13.00, £5.00 under 16. For an extra £1.00 you get a river cruise too. Buy tickets on the bus, or in advance from any London Transport or London Tourist Board Information Centre. Or ring London Plus on 071-828 7395.

RED BUSES

The famous red double-decker buses are a great way to see London during the day and with bus passes can be good value. Night buses leave Trafalgar Square to all over London and are a cheap way to get home after the tube closes.

THE UNDERGROUND (TUBE)

The underground wakes up at 05.30 Mon-Sat, 07.00 on Sun, and closes between 23.30 and 01.00. Stations display the times of the last tube, so make a note of it, particularly on Sunday night when they finish earlier, or be prepared for a taxi ride.

Wheelchair users can ring 071-918 3312 for the book 'Access to the Underground' which costs £1.00.

FARES

There are six underground zones and four for buses. Zone one is the centre. Bus zone four is equivalent to underground zones four, five and six. Bus passes, and Travelcards for buses and tube and trains, give unlimited travel. Buy them at stations and many newsagents. You need a passport size photograph for weekly and monthly ones. Under fives are free, under sixteens pay a 'children's fare' if travelling before 10pm. 14 & 15 year olds must get a free Child Rate Photocard.

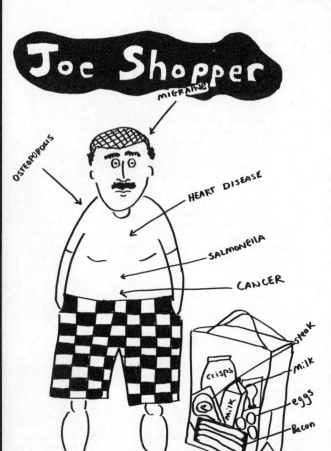

Remember to say you saw it in the Cruelty-Free Guide

Failure to have the correct ticket now carries a £10.00 on the spot fine. If you do forget to buy a ticket and meet an inspector it's best to plead ignorance, thank him or her for pointing out the error of your ways, apologise and offer to pay the correct fare if you have it.

TRAVELCARDS

Daily Travelcards can be used on buses, tubes and trains after 09.30 on weekdays and at any time weekend or bank holidays. They are not valid on N-prefixed night buses. A one day 6 zone adult Travelcard covers all London for £3.70, £1.40 child. Zones 1 & 2 covers central London for £2.70, £1.40 child.

Weekly Travelcards can be used at any time and on night buses. Zones 1-2 costs £13.00 per week or £50.00 per month. 6 zones is £29.50 for a week.

BUS PASSES

One day Bus Passes are £3.20 adults £1.00 children, for all four zones. They can be used after 09.30 in the morning.

NATIONAL BUSES

GREEN LINE services operate within 35 miles of London, eg to Hampton Court and Windsor. Their enquiry office is at Eccleston Bridge, off Buckingham Palace Road, SW1. Tel: 071-668 7261. Or contact their head office at Lesbourne Road, Reigate, Surrey, RH2 7LE. Tel: 07372 42411.

NATIONAL EXPRESS serves all of Britain and Europe from Victoria Coach Station, Buckingham Palace Road, SW1. It's 10 minutes walk from Victoria underground station. Fares are approximately half those of British Rail. Buy tickets in advance to be sure of a seat, either at the Coach Station Mon-Sun 06.00-24.00, or at some travel agents, who charge a small commission.

Information Dept open Mon-Sat 07.30-22.00, Sun 08.00-22.00. Tel: 071-730 0202. Credit card bookings Mon-Sat 09.00-20.00, Sun 06.00-12.00. Tel: 071-730 3499. There is a special emergency line 071-625 1278.

If you are a vegan, take food with you for a long journey. You could tank up on falafel and chips at the kebab shop by Victoria red bus station, next to the tube, or get some vegan flapjacks from the Treats shop inside the tube station.

LOCAL TRAINS

Local overground trains are operated by Network SouthEast. Tel: 081-928 5100. They share some stations with the underground newtork. Trains are expensive even by London standards unless you use a Travelcard.

NATIONAL TRAINS

British Rail trains leave from eight major stations.

Charing Cross, Victoria and **Waterloo** for south-east England. Information 071-928 5100. Credit Card Booking 0800-450-450.

Euston and **St Pancras** for the Midlands, north Wales, north-west England and west Scotland. Information 071-387 7070. Credit card booking Euston 071-387 8541 or 071-388 6061. St Pancras 071-837 5483.

King's Cross for east and north-east England and east Scotland. Information 071-278 2477. Credit ard booking 071-071-278 9431.

Liverpool Street for East Anglia and Essex. Information 071-928 5100. Credit card booking 071-928 5100.

Paddington for west and south-west England, south Midlands and south Wales. Information 071-262 6767. Credit card booking 071-922 4372

Trains are expensive compared to coaches but faster, especially high speed 'Inter-City' trains which have a buffet car. Second class fares are complex, with a huge choice of budget fares listed below in ascending order of cost. It pays to plan ahead.

SUPER APEX

Cheap return tickets to Darlington, Durham, Newcastle, Edinburgh, Motherwell, Glasgow, which are good places to change for your final destination. You have to book at least 14 days in advance but aim for eight weeks as tickets are limited.

APEX

Have to be booked seven days in advance and are also limited.

SUPERSAVER

No need to book in advance but they cannot be used on Fridays, over Christmas, or during peak hours.

SUPERADVANCE

Available on some long distance journeys where a Supersaver would not be valid. Must be booked by 12.00 midday before the day of travel. Numbers limited.

SAVER

These can be used on most trains outside rush hours for outward journeys and on all return journeys.

LEISURE FIRST

This is an off-peak first class ticket at half fare for those spending a Saturday night away. You must make your reservation by 16.00 the day before outward travel.

Super Apex, Apex, Super Advance and Leisure First tickets can be booked by credit card on FREEPHONE 0800-450 450.

If you are a vegan, take food with you especially on a non 'Inter-City' train. Casey Jones and Burger King do beanburgers which may be with cheese. You can get hummus and salad in pitta bread outside Victoria and King's Cross stations. At the time of writing, the one vegan meal available on Inter City trains is Thai vegetables with rice for £3.45.

CAR RENTAL

A car is almost totally useless for sight-seeing in the capital. It can be convenient, if very ecologically unfriendly, for seeing the rest of the country.

If you do not have a British driving licence then you'll need an international licence, unless you're from an EEC country other than Spain. Get it for £2.50 (and two passport size photos) from the Automobile Association (AA) 071-839 7077, or the Royal Automobile Club (RAC) 071-839 7050.

The main operators are Hertz and Avis. Local car hire agencies are cheaper. Ensure the car has 24-hour accident and repair cover. You'll pay £80 or less for a small car for the weekend with unlimited mileage. There is usually at least a £50 deposit. Seat belts must be worn and remember - we drive on the left hand side of the road. For further information buy a copy of the Highway Code from a newsagent.

CAR SHARING

If you live in London and really want to use a car to get around why not think about sharing one with other people. This can work out much cheaper than buying one, is far more sociable and a lot more friendly to the environment.

South London Vehicle Co-op have a vehicle to share. Costs are 10p per mile plus petrol, a monthly facility fee and a deposit in the form of a 'share'. Call 081-653 6119 (evenings), or 081-673 0262 (evenings or weekends).

CYCLING

Join the 1.5 million cyclists in London, burn off 5.5 calories per minute, park for free and pass all other road users during the rush hour, which lasts for most of the day. But don't leave home without a good lock. Bikes walk.

The definitive guide to cycling in London is 'On Yer Bike', £3.95. It has 24 pages of cycle routes covering central London and lists all London's bike shops. Get yours from The London Cycling Campaign, 3 Stamford Street, SE1 9NT, Tel: 071-928 7220. LCC organises social rides during the evenings and at weekends. Ring for details.

If you don't arrive on a bike you can hire one from:

GO BICYCLE
9 Templeton Place, SW5. Tel: 071-373 3657

*Open: Wed-Sat 09.30-18.00 and
more days in summer.
£10.00 per day, £20.00 weekend,
£40.00 per week. Deposit £150*
Visa and Access will do nicely.
They are in the car park of the
Hotel George. Insurance £1.00 per
day

ON YER BIKE

*52-54 Tooley Street, SE1. Tel: 071-
357 6958
Open: Mon-Fri 09.00-18.00, Sat
09.30-17.30*
Racers and three speeds £8.00 first
day, £6.00 next day, £15.00
weekend, £25.00 per week. £50.00
deposit. Mountain bikes £14.00
first day, £10.00 second day,
£25.00 weekends, £50.00 per week.
Deposit £200. Identification with
proof of address essential.

Alternatively you could pick up
a cheap secondhand bike at one of
the markets such as Brick Lane,
Camden or Portobello.

TAXIS

When black taxis are available the words 'For Hire' or 'Taxi' are lit
up in yellow in the front window. There is a pick-up charge which is
displayed when the driver resets the meter at the start of your
journey. Modern cabs can take five passengers and older ones just
four. They can be good value if you fill the seats.

Outside the central area, unmetered mini-cabs operate a cheaper
service. They are not however allowed to pick up passengers on the
street. You must phone or go to their office.

TIPPING

If not on the menu 10% is the norm in restaurants with table
service. There is no reason to tip taxi drivers though they often seem
to expect it as a right, especially if you've had the audacity to request a
south London destination.

THE RIVER

The Thames is not a working river anymore so there is little traffic
along it. One of the ways you can enjoy it is by taking a river trip or

cruise operated by a number of private companies, such as Catamaran Cruises. Tel: 071-987 1185. Best value is a Discoverer one day pass for £6.00 adult, £3.00 child, which can be used all day between any of the three piers at Charing Cross, Tower Bridge and Greenwich. Departures every 30 minutes from 10.30. They also offer a range of evening cruises and trips to the Thames Barrier.

If you want to go upstream to Hampton Court, Kew, Putney or Richmond, it's best to start your journey from Westminster Pier (071-930-4097) at the north east corner of Westminster Bridge.

Thames Passenger Services Federation can provide information on the operators who are members. Tel: 071-231-7122.

POST

Main post offices are open Mon-Fri 09.00-17.00, Sat 09.00-12.00. Smaller ones often close for lunch between 13.00-14.00. First class inland (under 60g) and EEC (20g) mail costs 25p, second class (60g) 19p. Stamps for non-EEC Europe destinations cost 30p, all other destinations (10g) 41p. Aerogrammes to anywhere in the world cost 36p from post offices and mean that you don't have to carry around writing paper and envelopes.

TELEPHONE

The days of weatherproof public telephone boxes are almost over. Now that competition has reached the industry you'll have to huddle under a hood and compete with the passing traffic while the wind roars up your trouser leg. The advantage is that when you do find a call box it's more likely to be working.

The main operators are British Telecom and Mercury, who both operate coin and card phones. Phonecards cost £2.00-£40.00 from newsagents, post offices and underground stations, or use a credit card (minimum 50p). Calls cost more on weekdays from 09.00-18.00. At weekends you pay local rate for long-distance calls - a real bargain

London phone numbers have area code 071 (central area) or 081 (outer area). Dial 071 if you are phoning from an 081 number and vice-versa.

International code	010
Emergency services	999
Operator	100
International operator	155
Directory Enquiries	192

You can use directory enquiries free from a phone box, or pay 45p on a private line.

WHAT'S ON MAGAZINES

Time Out is the most complete weekly listings magazine for London and costs £1.50. It has sections on art, books, children, clubs, comedy, dance, film, gay London, music, politics, sport, theatre, television and issues affecting Londoners. There is a visitors' section aimed at visitors called Around Town which lists special events each week. It covers eight days from Wednesday to Wednesday.

If £1.50 is the cost of your mid-day meal then grab one of the less detailed free listings magazines given away from street dispensers and on weekday mornings at central railway and tube stations. Or try The Big Issue from street vendors for 50p and help London's homeless.

SHOPPING

The Animal Free Shopper is a 180 page pocket-sized book listing all known products and services which contain no animal ingredients and have not been tested on animals. To get your copy send £4.95 + 65p postage to The Vegan Society, 7 Battle Road, St. Leonards-on-Sea, East Sussex, TN37 7AA.

THE WEST END

London's West End is the greatest shopping mall in the world, extending from Hyde Park to the Kingsway. There are thousands of boutiques, hundreds of restaurants and cafes, dozens of department megastores, not to mention over a hundred theatres and cinema screens. If you're in need of some retail therapy then London is the place for you and it's made all the more addictive because similar shops tend to be clustered together.

Covent Garden, WC2, is the mecca of weird and wonderful speciality stores and designer shops. In Charing Cross Road, WC2, you can browse in gigantic bookshops, smaller secondhand ones, and those catering for specific interests. Tottenham Court Road, W1, is full of computer, hi-fi and electronic goods.

Oxford Street, W1, extending from the top of Charing Cross Road, west for one mile to Marble Arch and Hyde Park, is home to the large department stores. Regent Street and Bond Street cater for those who spend more on their socks than most of us do on our shoes. The giant record stores Virgin, HMV and Tower Records are all in this area.

In Knightsbridge, SW3, you will find the internationally famous department store Harrods and up-market designer Chelsea is a short ride away. More down to earth fashion can be found in the boutiques of the King's Road, SW3, Camden Town, NW1, and Portobello Road, W11.

OUTER LONDON

Beyond the centre is local London, the villages absorbed by the relentless expansion of the metropolis, where Londoners do their daily shopping. You won't regret visiting some of the markets for real bargains and a unique slice of London life.

MARKETS

Here are some of our favourite markets. For more information look them up in the main section of the guide.
BERWICK STREET, W1 *Mon-Sat 09.00-17.00. Food and clothing.*
BRICK LANE, E1. *Sun 05.00-15.00. Everything secondhand.*
BRIXTON, SW9. *Mon-Sat 09.00-17.00 (not Wed pm). Fruit and veg.*

Remember to say you saw it in the Cruelty-Free Guide

CAMDEN PASSAGE, NW1. *Sat-Sun 10.00-17.00. Hippy chic: clothing, incense, ethnic jewellery, whacky street fashion.*
GREENWICH CRAFTS & OPEN AIR, SE10, *Sat-Sun 10.00-17.00. Crafts, clothes and bric-a-brac.*
LEATHER LANE, EC1. *Mon-Fri 10.30-14.00. Fruit and veg and clothes in the City.*
PORTOBELLO ROAD, W11 . *Mon-Sat 09.00-17.00. Street fashion, antiques and bric-a-brac.*
RIDLEY ROAD, E8. *Mon-Wed 09.30-15.00, Thu to 12.00, Fri-Sat to 17.00. Fruit and veg.*
SPITALFIELDS, E1. *Sun 09.00-14.00. Organic fruit and veg and bric-a-brac.*

CHARITY SHOPS

The fastest growing sector of the retail trade in the 90's, charity shops are now in every high street in London and full of incredible bargains. The biggest chain in London is Oxfam which also sells Fair Trade goods. Try 202 Kensington High St, W8 or 23 Drury Lane, WC2. Some people avoid the Imperial Cancer Research Fund and other charities who fund vicious vivisection experiments.

HEALTHY URBAN FORAGING

There are two kinds of shop all over London to refuel vegetarians and vitalize vitamin freaks.

'Healthfood' shops sell prepackaged wholefoods, vitamins and supplements, homeopathic medecines and herbal remedies, pills, cruelty-free cosmetics and sports supplements. Holland & Barrett are the biggest chain and are all over the city. They give 10% discount to card-carrying members of the Vegetarian Society (UK) or the Vegan Society. This should enable you to amply recover the cost of your subscription, this book, dinner for two, and a world cruise.

'Wholefood' shops tend to be staffed by the owners. Products are vegetarian and vegan, and sold from sacks and bins without unnecessary packaging. Some also sell organic foods, including fruit and veg, and perhaps wholemeal bread, cruelty-free toiletries, refrigerated takeaway foods, books and 'green' cleaning products.

We haven't included supermarkets or they'd fill half the book, but we consider Safeway, Tesco and Sainsbury's to have the best range of vegetarian, vegan and organic foods. Some supermarkets have their own 'suitable for vegetarians' labels, which may allow animal rennet cheese or battery eggs. The only seals of approval we trust are the Vegetarian Society's seedling-shaped V symbol, or the Vegan Society's sunflower.

l

WHOLEFOOD DELIVERY

Wholefood Express delivers fresh, organic produce and wholefoods throughout London. London North call 071-354 4923, London South call 081-674 8727. Minimum order £20.

BEAUTY PRODUCTS

The Body Shop chain spearheaded the backlash against animal tested cosmetics. However, certain of their beautifully packaged goodies contain slaughterhouse by-products. Read the ingredients and the Product Information Manual at the counter to check they're truly cruelty-free, ie vegan. For a comprehensive guide to cruelty-free cosmetics in Britain send a stamped addressed envelope to the British Union for the Abolition of Vivisection, 16a Crane Grove, London N7 8LB. Tel: 071-607 9533.

CLOTHES WITHOUT CRUELTY

Wild Things, WC2. Non-leather shoes, belts, jackets, t-shirts. Wild Things raises money for the Respect for Animals campaign against the fur trade. Also mail order.

Natural Shoe Store, WC2. Now selling non-leather, breathable Doc Marten shoes.

MAIL ORDER CLOTHES WITHOUT CRUELTY

Alchuringa, Unit 2, Stable Cottages, Derry Ormond Park, Derry Ormond, Lampeter, Dyfed SA48 8PA, Wales. Shoes and boots.

Ethical Wares, 84 Clyde Way, Rise Park, Romford, Essex RM1 4UT. Tel: 0708-739293. Non-leather hiking boots.

T'arus, 107 The Drive, Wellingborough, Northants NN8 2DD. Tel: 0933-277964. Non-leather shoes and belts.

Vegetarian Shoes,12 Gardner Street, Brighton, BN1 1UP. Tel: 0273-691913. Non-leather shoes, boots, clothes and accessories.

Veggie Jacks, 5 Gardner Street, Brighton. Tel: 0273-203821. Non-leather shoes, jackets, belts, bags and accessories.

WORST OF THE SHOPS

A booby prize goes to Boots the drugstore chain, which launched a campaign to promote their goods as not tested on animals. However, following raids by the the Animal Liberation Front we know that Boots still experiment on live animals to test their pharmaceutical products. For more information contact London Boots Action Group, c/o Alara, 58 Seven Sisters Rd, London, N7 6AA.

Another booby prize to McDonald's, who target children with TV advertising for their meatburgers, sugarshakes and caffeine-cola. Their pizzas have animal rennet cheese and the vegetable nuggets contain battery eggs. They say that "free range hens are outside and could catch disease". Can you think of anything more sick than a battery hen? But they do have the capital's cleanest free toilets. For more information on the anti-McDonald's campaign contact McLibel Support Campaign, 5 Caledonian Rd, London, N1 9DX.

BEST SHOPPING

STREET FASHION

King's Road, SW3
Oxford Street, W1
Camden Market, NW1
Kensington High Street, W8
Oxfam shops
Portobello Market, W11
Wild Things, WC2

HIGH FASHION

Bond Street, W1
Regent Street, W1
King's Road, SW3
Knightsbridge, SW3

WEIRD AND WONDERFUL

Anything Left Handed, Brewer Street, W1

Covent Garden General Store, WC2

MAGAZINES

Time Out. The definitive guide to what's on in London. Every Wed.
Vegetarian Living. Stacks of features on healthy living in the
    nineties, with ads for vegetarian guest houses all over Britain.
BBC Vegetarian Good Food. Healthy recipes and other features.
In Britain magazine. Free from the British Travel Centre at 12
    Lower Regent Street, W1.

VALUE ADDED TAX (VAT)

VAT is a sales tax of 17.5% which is levied on most goods. In
restaurants you will see VAT added at the bottom of the bill.

To allow visitors from abroad to avoid VAT, some shops operate a
Retail Export Scheme for purchases over a certain amount, usually
about £50.00, but you will need to show your passport and the money
is not deducted at the point of purchase but refunded by post.

BARGAINING

A must if you're buying secondhand gear but definitely on the
increase in a number of situations when you're making a major
purchase and where competition is particularly intense, such as
electronic goods in Tottenham Court Road and at markets.

Remember to say you saw it in the Cruelty-Free Guide

19

ETHNIC LONDON

The availability of vegetarian and vegan food in London owes a great deal to the diverse ethnic communities which have had a massive impact on British eating habits. Time Out magazine recently reported that London has more Indian restaurants than Bombay and Delhi put together.

Here we give a brief guide of where London's ethnic communities are to be found and the types of offerings they have for the cruelty-free gastronome. We list restaurants which you can find in the main part of the guide.

INDIAN

Indians are found in three main groups, although increasingly widely dispersed throughout the capital. Southall, near Heathrow airport, is home to a Sikh community. The East End, particularly around Spitalfields and Brick Lane, is home to many Bengalis, whilst West London around Wembley has a large Gujarati community. Indian cuisine in all its various guises has probably done more than any other to make life a joy for the vegan or vegetarian in London. Indian restaurants are now so popular that you'll find them on every high street.

SIKHS IN SOUTHALL

In Southall, the main area of interest is around The Broadway and South Road where many people, especially women, wear traditional costume. The foodstores have a great selection of traditional culinary ingredients, such as flours for making different flat-breads, chutneys, pickles, pulses, peas, grains, varieties of rice, fresh herbs and spices and vegetables such as okra, spinach, green beans, cauliflower and root vegetables.

There are many cheap cafes and simple restaurants in the area, though because the prevailing cuisine is North Indian you will find a lot of meat on the menu. Try A Sweet, Moti Mohal, Gil Sweet Mart, or Shahanshah, all in Southall, Middlesex.

BENGALIS IN BRICK LANE

The area around Brick Lane, E1, has been home to immigrants and minorities for hundreds of years. Huguenots, Irish Catholics, Jews and more recently Bengalis have all settled here. The area is smaller than Southall but very well known for its unique streets and the busy market in Brick Lane.

We have not singled out particular restaurants because there are so many of them — 21 in Brick Lane alone and others in the adjoining side streets. Take a walk one evening and choose one for yourself. They are mostly cafe style or cheaper Tandooris.

GUJARATIS IN WEMBLEY

Wembley has a Saturday and Sunday street market selling all the best Indian fruit and vegetables and numerous other goods. Gujarati food is less oily and, coming from a Hindu community, more vegetarian than North Indian. Many Gujaratis have lived in East Africa and you will find ingredients from that continent like corn and casssava. Try Maru's Bhajia House or Sakonis in Wembley, Middlesex.

SOUTH INDIAN CUISINE

There are a large number of Asian vegetarian restaurants in London based on a Southern Indian cuisine which is hotter and spicier than that of the North and generally cheaper too. The largest concentration of them is in Drummond Street, NW1, to the west of Euston Station, all serving excellent, cheap food.

Amongst the specialities are dosa (a large pancake made from split peas and rice), iddlies (steamed rice cakes), spicy vegetable savouries, nuts, peas and grains. A thali is a combination of about eight small dishes served on one large platter, and can be made vegan. Try:

Chutneys, NW1
Diwana Bhelpoori, NW1
Mandeer, W1
Ravi Shankar, EC1
Sabras, NW10
Shahee, SW16.

The Young Indian Vegetarian Society is listed under local groups at the end of this guide.

PAKISTANI

If you want to sample the best Pakistani food you're probably better off in the West Midlands Balti Houses. Balti dishes are made by stir frying in a small wok-like pan and adding a previously prepared spicy sauce. It is usually served with nan or other flat-breads. There are few true Pakistani restaurants in London and the Balti craze, which anyway is heavily meat based, is only slowly reaching us. Try:

Sapna, Wembley, Middlesex
Amina Tandoori Balti House, N16
Planet Poppadom, due to open on the King's Road, SW3 in June 94.

CHINESE

Chinatown is sandwiched between Leicester Square, Shaftesbury Avenue and Wardour Street. Right in the middle are the Gerard Street oriental arches which are the centre of the Chinese New Year celebrations in late January or early February.

The area is packed with Chinese restaurants and foodshops and is a

maru's bhajia house

230 Ealing Road
Alperton
Tel: 081 903 6771
Tel: 081 902 5570

Snacks, Toasted Sandwiches,
Fresh Juices, Milk Shakes,
and Hot Drinks

Also available:
PANI PURI, KACHORI, BOMBAY BHEL
We are open:
Tuesday to Friday 12 noon to 8.45pm
Saturday and Sunday 12 noon to 9.45pm
Monday closed except on Bank Holidays

great place to buy presents. Neal Street East, WC2, is a good place to go to get a lot of Chinese and oriental paraphernalia under one roof, though it is actually in Covent Garden and decidedly westernised.

The foodshops and supermarkets on Gerard Street and Newport Place have cheap rice, noodles, soy sauce, spices, water chestnuts, Chinese beer, and eastern vegetables such as mooli and lotus roots. But you will be swamped by the range of meat and fish products and the sight of dead carcasses roasting on spits.

Vegetarians returning from a visit to China will always testify to the wide variety of vegan and vegetarian food consumed there. Most Chinese restaurants in London have a high proportion of meat and fish dishes. Though you will almost always find a range of vegetarian food and often a separate vegetarian menu. Chinese food added a new dimension to veggie cuisine when it first became popular in the 50's and 60's, bringing a more communal approach to eating and faster methods of cooking that retain the goodness of the food, enhance colour and appearance and use very little dairy produce.

Chinese cuisine has probably done more than any other to introduce bean curd (tofu) in all its forms as an essential item in a healthy diet. Producing it in shapes and textures that resemble meat and fish dishes means that committed veggies may find themselves ordering dishes with names like Peking Duck and Pork with Green Peppers.

Vegetarian Cottage, NW3. London's first Chinese vegetarian restaurant, opened only a year ago and serves a wonderful range of non-meat meals and desserts. For a fast food Chinese noodle meal try The New Culture Revolution, N1, which is cheap by Islington's standards.

ITALIAN

People of Italian descent have lived in London as bankers, merchants, street entertainers, political refugees, restaurateurs, artisans and labourers since Roman times. Italians are now dispersed throughout London.

Italian cuisine was probably the first 'foreign food' to be accepted by the English. Soho is a good area for Italian coffee bars and restaurants, especially around Frith Street, Compton Street, Old Compton Street, Moor Street and Charlotte Street. They range from the very cheap to the very expensive. Italian restaurants do not usually offer a great choice for the cruelty-free connoisseur but there are often a few simple dishes that are vegan, if only spaghetti with tomato sauce. For a quick cheap meal in the West End try Pollo, W1.

Italian delicatessens stock many animal-free foods including pasta (the fresh variety is usually made with egg), sun-dried tomatoes, olive oil, exotic vegetables such as aubergines, olives, artichokes in oil or pickled in vinegar, herbs, spices and a whole variety of special breads.

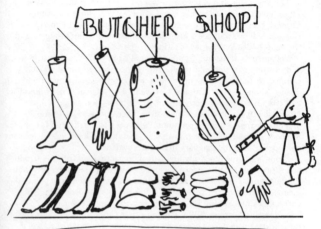

Don't miss the ciabatta bread made with olive oil and so popular that it can now be found in supermarkets.

For a vegan flavour of Italy stop off at a wholefood shop for some cheese-free pesto, sun-dried tomato or organic spaghetti sauce, all of which make a great quick meal with pasta.

PIZZA

The massive pizza market in the UK is an American product with an Italian influence. Pizza is the perfect fast food for the retailer being cheap to produce, quick to prepare and requiring virtually no washing-up. There are four main pizza chains in London: Pizza Express, Pizza Hut, Deep Pan Pizza Co. and Pizzaland. None of them offer much for vegans or replied to our written enquiry about rennet-free cheese for vegetarians, although we do know that Deep Pan Pizza Co. use vegetable rennet in all their vegetarian pizzas and that Pizza Hut pizza bases are now vegan. They often have an all-you-can-eat salad bar.

If you hang out with a vegan you might prefer to try a restaurant which gives a better choice of pasta. Try Ecco's, SW4, or Est, W1.

GREEK, TURKISH, CYPRIOT

Most people of Greek or Turkish extraction living in London originate from Cyprus. Early settlers came to work in the clothing, leather and catering industries and settled in Camden Town and Hackney.

The largest waves of immigration followed the lead up to independence from Britain and in the Turkish invasion in 1974. The majority now live and work on the 'Haringey ladder', a rectangular patchwork of streets just north of Finsbury Park and adjoining Green Lanes.

Green Lanes is distinctive for its takeaways, restaurants, grocers, patisseries, delicatessens, and cafes. The latter adorned with the name of the local football team. These cafes are principally populated by men passing the time of day over a game of backgammon and a 'never say sleep' coffee or Metaxa brandy. They are not really meant for outsiders and rarely frequented by women.

Mediterranean fruit and veg is widely available and cheap. Other delicacies are stuffed vine leaves, olive oil, and sticky sweets and cakes, most of which contain cheese or egg unfortunately.

Whilst Green Lanes has a massive takeaway trade, most Turkish or Greek restaurants are in Central London. You should find at least one cooked vegan meal such as a bean dish which can be eaten with hummus, aubergine, salad, vine leaves and bread —if you need to eat all that in one go. Try: Kalamaras, W2.

More commercially minded restaurants throw in some very tongue in cheek and raucous entertainment which can include plate smashing, a magic show, a disco and belly dancing — not everyone's cup of tea.

For a more distinctly Turkish experience you could visit Stoke Newington where there are several Turkish shops and eateries. Try: Anglo Anatolian Restaurant, N16.

IRISH LONDON

The Irish are the only large immigrant group in London that is still growing, mainly due to poor employment prospects at home. They number a quarter of a million and are widely dispersed around the capital's working class districts, principally Kilburn, Paddington, Hammersmith and Camden.

Historically the main periods of Irish immigration were 1847-8 following the failure of the potato crop and in the 1950's when Irish people were used, along with other immigrant groups, to fill low paid jobs in the construction, manufacturing, health, transport and catering industries

Apart from the chunky soda bread available from the Irish bakeries on Kilburn High Road, traditional Irish food has little to offer the cruelty-free eater. Irish whiskey, single malts and blended, is made from barley and cereals and is famous throughout the whisky drinking world. The most well-known brand is Jamesons. Guinness, the country's traditional dark beer, is, in all its forms, fined with fish bladder. The only consolation for the Guinness loving vegetarian is that it's supposed to taste better in Dublin anyway — not much of a consolation.

Whilst the food and Guiness may not grab you, Irish culture has been an important influence on London's social scene and you should not go home without sampling some of it. There are loads of pubs and clubs in which to hear traditional and modern Irish music which is a mixture of rock, country and folk. Try:

Archway Tavern, Archway Roundabout, N6. Tel: 071-272 2840. Tube: Archway. Free Mon-Wed, £1.50 Thu-Sat.

National Ballroom, 234 Kilburn High Road, NW6. Tel: 071-328 3141. Tube: Kilburn. £5.00-£7.00.

Biddy Mulligans, 205 Kilburn High Road, NW6. Tel: 071-624 2066. Tube: Kilburn. Every night, free.

The Victoria, 203 Holloway Road, N7. Tel: 071-607 1952. Tube: Highbury & Islington. Free music Sat and Sun. Look out for a band called Chanter.

The Swan, 215 Clapham Road, Stockwell, SW9. Tel: 071-978 9778. Tube: Stockwell. Free Sunday lunchtimes. £2.00-£5.00 evenings.

Sir George Robey, 240 Severn Sisters Road, N4. Tel: 071-263 4581. Tube: Finsbury Park. £3.00-£5.00. Some Irish music but a lot of 'grunge' played there too.

Mean Fiddler, 24-28 Harlesden High Street, NW10. Tel: 081-961 5490. Willesden Junction BR. Irish bands often play here when in town

but it's primarily an 'indie' venue. £4.00-£8.00 every night.
An Irish music festival or Fleadh is held every year in July and
features some of the country's best musicians.

JEWISH LONDON

Jews settled in London in the 19th century following persecution in
Russia and Eastern Europe. Their numbers increased in the 1930's
with people fleeing Nazi Germany. The early immigrants settled
mainly in the East End around Whitechapel, Spitalfields and Mile
End. Many worked in the clothes and shoe industries. As their
circumstances improved, many moved out to Golders Green, Stamford
Hill and Edgware and the suburbs of North London. Jewish people in
London now number about 200,000.

Orthodox Jewish cuisine has made a unique contribution to the
variety of animal-free foodstuffs. In Jewish law one is not permitted to
eat dairy products and meat at the same meal. Therefore Kosher
restaurants which serve meat have no dairy products, and conversely,
Kosher dairy restaurants have no meat. Many kosher products are
'parve' and contain neither meat nor dairy so that they can be eaten
with either, and are therefore usually vegan. This is slightly compli-
cated by the fact that eggs and fish are not considered to be either
dairy or meat so could appear in either type of restaurant. The golden
rule is to always check the ingredients.

Delicious Kosher vegan products include Tomor margarine, Toffutti
ice-cream, Toffutti cream cheese and sour cream, non-dairy creamer for
teas and coffee, parve whipped cream and Elite plain chocolates. They
are all available from wholefood shops.

Other culinary delights include falafel, a fast-food in Israel made
from crushed chickpeas that are pressed into balls, deep fried and
served with salad and pitta bread. They are widely available from
delicatessens and takeaways specialising in Mediterranean food.
Hummus is a gorgeous crushed chickpea and tahini dip or sandwich
filling that you can buy in supermarkets and Mediterranean takeaways.

Bagels, unleavened bread rolls which are cheap and wholesome, are
something of an institution in London. Get them fresh and with a
filling if you wish at:

    Brick Lane Beigel Bakery, E1
    Ridley Bagel Bakery E8
    Sharon's Bakery, N16

London has its own Jewish Vegetarian and Ecological Society, 853-855
Finchley Road, NW11 8LX. Tel: 081-455 0692. The Jewish Vegetarian
quarterly magazine costs £1.25. There are regular meetings with guest
speakers - ring for details. They have a restaurant—The Greenery on
the premises. They also stock two great Jewish vegetarian cookbooks.

AFRICAN AND CARIBBEAN

The first Africans in London were probably Roman soldiers. Numbers increased with the slave trade in the 18th century, expanding foreign trade in the 1880's, the second world war, and most noticeably in the 1950's and 60's when Caribbeans and West Africans were recruited to fill low paid jobs in an expanding British economy.

London's black population now numbers over 450,000 with the most important centres being Brixton, Hackney and Brent. A smaller, Trinidadian dominated black community around Notting Hill Gate and Portobello stages the Notting Hill Carnival. The carnival is the largest street festival in Europe and takes place over the August Bank holiday. Festivities now wind down at 6pm each night because of violence in previous years. However, the show still goes on and 1993's was one of the best yet. Steel bands and massive sound systems pump out soca, reggae and calypso and there are lots of stalls selling food and drink. If you did nothing else but go to carnival during your visit to London you would not be disappointed.

Although Caribbean and particularly African cuisine in London is heavy on meat and fish, the influence of Rastafarianism, which is nearly totally vegan, and economic necessity mean that there are usually goodies for the cruelty-free eater. Restaurants specialising in Caribbean cuisine often have vegetarian options, though this is not always the case with African restaurants and vegans should always ring before going.

African and Caribbean greengrocers usually stock breadfruit, limes, mangoes, guavas, yams, sweet potato, callalloo, plantain, coconut cream and milk, cassava, black-eyed beans, hot pepper sauces and other treats.

Brixton, traditionally a predominantly Jamaican area, with its market and surrounding shops, has historically been the best place for African and Caribbean ingredients, although Ridley Road Market, E8, and Kingsland High Street, E8, have now taken over. Good restaurants include:

Blue Gardenia, E6
Brixtonian Restaurant, SW9
Calabash, WC2 and Le Caribe, N16

SPANISH

Spanish 'tapas' bars became fashionable in London in the 1980's and many have managed to survive the recession of the 90's in one form or another. They often resemble wine bars or brasseries and serve wines and bottled beers. The tapas are small savoury dishes that are great for snacking on. Whilst the majority of them are meat or fish based you can find some that are vegan or vegetarian and they are always cooked in olive oil rather than butter or margarine. Common dishes include chilli potatoes, spinach and pine nuts, spiced green beans, olives, assorted nuts, and spiced mushrooms. Try:

The Finca, N1
The Gallery, SW8
Meson Don Phillipe, SE1

THAI

The exotic richness and subtlety of Thai food has made a big impact on the London restaurant circuit. Although meat and fish dominate the menus, there is usually no shortage of excellent vegetarian and vegan options. Thai food bridges the Indian/Chinese culinary divide with the main ingredients being lemon grass, banana leaf, coconut milk, hot chillies, peanut butter sauce, bean curd, sticky glutinous rice, white and wild rice, noodles, yellow and black bean sauces, seaweed and crispy vegetables. Puddings are made with a selection of the above and embellished with exotic fruit such as lychees. Try:

Bahn Thai, W1
Sri Siam, W1
Thai Garden, E2
Yum Yum, N16

MALAYSIAN AND INDONESIAN

Malaysian and Indonesian food is like a halfway house between Thai and Chinese, with Satay (peanut butter sauce) as a typical favourite. Try:

Indorasa, SW2
Makan, W10
Melati, W1
Mutiara, SE1

JAPANESE

Vegetarian options in Japanese restaurants in London are usually minimal, and always at the bottom of the menu. Much of the cuisine is based around seafood, slivers of meat and white rice. Macrobiotics is based on Japanese vegetarian wholefoods such as brown rice and other grains, beans, soya products such as tofu, tempeh and miso, steamed vegetables and seaweeds. The centre of the macrobiotic world is the East West Gourmet Restaurant, EC1. For a taste of Tokyo fast food style try Wagamama noodles bar, WC1, or takeaway at Sushi & Sozai, W1. Also Ajinura, WC2.

There are two Muji shops, in W1 and WC2, where you can buy all sorts of modern Japanese goods.

LEBANESE

Lebanese food has a lot to offer vegans and vegetarians, and shares many ingredients with other Mediterranean cuisines. Hummus, chickpeas, tahini, pureed vegetables, garlic and lemon are all widely used. Tabouleh is a traditional salad dish made from fresh parsley, crushed wheat, olive oil, garlic and lemon. Meals are served as a number of small dishes called meze. There are some great Lebanese restaurants in W8 including Al Basha and Byblos, which offers a vegan meze and gives discount to members of the Vegan Society. Also La Reash Cous Cous House, W1V.

BRITISH PUBS AND ALCOHOL

Here's what no vegetarian wants to hear - traditional British beer, often called real ale because of its indigenous ingredients and method of production, is almost never vegetarian. This is because of the use of isinglass (fish fining) to clear the beer. It is safer to stick to bottled, canned or keg beer. Or better still, lagers, which are more likely to be chill filtered.

Wine is even more problematic as it can be cleared using a whole range of animal products including: milk, eggs, fish oil and pigs blood. You can mail order vegetarian and vegan wines and beers and arrange tastings with Water 2 Wine. They run the Vegetarian Wine Club and can be contacted on 081-905 5515. Vinceremos or Vintage Roots also do mail order and their details are given in the 'Action' chapter under 'Miscellaneous'. For a free leaflet on organic wine, which is not always vegan, send a sae to The Soil Association, 86 Colston Street, Bristol BS1 5BB. Tel: 0272-290661. Next to the Green Leaf Bookshop at the top of Christmas Steps (see the chapter on Bristol).

In London Sedlescombe Vineyard retail organic wines and champagnes on Sunday mornings from a stall in Spitalfields Organic Market, E1. You can make a trip to the vineyard which is eight miles north of Hastings. It is open every day from April to December from 10.00-18.00 and Jan-Mar weekends 12.00-17.00. They have accommodation so you don't have to stagger home after a torrid tasting. For more details send sae to Sedlescombe Vineyard, Cripps Corner, Sedlescombe, Nr Robertsbridge, East Sussex. Or phone 0580-830715.

The good news about British pubs is that there has been a huge increase in the amount of vegetarian and even occasionally vegan food on offer, especially in the south east. The JD Wetherspoon chain have 50 pubs in London offering vegetarian delights such as Avocado Beanfeast with garlic or granary bread and Pasta Flora, (£3.45-£4.45) and spicy vegan vegetable chilli (£3.25). Also salads for £4.25. Vegetarian cheese is used in all vegetarian dishes and everything is clearly marked on the menu. For a list of JD Wetherspoon pubs, send a sae to 735 High Road, London N12 0BP. Tel: 081-446 9099.

Remember to say you saw it in the Cruelty-Free Guide

LESBIAN AND GAY LONDON

LLGC (London Lesbian & Gay Centre)
67-69 Cowcross St, EC1. Tel: 071-608 1471
Open: Mon 17.30-23.00, Tue-Thur 12.00-23.00, Fri-Sat 12.00-02.00,
Sun 12.00-23.00 Tube: Farringdon
Big social centre where you can eat, dance, work out, or join many
different groups.

FIRST OUT COFFEE SHOP
52 St.Giles High St, WC2. Tel: 071-240 8042
Open: Mon-Sat 11.30-23.30, Sun 13.00-19.30
Tube: Tottenham Court Rd.
Great vegetarian lesbian/gay cafe between Oxford Street and Covent
Garden. Open late and handy for the nearby gay nightclubs.

SILVER MOON WOMEN'S BOOKSHOP
68 Charing Cross Rd, WC2. Tel: 071-836 7906
Open: Mon-Sat 10.30-18.30
Tube: Leicester Square.
Feminist and lesbian books.

GAY'S THE WORD BOOKSHOP
66 Marchmont St, WC1. Tel: 071-278 7654
Open: Mon-Sat 11.00-19.00, Sun 14.00-18.00
Tube: Russell Sq.uare.
Lesbian and gay books.

PAPERS
There are four free papers available at the above shops or in clubs and
bars: Capital Gay (men), Pink Paper (men and women), Boyz (men),
MX. The bookstores have gay guidebooks to the capital such as London
Scene.

GAY TIMES
£2.00 at the start of each month from newsagents, eg WH Smith or
Menzies in British Rail stations.

TIME OUT
London's weekly what's on magazine has two pages of lesbian and gay
listings.

LESBIAN AND GAY SWITCHBOARD
Tel: 071-837-7324. 24 hour advice and information.

LESBIAN LINE
Tel: 071-251-6911 Open: Mon & Fri 14.00-22.00, Tue-Thur 19.00-22.00.
Advice and information.

TV/TS HELPLINE
Tel: 071-729-1466 Open: Tue 14.00-18.00, Fri-Sun 20.00-22.00

GAY VEGETARIANS AND VEGANS
GV, c/o Gemma, BM Box 5700, London WC1N 3XX.
Men and women meet regularly. Send self-addressed envelope or
international reply coupon.

Remember to say you saw it in the Cruelty-Free Guide

INNER LONDON POSTCODES

WEST END

WC1	Bloomsbury, Russell Square
WC2	Covent Garden, Charing Cross Road, Holborn, Leicester Square, Strand
W1	Edgware Road, Great Portland Street, Oxford Street, Baker Street, Marble Arch, Piccadilly, Tottenham Court Road, Soho, Mayfair, Park Lane, St Christopher's Place

CITY

EC1	Farringdon, Smithfield, Old Street, Angel, Clerkenwell
EC2	City, Barbican, Moorgate, Liverpool Street
EC3	Tower of London, Aldgate, Fenchurch Street
EC4	Fleet Street, Old Bailey, Blackfriars, St Paul's

SOUTH WEST INNER

SW1	Pimlico, St James's, Sloane Street, Westminster, Victoria, Belgravia
SW3	Knightsbridge, Chelsea, King's Road
SW5	Earl's Court
SW6	Fulham, Fulham Road, Parson's Green
SW7	Gloucester Road, South Kensington
SW10	West Brompton

CENTRAL LONDON

THE CITY (EC1, EC2, EC3, EC4)

EC1	*Smithfield, Old Street, Angel, Clerkenwell,*
	Farringdon, Shoreditch
EC2	*Barbican, Liverpool Street, Moorgate, City*
EC3	*Tower of London, Aldgate, Fenchurch Street*
EC4	*St Paul's, Fleet Street, Old Bailey, Blackfriars*

The Square Mile of the financial capital is brimming with British John Steed lookalikes sporting pinstriped suits and brollies. The main attractions are suitably serious. From noon till 14.00 myriad sandwich bars slice and spread lunch right before your eyes. At night and weekends this business district is as empty as Dewhurst's bank account.

EC1 SMITHFIELD, OLD STREET, ANGEL

ATTRACTIONS

WHIRL-Y-GIG
Shoreditch Town Hall, 380 Old Street, EC1. Open: 20.00-24.00
London's wildest New Age nightclub. Psycho-active drinks and veggie/vegan food from the Tranz-Peez Cafe. Bring your own alcohol. DJ Monkey Pilot spins the new world and ambient sounds. The decoration by Happy Hang-ups has to be seen to be believed as an old town hall is transformed into something resembling a cross between an Arabian bazaar and a Bedouin tent. The evening finishes off with a parachute dance. £7.00, £5.00 concessions. An out-of-body experience.

HORRORS

SMITHFIELD MARKET
Central Market, EC1. Tube: Farringdon
Boo! Hiss! The largest meat market in Europe. Venture here only to anti-meat demos, and to forage at:

VEGETARIAN RESTAURANTS & CAFES

CRANKS SMITHFIELD
5 Cowcross Street, EC1M 6DR. Tel: 071-490 4870
Open: Mon-Fri 07.00-15.00
Tube: Farringdon
Vegetarian. Health Food. Yumlicious veggie grub and herb teas.

EAST WEST GOURMET VEGETARIAN RESTAURANT

188 Old Street, St. Lukes, EC1V 9BP. Tel: 071-250 1051
Open: Mon-Sat 11.00-21.00, Sun 11.00-17.00
Tube: Old Street (exit 6)

99% Vegan. Macrobiotic. 10 vegan macrobiotic dishes and devilish desserts. Main meal £4.50-£6.00 for noodles with tofu, brown rice with mixed veg and salad, or something like aduki and ginger stew or tofu and rice croquettes. Desserts £0.85-£2.00. Vegans should beware of buttermilk in some of the bread. Licensed for beer and wine. A favourite eating place of London Vegans. Also has a book shop during the day and lots of well cool classes like shiatsu, tai chi, macrobiotic cooking and yoga in the East-West Centre, headquarters of the Community Health Foundation.

RAVI SHANKAR'S

422 St. John's Street, EC1. Tel: 071-833 5849
Open: Daily 12.00-14.30 (Sun 16.30),18.00-23.00
Tube: Angel

Vegetarian. South Indian. Famous restaurant owned by the same people as the other Ravi Shankar in NW1 and with a similar menu. All 38 dishes are vegetarian specailities from Kerala, including the £5.95 thali, and only vegetable ghee is used. Average £5.50. Bring your own alcohol, free corkage. Booking advised. Lunch buffet £3.95. Evening a la carte.

OTHER RESTAURANTS

AXIOM CAFE

22 Underwood St, near City Rd, EC1. Tel: 071-490 2924
Open: Mon-Fri 8.30-14.00
Tube: Old Street

90% Vegetarian. New cafe in office block next to Friends of the Earth headquarters, with good vegetarian lunches from £2.45. Vegans can have spring rolls, bhajias, nutty mushroom pasty, chickpea roti, veg and lentil or mushrrom rissole for an average £1.25. Soup may be vegan £1.85. Salads £1.25.

SHOPS

FRESHLANDS WHOLEFOODS

196 Old Street, EC1V 9BP. Tel: 071-250 1708.
Open: Mon-Fri 09.00-19.00, Sat 09.00-17.00.
Tube: Old Street, exit 6.

Large wholefood, organic fruit and veg, and macrobiotic store by the East-West Centre. Vegan and vegetarian pies, pastries and sand-wiches. Downstairs sells cosmetics, toiletries and vitamins.

HATTON GARDEN
Wall to wall jewellery shops, even open on Sunday.

LONDON DISTRIBUTORS
47 Farringdon Road, EC1M. Tel: 071- 404 5237.
Open: Mon-Fri 08.30-17.00.
Tube: Farringdon.
Health food shop. Sandwiches are not vegan, but they have vegan
flapjacks.

RYE WHOLEFOODS
35a Mydletton Street, EC1R. Tel: 071- 278 5878.
Open: Mon-Fri 09.30-18.00, Sat 10.30-16.00.
Tube: Angel, Farringdon.
Small stock of wholefoods and a great takeaway section with 20
vegetarian hot dishes, 10 of them vegan, £1.50. Limited hot food on
Sat.

BARBICAN, LIVERPOOL STREET (EC2)

ATTRACTIONS

THE BARBICAN ARTS CENTRE
Silk Street, EC2. Tel: 071-638 4141 general information, 071-628 2295 /
9760 24 hr information
Open: Daily 10.00-23.00
Tube: Barbican (not Sundays), Moorgate
Vast arts complex with free music lunchtimes and early evenings,
three cinemas, exhibition halls, an art gallery, cafes and bars. Home to
London Symphony Orchestra and Royal Shakespeare Company.

BROADGATE CENTRE
Eldon Street EC2. Tel: 071-588 6565 Open: 24 hours.
Tube: Liverpool Street. Free.
Bars, shops, restaurants for the well-off. Outdoor ice-skating in winter
(£3.00 adults, £1.50 children), performance space in summer.

BANK OF ENGLAND MUSEUM
Bartholomew Lane, off Threadneedle Street, EC2.Tel: 071-601 5545
Open: Mon-Fri 10.00-17.00. Tube: Bank
Free films and tours of the central bank of the UK should raise the
interest of aspiring yuppies.

MUSEUM OF LONDON
150 London Wall, EC2. Tel: 071-600 3699 Open: Tue-Sat 10.00-18.00,
Sun 14.00-18.00 Tube: Moorgate, St Paul's Adults £3.00, children
£1.50.
The story of London. Restaurant, shop, wheelchair access.

VEGETARIAN RESTAURANTS

THE PLACE BELOW

Crypt of St Mary-le-Bow Church, Cheapside, EC2. Tel: 071-329 0789
Open: Mon-Fri 07.30-15.30, also Thur-Fri 18.30-21.30.
Tube: St Paul's, Bank
Vegetarian. Fast food and exotic. Great vegetarian fast lunches and exotic evening dinners, with a couple of vegan dishes. Book for evening and bring your own booze.

SHOPS

THE BODY SHOP

22-23 Cheapside, EC2 6AB. Open: Mon-Fri 09.00-17.30.

THE BODY SHOP

West Concourse, Unit 5-6 The Mall, Liverpool St. Station, EC2M 7PY.
Open: Mon-Fri 07.30-19.30, Sat 10.00-16.00.

EC3 TOWER OF LONDON, ALDGATE

ATTRACTIONS

LEADENHALL MARKET

Whittington Avenue, EC3.
Open: Mon-Fri 07.00-15.00
Tube: Bank
Attractive vegetables in this covered market but the stench of dead fish on display is definitely not for the tender stomach or nostril. Loads of city types in the local bars and restaurants.

TOWER OF LONDON

Tower Hill, EC3. Tel: 071-709 0765. Open: Mar-Oct Mon-Sat 09.30-18.30, Sun 14.00-18.15; Nov-Feb Mon-Sat 09.30-17.00
Tube: Tower Hill, Tower Gateway (Docklands Light Railway)
£6.00 adults, £3.70 children, under fives free.
Royals now get the chop in the tabloids, but veggies can still ogle beefeaters and the crown jewels.

TOWER BRIDGE

Tel: 071-407 0922. Open: Apr-Oct 10.00-14.30, Nov-Mar 10.00-18.30.
The bridge that raises for ships and the one the Americans thought they had bought. Walk across from the Tower of London to the South Bank for free. Go aloft for £3.50 adults, £2.50 children, and get a stunning view over the river Thames. (see also SE1)

VEGETARIAN FOOD

FUTURES VEGETARIAN TAKEAWAY

8 Botolph Alley, Eastcheap, EC3R 8DR. Tel: 071-623 4529
Open: Mon-Fri 07.30-10.00, 11.30-15.00. Closed Sat, Sun
Tube: Monument, Bank

Vegetarian takeaway. Telephone ordering. Main course such as curry £3.10. Pizza or quiche £1.78. Hot or cold desserts £1.50. There are usually 2 or 3 clearly labelled vegan dishes each day and soups. The menu changes daily and city slickers can call it up on their Reuters information screen.

EC4 ST PAUL'S, FLEET STREET

ATTRACTIONS

CITY OF LONDON TOURIST INFORMATION CENTRE

St Paul's Church Yard, EC4. Tel: 071-260 1457
Open: Daily 09.30-17.00 (Oct-Mar closed Sun)

ST PAUL'S CATHEDRAL

St Paul's Church Yard, EC4. Tel: 071-248 2705
Open: Mon-Fri 10.00-16.15, Sat 11.00-16.15
Tube: St Paul's

Church of England. Free or donations, charges for inner rooms and guided tours. Great views of the city from the dome. Shop. Phone for times of organ recitals.

THE OLD BAILEY

Newgate Street, EC4. Tel: 071-248 3277.
Open: Mon-Fri 10.30-13.00, 14.00-16.00.
Tube: St Paul's. Free.

Courtroom open to the public. Real-life Rumpole with no charges for you. And here are the rules if you want to stay out of the dock: no large bags, nothing electrical, no food, no under 14's. Nearby, at the High Court in Fleet Street, near Aldwych, is the vegetarian trial of the century - McDonald's versus London Greenpeace. For further information send two stamps to McLibel Support Campaign, London Greenpeace, 5 Caledonian Road N1.

SHOPS

LEATHER LANE MARKET

Open: Mon-Fri 10.30-14.00.
Tube: Chancery Lane.

Fruit, veg and clothes at the western extremity of the City.

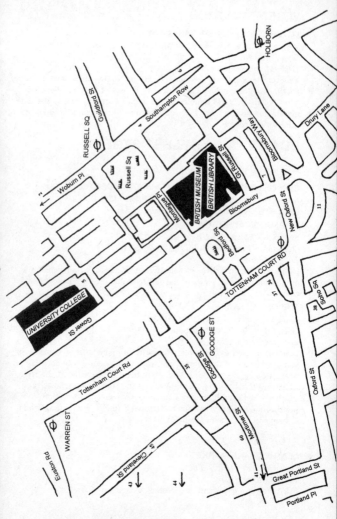

Remember to say you saw it in the Cruelty-Free Guide

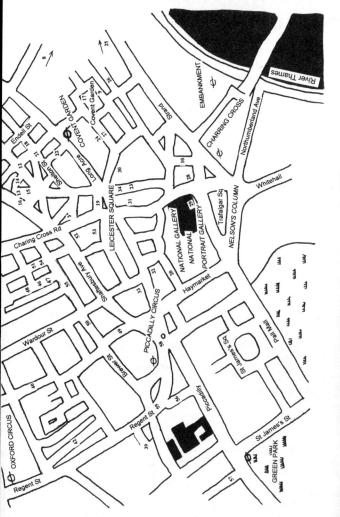

WEST CENTRAL LONDON

WC1	*Bloomsbury*
WC2	*Covent Garden*
	Trafalgar Square
	Leicester Square
	Charing Cross Road

Centered around the vegetarian paradise of Covent Garden, there's enough in the WC area for several weekend visits. Bloomsbury's main attraction is the huge and totally free British Museum. Covent Garden has the greatest concentration of cruelty-free eating places in Britain and lots of weird, whacky and just plain wonderful shops. Base yourself here and venture out for a stroll along the river, around pigeon infested Trafalgar Square and the National Gallery, or into the glitzy cinemas and nightclubs of Leicester Square. The northern end of Charing Cross Road is wall to wall bookshops.

WC1 BLOOMSBURY

ATTRACTIONS

LONDON VEGANS

London Vegans, who produced Vege-Tables, the forerunner of this book, meet on the last Wednesday of the month (except December) from 18.30 till 21.00. Come and join us for a discussion, a snack, to pick up some leaflets or books, a free copy of the London Vegans What's On Diary, and a drink in the pub afterwards. We'll be at Millman Street Community Rooms, 52 Millman Street, east of Russell Square underground. Entrance at the back of the building via a small alley. Call in advance for more details - see our listing under local groups at the end of this guide. We organise many social events and also go out campaigning. We meet many of our friends through London Vegans and so could you.

THE BRITISH MUSEUM

Great Russell Street, WC1. Tel: 071-636 1555, Information Desk 071-323 8299, recorded information 071-580 1788. Open: Mon-Sat 10.00-17.00, Sun 14.30-18.00. Tube: Tottenham Court Rd. Free.
More antiques than Lovejoy in the biggest of London's 150 museums, including Egyptian mummies, Greeks, Romans and other British Empire loot. Not forgetting the Cheshire bog man, who didn't die unblocking the gents in Chester, but is in fact the well-preserved 2,000 year old victim of murder. Free talks and lectures Tue-Sat. Cafe with vegetarian food.

VEGETARIAN RESTAURANTS

GREENHOUSE

Drill Hall, 16 Chenies Street, WC1E 7EX. Tel: 071-637 8038
Open: Mon 10.00-22.00 (women only 20.00-22.00), Tue-Fri 10.00-22.00,
Sat 12.00-22.00.
Tube: Goodge Street.
Vegetarian. Global food. Wholefood restaurant with wholesome
portions. Main meal £3.85. All soups and most starters are vgan.
Everything is home-made. Free corkage. No bookings. Can get very
busy especially at lunchtimes but the place you're most likely to meet
famous thespians in the toilet.

THE PLACE THEATRE CAFE

17 Duke's Road, WC1H 9AB. Tel: 071-383 5469 cafe, 071-387 0031 box
office.
Open: Mon-Sat 10.00-16.00 (20.00 if a performance), Sun 10.00-16.00
but only if a performance.
Tube: Euston.
Vegetarian. Wholefood. Counter service cafe in the basement of the
theatre and managed by the same people as the cafe at St Martins-in-
the-Field. Menu changes daily but is the same for lunch and evening
meal. Soups are usually vegan and cost £1.25. Main courses include
pasta, pizza, pies and casseroles (the latter usually vegan) and cost
£2.85-£3.25. Cakes and flapjacks are 50p-85p. The cafe predominantly
serves drama students who attend classes at the theatre, but there is
also some passing trade from office workers.

OTHER RESTAURANTS

CHAMBALI

146 Southampton Row, WC1. Tel: 071-837 3925
Open: Every day 12.00-15.00, 18.00-23.30
Tube: Holborn
Omnivorous. North Indian. Lots of vegetarian food. Thali £10.80,
vegetable biryani with curry sauce £7.85.

CRYPT CAFE

2 The Cloisters, Christ the King Church, Gordon Square, Bloomsbury,
WC1H 0AG. Tel: 071-383 5553
Open: Closed in summer and in university holidays.
Tube: Russell Sq.
70% vegetarian wholefood. Good cheap wholesome fare in this
atmospheric underground cavern. Only £3.00 for a main course and the
soups are always vegan. Best outside the 12.00-15.00 lunchtime slot
which can get very crowded with students from the university. No
smoking in 50% of the building.

THE OCTOBER GALLERY RESTAURANT

24 Old Gloucester Street, WC1N 3AL. Tel: 071-242 7367
Open: Tue-Sat 12.30-14.30
Tube: Holborn, Russell Square
Omnivorous. Always vegetarian soups, a salad and a main dish such as veg pasta bake, Algerian black-eyed bean stew with coconut and spinach, or spinach roulade. Occasional vegan dishes and lots of soups like spinach dhal or parsnip and ginger. Main course £3.60-£3.80, salad £1.20, soup £2.00.

WAGAMAMA

4 Streatham Street, off Bloomsbury Street, WC1A 1JB.
Tel: 071-323 9223.
Open: Mon-Sat 18.00-23.00 & Mon-Fri 12.00-14.30, Sat 12.30-15.00.
Tube: Tottenham Court Road
Omnivorous. Japanese. Central London's coolest fast food noodles bar. The experience of Wagamama is well worth the inevitable queue and anyway you can have a can of Saporo lager while you mingle with other would-be diners. Low lighting, cream walls, no decoration and rows of tables make this look like an upmarket school canteen - but you never got food like this in school. Veggie and vegan choices are limited but delicious. A pure wagamama served in a large bowl contains a noodle dish with seasoned green vegetables and tofu, a side dish of carrot, garlic, cabbage and water chestnut grilled dumplings and a raw energy juice drink. It will set you back £6.50. A delicious Yasi Chilli Men is a Thai style noodles dish with assorted vegetables and a tofu chilli sauce. Raw energy juice is £1.60, salad £4.00, Japanese Green Tea £1.00. Free postcards of the restaurant. No booking.

SHOPS

ALARA WHOLEFOODS

58 Marchmont Street, WC1N 1AB. Tel: 071-837 1172.
Open Mon-Sat 09.00-18.00 (Fri till 18.30, Sat from 10.00).
Huge takeaway section, loads of vegan products, organic produce including beers, wines and bread. Also a selection of cruelty-free cosmetics and food supplements. A street with a real sense of community, enhanced by a number of takeaway food shops and cafes— was all of London like this once?

THE BODY SHOP

18 High Holborn, WC1V 6BX. Tel: 071-831 2515. Open: Mon-Fri 8.30-18.00.

HOLLAND & BARRETT

34 Brunswick Centre, Russell Square, WC1N 1AU.
Tel: 071-278 4640. Open: Mon-Sat 9.30-17.30. Health food & takeaway.

HOLLAND & BARRETT

319 High Holborn, WC1V. Tel: 071-242 0459. Open: Mon-Fri 08.00-18.00. Closed weekend.

WHOLLEY'S HEALTH FOODS

33 Theobalds Road, Holborn, WC1X 8SP. Tel: 071-405 3028.
Open: Mon-Fri 07.00-15.30. Closed Sat, Sun.
Tube: Holborn.
Health Food. Omnivorous. Takeaway only with salads and soups. Fax your order through on 071-430 2417.

WC2 COVENT GARDEN

The best area of London for cruelty-free munchies and shopping. In fact there are a vegan baker's dozen (yes thirteen!) great vegetarian eateries within five minutes walk of the tube station. The perfect place to spend an afternoon wandering the streets. There are two focal points for veggies, Neal's Yard and the covered market.

The area around Neal's Yard, Long Acre and Neal Street is jam packed with unique and amazing shops. Stock up at Neal's Yard wholefood shop. Behind is Neal's Yard itself, with several daytime vegetarian cafes and New Age shops, including an apothecary (natural remedies), desk top publishing service, rubber stamp shop, and meeting rooms for green events. Just around the corner is the Food for Thought cafe. Strolling east you'll come to the London Ecology Centre, containing the World of Difference green shop and the Yours Naturally vegetarian cafe. A little further brings you to the shop Wild Things, run by Respect for Animals (formerly Lynx) and selling non-leather shoes, clothes and other vegan goodies to help fund the campaign against fur.

At the south end of Neal Street is the covered market, with lots of shops and a Cranks cafe. Nearby you'll see London's best jugglers, street theatre and musicians. On the south side of the market you can join the Youth Hostel Association and plan your dream holiday at the YHA Adventure Shop in Southampton Street.

ATTRACTIONS

JUBILEE HALL SPORTS CENTRE

30 The Plaza, Covent Garden, WC2. Tel: 071-836 4835, 071-836 4007.
Open: Mon-Fri 06.30-22.00, Sat-Sun 10.00-17.00.
Tube: Covent Garden
Big gym, huge classes, mixed. Next to the Transport Museum. Largest weights room in London. £5.00 for one day of gym and sauna, £4.00 aerobics class. £40.00 for a month, or £55.00 with unlimited classes. Single sex saunas. Sunbed £6.00 for 20 mins. Best to book for sports massage, weights instruction, osteopathy, aromatherapy, reflexology.

Remember to say you saw it in the Cruelty-Free Guide

Buy your gear in the small sports clothes shop open Mon-Fri 12.00-14.00, 17.00-20.00, Sat 12.00-15.30.

Whether you've just worked out or you've simply dropped in to see some sweat (no admission charge), you can watch the gym from the Jubilee Hall Cafe which is 95% vegetarian. They serve mainly salads for £2.00, or quiche and salad £3.75. Jacket potato with one vegan filling £1.99, two £2.70, three £3.20. Cakes and vegan hand-made flapjacks 80p. £1.40 for half a pint of freshly squeezed orange, apple, carrot or mixed juice. Tea 45p, cappuccino 85p, herbal tea 55p or 60p for a pot. Cafe open Mon-Fri 08.15-21.15, Sat 11.00-16.15, Sun 12.00-16.00.

Other places to stay in trim in Covent Garden are:

Oasis swimming pool, 32 Endell St. Tel: 071-831 1804.

Pineapple dance studio, 7 Langley St. Tel: 071-836 4004.

The Sanctuary, 11 Floral St. Tel: 071-240 0695. A gorgeous health club for women only.

LONDON TRANSPORT MUSEUM

39 Welling Street, WC2. Tel: 071-379 6344
Open: daily 10.00-18.00. £3.95 adults. £2.50 children, students, senior citizens and disabled. Family ticket for two adults and two children £10.00, under fives free.
Tube: Covent Garden.

Real life and model trains, trams, buses and other public transport memorabilia, and a shop. Simulators for the young and young at heart and a fine display of posters. Wheelchair access. The London Transport Cafe in the building is open to non-visitors and has some vegetarian food like ploughman's pies, or courgette, basil and tomato tart with vegetarian pasta salad for £2.90. Tea 80p, coffee 90p, fruit tea 80p.

VEGETARIAN RESTAURANTS AND CAFES

BUNJIES COFFEE HOUSE

27 Litchfield Street, Covent Garden, WC2H 9NJ. Tel: 071-240 1796.
Open: Mon-Sat 12.00-23.45. Sunday 17.00-23.00.
Tube: Covent Garden, Leicester Square

Widely known and atmospheric vegetarian basement cafe, with intimate folk and poetry cellar on Tue, Wed and Sat. Basic international cuisine, average £3.50. Vegans can have ratatouille or curry with brown rice. Bring your own alcohol, licence applied for.

THE CAFE, STUDENTS' UNION LSE

London School of Economics, East Buildings, Basement, Houghton Street, Aldwych, WC2 2AE. Tel: 071-955 7164
Open: Mon-Fri 09.00-18.00 term, 10.00-15.00 vacations
Tube: Aldwych, Temple

Vegetarian. International. Average £3.50. Cafe and takeaway. Very cheap, simple vegetarian food and drinks. You'll feel more comfortable if you look like a student. Ask the students where to go or you'll never find it. Right-wing students are trying to force the cafe to serve meat, so please support our friends by eating there and encourage them to stick to their principles. There are plenty of other cafes in the university for the carnivores.

Always two vegan main dishes. All cakes are vegan and sugar free.

CRANKS COVENT GARDEN

The Piazza, Covent Garden, WC2. Tel: 071-379 6508
Open: Mon-Sat 09.30-20.00 (sometimes later), Sun 11.00-19.00
Tube: Covent Garden

Vegetarian. Health Food. Juice bar and takeaway upstairs, vegan and veg-eat-dairy-an cafe downstairs. Right in the heart of the shops and near the crafts market. Average £3.00. One of the Cranks chain selling earthy and diverse good quality wholefood.

FIRST OUT COFFEE SHOP

52 St. Giles High Street, St. Giles, WC2H 8LH. Tel: 071-240 8042. Open:
Mon-Sat 11.00-23.15, Sun 14.00-19.00
Tube: Tottenham Court Road

Vegetarian. Continental. Classy lesbian and gay coffee house serving vegetarian meals with vegan options. Average £3.00. Licensed for alcohol. Menu changes daily.

FOOD FOR THOUGHT

31 Neal Street, Covent Garden, WC2H 9PR. Tel: 071-836 0239
Open: Mon-Sat 9.30-20.00, Sun 10.30-16.30.
Tube: Covent Garden.

Vegetarian. International. Lively, ever popular vegetarian restaurant serving deliciously different delights from around the world. Vegan and gluten free options always available. Menu changes daily and is prepared entirely on the premises using only fresh quality produce. No deep freezing, no microwaving, no artificial additives. Excellent value for money: under £5.00 for a two course meal. Free corkage. No smoking. Takeaway, delivery and tailor-made catering service available: Phone 071-836 9072.

NEAL'S YARD BAKERY TEAROOM

6 Neal's Yard, Covent Garden, WC2H 9DP. Tel: 071-836 5199
Open: Mon-Fri 10.30-19.30 (close 17.00 Wed), Sat 10.30-16.30. Closed
Sunday.
Tube: Covent Garden

Vegetarian. Health food. Good range of vege-favourites. Average £5.00. Buy your meal from the display downstairs either to take away, or sit down in the cafe upstairs and grab tomorrow's loaf on the way out. Good place for comparing your bargains.

Cranks

Select from a delicious range of freshly prepared foods, served in contemporary and comfortable surroundings.

NEAL'S YARD DINING ROOM

First Floor, 14 Neal's Yard, Covent Garden, WC2H 9DP.
Tel: 071-379 0298. Open: Mon-Sat 12.00-17.00 (till 20.00 Wed) winter,
12.00-20.00 summer.
Tube: Covent Garden
Vegetarian. International. Also called World Food Cafe. Good meal for £7.00 and you can watch veggie shoppers in the yard below. Many dishes are vegan and there are fruit salads in the summer.

NEAL'S YARD SOUP & SALAD BAR

2 Neal's Yard, Covent Garden, WC2H 9DP. Tel: 071-836 3233
Open: Mon-Thur 11.00-19.00. Fri, Sat 11.00-17.00.
Tube: Covent Garden
Vegetarian. Health Food. Average £5.00. Grab some munchies from the counter and chill out under the sun at an outside table.

SHAN RESTAURANT

200 Shaftesbury Avenue, Covent Garden, WC2H 8JL.
Tel: 071-240 3348 Open: Mon-Sat 11.30-19.30
Tube: Covent Garden, Tottenham Court Road
Vegetarian. Indian. 50 of the 69 dishes are vegan. Some dishes may have butter ghee. Average £5.00. Deluxe thali £4.99 is dhal soup, mixed veg curry, bean curry, chana curry, brown or white rice,

chapattis, popadoms, salad, lassi or cold drink, raita and sweet. Set lunch £3.45 for veg curry, brown or white rice, chapattis. You can bring your own wine during licensing hours and pay 75p corkage. Rather basic but dirt cheap.

TAKE 5 FAST FOOD
Jubilee Hall Market, Covent Garden, WC2.
Open: Every day 8.00-18.00
Tube: Covent Garden
Vegetarian. International. Average £3.00. Counter service for eat-in or takeaway. Two vegan dishes every day. Casserole and stir-fry always vegan, occasionally vegan bake. No sweets.

YOURS NATURALLY VEGETARIAN CAFE
London Ecology Centre, 45 Shelton Street, Covent Garden, WC2H 9HJ.
Tel: shop / cafe 071-379 4324.
Open: Mon-Sat cafe 10.00-18.00, shop 10.00-20.00.
Tube: Covent Garden
Vegetarian. Wholefood. Average £2.50. Vegecological cafe in the London Ecology Centre with a range of low cost vegetarian and vegan dishes. The centre itself sells 'green' products and stocks a number of animal rights publications.

OTHER RESTAURANTS

AJIMURA JAPANESE RESTAURANT
51-53 Shelton Street, Covent Garden, WC2H 9HE.
Tel: 071-240 0178.
Open: Mon-Sat 12.00-23.30
Tube: Covent Garden, Leicester Square
Omnivorous. Japanese. Average £5.00. Table and takeaway service. Good selection of vegetable dishes including: vegetable tempura, vegetable sushi, salad and tofu steaks, many of which are also vegan.

CAFE PACIFICO
5 Langley Street, Covent Garden, WC2H 9JA. Tel: 071-379 7728
Open: Mon-Sat 12.00-23.45, Sun 12.00-22.45.
Tube: Covent Garden
Omnivorous. Mexican. Average £8.00. Nothing for vegans but the usual selection of enchilladas, burritos, pizza and tortilla for veggies. Lively place for revellers on Fridays and Saturdays.

CAFE PELICAN
45 St. Martins Lane, Covent Garden, WC2N 4EJ.
Tel: 071-379 0309
Open: Mon-Sat 11.00-02.00. Sun 11.00-24.00.

Tube: Leicester Square, Covent Garden
Omnivorous. French. Average £6.95. Table service. Separate bar/
brasserie and restaurant menu available with an international flavour
and lots of vegetarian food but nothing vegan.

CALABASH

The Africa Centre Basement, 38 King Street, WC2E 8JS.
Tel: 071-836 1976
Open: Mon-Fri 12.30-15.00, Mon-Sat 18.00-22.30
Tube: Covent Garden
Omnivorous. African. £16.00 three course. Good choice for veggies, but
vegans are advised to ring in advance. A variety of unusual wine and
beers. African bands in club above on Fri and Sat. African craftshop is
open in the same building during the day.

INDIA CLUB

143 Strand, Aldwych, WC2R 1JA. Tel: 071-836 0650
Open: Every day 12.00-14.30, 18.00-22.00.
Tube: Aldwych, Charing Cross, Embankment
Omnivorous. Indian. Average £6.00. North and South Indian
combinations at very reasonable prices in friendly restaurant with a
separate bar downstairs.

NANKING FAST FOOD

Jubilee Hall Market, 1A Tavistock St, WC2.
Tel: 071-379 4372
Open: Daily 10.00-18.00
Tube: Covent Gdn.
Omnivorous. Chinese. Eat in or takeaway. Quite a few vegan options
amongst the ten vegetarian dishes for £2.50. Telephone orders
welcome. Free local delivery over £10.00.

PLUMMERS

33 King Street, Covent Garden, WC2E 8JD. Tel: 071-240 2534
Open: Mon-Fri 12.00-14.30, Mon-Sat 17.30-23.30, Sun 18.00-22.00.
Tube: Covent Garden
English. Omnivorous. Three vegetarian dishes on the menu. One
course set menu £8.45, two courses £11.55, three courses £13.95. All
cheese has animal rennet.

SHOPS

THE BODY SHOP

Unit 18, Central Avenue, The Market, Covent Garden WC2.
Open: Mon-Sat 10.30-19.00 (Wed from 11.00), Sun 11.00-18.30.
Cruelty-free cosmetics chain founded by Anita Roddick.

THE BODY SHOP

The Floral Centre, 23 Long Acre, WC2E 9LZ.
Open: Mon-Sat 10.30-19.00, Sun 12.00-18.00.
Tube: Covent Garden.

BOOKS ETC

26 James St, WC2. Tel: 071-379 6947.
Open: Mon-Sat 10.00-22.00, Sun 12.00-19.00.
Tube: Covent Garden.
Late night bookshop by the tube station.

CHEONG LEEN

4-10 Tower St, WC1. Tel: 071-836 5378. Open: Mon-Sat 10.00-18.30.
Tube: Tottenham Court Rd.
Big Oriental supermarket.

COVENT GARDEN GENERAL STORE

105-111 Long Acre, WC2. Tel: 071-240 0331.
Open: Mon-Sat 10.00-23.00, Sun 11.00-21.00.
Tube: Covent Garden.
Late night shopping for the silliest gizmos. Great fun for browsers.
(The restaurant in the basement has a limited choice for vegans with
some salads and baked potatoes. Open: 10.00-19.30, every day.)

GOLDEN ORIENT

17 Earlham Street, Covent Garden, WC2H. Tel: 071-836 5545.
Open: Mon-Sat 10.00-18.00.
Tube: Covent Garden.
Health food shop with vegetarian sandwiches for £1.10. Also salads,
and some vegan snacks such as pakoras, bhajias and tandoori cutlets.

LONDON ECOLOGY CENTRE

45 Shelton Street, Covent Garden, WC2H 9HJ. Tel: 071-497 2723.
Open: Mon-Sat 10.00-20.00.
Tube: Covent Garden.

Literature and gadgets for ecologists and vegetarians. Lots of recycled animal-, people- and planet-friendly goods. Great place to meet up with a friend.

MUJI

38 Shelton Street, Covent Garden, WC2H 9HJ. Tel: 071-379 1331.
Open: Every day 10.30-19.00 (19.30 Thu-Fri).
Tube: Covent Garden.
The larger of the two Muji shops selling a whole range of simply designed, stylish goods from Japan. They have every sort of container for everything that you'd want to get organised, as well as clothes, household wares and stationery. You can even buy a designer cycle here.

NATURAL SHOE STORE

21 Neal Street, WC2. Tel: 071-836 5254.
Open: Mon-Tue 10.00-18.30 Wed-Fri 10.00-18.00, Sat 10.00-19.00, Sun 12.00-17.30.
Tube: Covent Garden.
Now selling non-leather, breathable Doc Marten shoes.

NEAL STREET EAST

5 Neal Street, WC2. Tel: 071-240 0135/6,
Open: Mon-Sat 10.00-19.00.
Chinese and oriental goods including clothing, books, cards, ornaments, origami, household and kitchen stuff.

NEAL'S YARD WHOLEFOODS

21 Short Gardens, WC2H. Tel: 071-379 8553.
Open: Mon-Sat 9.00-18.00 (18.30 Sat), Sun 10.00-17.30.
Tube: Covent Garden.
Big and busy wholefood store plus lots of high-energy snacks like dried fruit, nuts and trail mix.

WILD THINGS

79 Long Acre, WC2E 9NQ (Drury Lane end). Tel: 071-836 9702.
Open: Mon-Sat 10.00-18.00.
Tube: Covent Garden.
Non-leather shoes, belts, jackets, t-shirts. If your size is out of stock then leave your phone number and they'll call you when it's ready (no cash up front). Great Lynx and Respect posters for your flat, cards, wallets, postcards. Honesty cosmetics. Vegan chocolates. Don't be put off by some of the prices as Wild Things raises money for the Respect for Animals campaign against the fur trade. Also mail order.

WORLD OF DIFFERENCE

London Ecology Centre, 21 Endell Street, Street, Covent Garden, WC2H 9BJ. Tel: 071-379 8208.
Open: Mon-Sat 10.00-18.00.

Tube: Covent Garden.

The green shop in the heart of London. Low energy lightbulbs, sun and wind energy sources, non-toxic paints, recycled paper, Traidcraft goods, books and magazines. Also a full range of animal rights books including this one.

YHA ADVENTURE SHOP

14 Southampton St, WC2. Tel: 071-836 8541.
Open: Mon-Wed 10.00-18.00, Thu-Fri 10.00-19.00, Sat 9.00-18.30.
Tube: Covent Garden, Charing Cross. Between the market and The Strand.

Huge camping and travel store with rucsacs, outdoor wear, tents, sleeping bags (including vegan ones without duck feathers), cooking kit, skiing, cycling, books, maps, climbing. The 12,000 items in stock have all been thoroughly tested and the friendly, helpful staff know them all. They guarantee to beat any competitor's price. 10% discount to Youth Hostels Association members. The only thing we could not find there were vegan hiking boots, which you can get by mail order from the addresses in our chapter on shopping.

WC2N TRAFALGAR SQUARE

The square is overseen by the monument to Lord Nelson, conqueror of the French navy at the battle of Trafalgar. His main enemy this century has been the defecating pigeons who share the square. Check out the National Gallery and the pigeon spotters around Nelson's Column. Trafalgar Square is the venue for mayhem and madness on New Year's eve and the finishing point for many major demonstrations.

ATTRACTIONS

NATIONAL GALLERY

Trafalgar Square north side. Tel: 071-839 3321
Open: Mon-Sat 10.00-18.00, Sun 14.00-18.00
Tube: Leicester Square, Piccadilly Circus. Free.

The biggest of the Big Smoke's 600 art galleries, where you can plan your tour on a computer. A major gallery of European paintings from the last 700 years. Shop. Free guided tours Mon-Sat. Cafe and restaurant on site, see restaurants below. Reach out to your favourite artist via the touch-screen computer information system in the Micro Gallery. Wheelchair access.

NATIONAL PORTRAIT GALLERY

2 St Martins Place, WC2. Tel: 071-306 0055
Open: Mon-Fri 10.00-18.00, Sat 10.00-18.00, Sun 12.00-18.00
Tube: Leicester Square, Charing Cross. Free.

Largest collection of portraits in the world and now a new twentieth century gallery. Bookshop. Wheelchair access via Orange Street.

VEGETARIAN CAFE

CRANKS CHARING CROSS

8 Adelaide Street, WC2. Tel: 071-836 0660
Open: Mon-Fri 8.00-19.00, Sat 9.00-18.00, closed Sunday
Tube: Charing Cross.
Vegetarian. Health Food. Yummy vegetarian cafe by Trafalgar Square. Average £4.00. Eat in or takeaway. There are always two vegan sandwiches, soup, cake and one savoury dish.

OMNIVOROUS RESTAURANTS

FIELDS RESTAURANT

The Crypt, 5 St Martins Place, WC2N 4JH. Tel: 071-839 4342
Open: Mon-Wed 10.00-16, Thu-Sat 10.00-21.30, Sun 10.00-18.30.
Tube: Charing Cross
Omnivorous. International cuisine with lots of cheap vegetarian food, but not always a vegan option. Approximately £5.00 for a two course meal. An enterprise of the church.

NATIONAL GALLERY CAFE

Trafalgar Square, WC2N 5DN. Tel: 071-839 1760
Open: Mon-Sat 10.00-17.00, Sun 14.00-17.00
Tube: Charing Cross, Leicester Square
Omnivorous. Average £5.10 for a main dish. Self-service cafe salads, soups, sandwiches and hot meals. Very helpful and will prepare a vegan dish if asked in advance.

NATIONAL GALLERY RESTAURANT

Trafalgar Square, WC2N 5DN. Tel: 071-839 1769
Open: Mon-Sat 10.00-17.00, Sun 14.00-17.00
Tube: Charing Cross, Leicester Square
Omnivorous. Average £10.00 for a three course meal. Waiter service. Overlooking Trafalgar with vegetarian as standard but no vegan options.

SHOPS

HOLLAND & BARRETT

Unit 16, Embankment Shopping Centre, Villiers Street, WC2N.
Tel: 071-839 4988.
Open: Mon-Fri 08.00-19.00, Sat 09.00-18.00.
Health foods and vegetarian takeaway.

WEIDER HEALTH & FITNESS

Unit 8c, 4 Adelaide Street, WC2N. Tel: 071-240 1363.

Open: Mon-Sat 9.00-18.00 (17.30 Sat).
Tube: Charing Cross.
In the subway. Health food, clothes, bodybuilding and fitness equipment, seminars.

WC2/W1V LEICESTER SQUARE

Traffic-free Leicester Square is the start of clubland, with The Hippodrome, Empire and Maximus discos and lush cinemas. Nearby is Stringfellows nightclub in St Martin's Lane. Try the Half Price Theatre Ticket Booth for cheaper entry to tonight's plays (Mon-Sat 12.00-18.30, cash only). If you think £7.00 is over the top for a cinema, try heading for the multi-screen one in the Trocadero at Piccadilly Circus, or check Time Out magazine for Monday night reductions.

VEGETARIAN RESTAURANTS

CRANKS LEICESTER SQUARE

17 Great Newport Street, WC2H 7JE. Tel: 071-836 5226
Open: Mon-Sat 10.00-22.00, Sun 12.00-19.00
Vegetarian. Healthfood cafe. Healthy and hearty food for an average £4.00, or just have a coffee. Extremely friendly and a good place to write postcards in the evening while you wait for a friend.

WOODLANDS VEGETARIAN RESTAURANT

37 Panton St, SW1Y 4EA. Tel: 071-839 7258
Open: Mon-Sat 12.00-15.00, 17.30-23.00, Sun 18.00-23.00
Tube: Piccadilly, Leicester Square
Vegetarian. South Indian. Big menu with plenty for vegans. Thali £9.95. Iddlies and dosa are very popular for £3.95 and £2.75. Pilau rice £2.95, mixed veg curry £3.25. Desserts include almond halva and carrot halva. Staff not always clear about vegan options. Technically in SW1, Panton St connects the Haymarket to the southwest corner of Leicester Square. This is the chief of three excellent vegetarian restaurants. If you liked it, don't miss the ones listed under Oxford Street, W1, and Wembley, Middlesex.

OMNIVOROUS

CAFE SANTÉ

17 Garrick Street, WC2.Tel: 071-240 7811
Open: Mon-Thu 08.00-02.00, Fri-Sat 10.00-04.00, Sun 11.00-23.00
Tube: Leicester Square
Omnivorous. Cafe. Chic, 50% vegetarian wholefood cafe just outside Leicester Square where you can read the daily papers for free. Light meals, rolls, sandwiches, herbal drinks, coffee, and snacks from the counter. No alcohol. Eat well and look good. Only morsels for vegans.

GABY'S CONTINENTAL BAR
30 Charing Cross Road, Soho, WC2H 0DB. Tel: 071-836 4233
Open: Mon-Sun 8.00-23.00
Tube: Leicester Square
Omnivorous. Middle-Eastern. Average £5.00. Table and takeaway.
Cheap and basic Greek and Lebanese cafe-cum-restaurant on the edge
of Leicester Square, with a wide selection of the most popular food
from that part of the world. Large meals and snacks available.

THE OLIVE TREE
11 Wardour Street, Leicester Square, W1V 3HE.
Tel: 071-734 0808.
Open: Mon-Sat 11.00-23.00, Sun 11.00-22.00.
Tube: Piccadilly Circus, Leicester Square
Omnivorous. Middle Eastern/North African. Average £5.00. Counter
service. Very popular budget restaurant with separate veggie menu
and plenty of vegan options. Dishes include: moussaka, dolmades
(stuffed vine leaves), imanbaialdi (stuffed aubergine), couscous,
goulash with bean curd and heaps of salads.

PIAZZA
92/3 St Martin's Lane, WC2N 4AP. Tel: 071-379 5278
Open: Every day 08.00-23.00 (24.00 Sat)
Tube: Leicester Square
Omnivorous. Italian. Lots of pasta £4.40, takeaway £2.50. Salad £2.50,
takeaway £1.50.

YET MORE MUNCHIES
At the northeast entrance to Leicester Square you'll find a 24-hour
chip shop which sells falafels and hummus in pitta bread. There is all-
you-can eat cabbage salad with it, so eat inside and pile the cabbage on
your plate. A kebab shop off the southeast corner sells falafels for
£1.70 (£1.80 eat in) and vegetarian kebab (hummus and salad in pitta)
for £1.50. The Pizza Hut in Leicester Square has an all-you-can-eat
salad bar with a lot more for vegans than just cabbage, and the
American style Garfunkels restaurant has plenty for vegetarians.

SHOPS

HEALTH FLAIR
65 Charing Cross Road, WC2H 0NE. Tel: 071-287 0940.
Open: Mon-Fri 11.30-19.45, Sat 12.00-19.30.
Tube: Leicester Square.
Vegetarian. Health food shop with lots of clearly labelled vegan
takeaway food. Average £2.00. Slightly north of Leicester Square on
the west side of Charing Cross Road, before you get to all the
bookstores. Also sells body building supplements, flower remedies.

WC2H CHARING CROSS ROAD

Heading north from Leicester Square, bookworms will need a rucsac, librarians a truck. There are multistorey book superstores and also specialist bookshops like Sportspages (sport) and Books For A Change (alternative living). You can spend days browsing without spending a cent, or stock up on reading for several lifetimes. 'Ere we go....

SHOPS

BOOKS FOR A CHANGE

2 Charing Cross Rd, WC2H 0BB. Tel: 071-836 2315.
Fax: 071-497 1036.
Open: Mon-Fri 10.00-18.30, Sat 10.00-18.00.
Tube: Leicester Square
Sells animal rights and vegan volumes including American titles.

SPORTS PAGES

Shopping Centre, Cambridge Circus, Charing Cross Rd, WC2. Tel: 071-240 9604.
Sports books and videos.

ZWEMMER

72 Charing Cross Rd, WC2H 0BB. Tel: 071-240 1559.
Art books at the Oxford University Press bookshop.

FOYLES

119 Charing Cross Road. Tel: 071-437 5660. Tube: Leicester Square.
Open: Mon-Sat 9.00-18.00 (till 19.00 Thur).
Mega-bookshop on many floors selling just about every book.

WATERSTONES

121 Charing Cross Road. Tel: 071-434 4291. Tube: Tottenham Court Road. Open: Mon-Sat 9.30-20.00, Sun 12.00-19.00.
Two more gi-normous shops with a mouth-watering seven floors of books.

W1 THE WEST END

Tottenham Court Road
Chinatown and Soho
Piccadilly Circus
Oxford Street

The West End, bounded by Covent Garden on the east and Hyde Park on the west, is jammed with shops, restaurants, cafes, pubs, clubs, cinemas, theatres and famous landmarks like Piccadilly Circus. It's the entertainment capital of Britain and a great place to blow your hard earned loot. There's so much to see that you could spend a month wandering the streets and just scratch the surface. At lunch-time and 5.00pm the streets and tubes fill with workers from the four or five storey offices above the thousands of shops.

We've divided the West End into four sections clustered around a well known street or streets. Spend a couple of hours checking out computers and hi-fi in Tottenham Court Road, shopping for cheap and exotic supplies in Chinatown supermarkets, or strolling around touristy Piccadilly. Music lovers of all tastes head for the Virgin Megastore and HMV in Oxford Street, and Tower Records at Piccadilly. Enjoy an afternoon shopathon in Oxford Street, which will leave your limbs as knackered as a lie detector at a vivisectors' conference. But then you can deservedly wend your way to one of the myriad veggie grubstops either nearby or in Covent Garden.

Vegetarians in W1 will be delighted to find ten totally vegetarian restaurants and cafes. (not to mention as many again in nearby Covent Garden) We can't speak too highly of the bargain all-you-can-eat lunches at Country Life (Piccadilly, closed Saturday) or Mandeer (Tottenham Court Rd, closed Sunday).

W1P TOTTENHAM COURT ROAD

Continuing north from Charing Cross Rd, Tottenham Court Road is an electric avenue of computer and gadget stores. Discounts available especially for cash purchases. The gigantic Dillons bookshop has 80,000 titles in 500 categories. Irrepressible Richard Branson's vast Virgin Megastore is a must-see at 14 Oxford Street, and close by is a five-screen cinema showing recent big films if you need a rest.

VEGETARIAN RESTAURANTS

CRANKS TOTTENHAM STREET

9-11 Tottenham Street, off Tottenham Court Road, W1P 9PB.
Tel: 071-631 3912
Open: Mon-Fri 8.00-19.30, Sat 9.00-19.30. Closed Sun.
Tube: Goodge Street
Vegetarian. Health Food. Yet another of the seven excellent Cranks
wholefood veggie cafes in Central London. Average feed £3.50.

MANDEER WHOLEFOOD VEGETARIAN RESTAURANT

21 Hanway Place, off Tottenham Court Road, W1P 9DG.
Tel: 071-323 0660, 071-580 3470.
Open: Mon-Sat 12.00-15.00, 18.00-22.30.
Tube: Tottenham Court Road
Vegetarian. Indian wholefood. For a special occasion blow an average
of £12.00, or £8.00 for a basic Thali, in this restaurant. They can do
special diets or without spice, garlic or onion on separate stoves.
Organic wine. At lunchtimes there's a bargain canteen section where
for £3.65 you can lay waste to a Veganosaurus Rex sized platter of
bhajia, samosa, brown rice, veg, chickpeas and dhal. Fab value,
generous portions, and you can chat to other veggiesaurs at the long
table. Everything is vegan except yoghurt. 10% discount to Vegan
Society members.

MINARA VEGETARIAN RESTAURANT

1 Hanway Place, off Tottenham Court Road, W1. Tel: 071-323 0660
Open: Mon-Sat 12.00-15.30, 17.30-23.00
Tube: Tottenham Court Road
Vegetarian. North and South Indian. Very cheap and close to the
Mandeer and Tottenham Court Road tube station. Curry and rice set
lunch for £2.50. Evenings £7.00 for a meal chosen from a large
vegetarian menu.

NON VEGETARIAN RESTAURANTS

RAGAM SOUTH INDIAN RESTAURANT

57 Cleveland Street, W1P 5PQ. Tel: 071-636 9098
Open: Every day 12.00-15.00, 18.00-23.30
Tube: Great Portland Street, Goodge Street
Omnivorous. South Indian. Extensive and reasonably priced vegetarian menu with starters at £1.70, main courses such as dosa, vada and
uttapam for £3.80. Eat in or takeaway. If there is a queue the waiters
will direct you to the local pub which is four doors away and collect you
when there is a free table.

SHOPS

DILLONS

82 Gower Street. Tel: 071-636 1577.
Open: Mon-Fri 09.00-19.00 (09.30 Tue), Sat 09.30-18.00.
Tube: Goodge Street.
A huge bookshop with a staggering 80,000 book titles in 500 categories should keep you browsing for hours.

HOLLAND & BARRETT

19 Goodge Street, W1P 1FD. Tel: 071-580 2886.
Open: Mon-Sat 09.00-18.00 (17.00 Sat).
Tube: Goodge St.
Health food, sandwiches, cakes, drinks.

SOLOMON'S MINE

37 Tottenham Street, W1P. Tel: 071-636 1458.
Open: Mon-Fri 09.30-17.00.
This 11-year-old wholefood shop, takeaway and grocer with a vegetarian proprietor is a real find. Free-range eggs used and sold, vegan snacks always available, lots of character.

VIRGIN MEGASTORE

14-30 Oxford Street. Tel: 071-631-1234.
Open: Mon-Sat 09.30-20.00 (Tue from 10.00), Sun 09.30-18.00.
Tube: Tottenham Court Road.
Richard Branson's massive music emporium is a music lover's paradise and almost as famous as him.

W1V CHINATOWN AND SOHO

Nestling by seedy Soho, Gerard Street's oriental arches host Chinese New Year celebrations in late January or early February. Sundays feel like Hong Kong as the Chinese flock here. Admire lacquer work, origami products, hand painted oriental designs, ceramics, martial arts equipment, masks, pots and pans, artificial flowers and traditional musical instruments. Grocers and supermarkets have cheap rice, noodles, soy sauce, spices, tofu, water chestnuts and eastern vegetables, but your stomach will churn at the sight of carcasses roasting on spits. Chinese restaurants are pretty meaty, though you will usually find vegetarian dishes or a separate vegetarian menu.

ATTRACTIONS

RONNIE SCOTTS JAZZ CLUB
47 Frith Street, Soho, W1. Tel: 071-439 0747.
Open: Mon-Sat 20.30-03.00
Tube: Leicester Square, Piccadilly Circus £12.00.
Unmissable for jazz music fans, strong world music presence, smokey and expensive. Always book in advance to ensure you get a table, then sit back as your drinks are brought to you. Upstairs is The Salsateca, a great little club with Latin, world and dance music.

VEGETARIAN RESTAURANTS

GOVINDA'S PURE VEGETARIAN RESTAURANT
9-10 Soho Street, W1V 5DA. Tel: 071-437 3662, Fax: 071-439 1127 Open: Mon-Sat 11.00-20.30
Tube: Tottenham Court Rd
Full meal for under £5.00. All-you-can-eat buffet of main dishes £3.99 Mon-Fri 15.00-18.00. All-you-can-eat happy hour £2.99 Mon-Sat 19.30-20.30, not including sweets and drinks. Eastern and wholefood cuisine. All dishes freshly prepared on the premises. No fish, meat, eggs, gelatine, rennet, chocolate, refined sugar, garlic, onions or preservatives used in any dishes, no smoking, no alcohol allowed on the premises - but you can still enjoy yourself. You'll be pushed to eat cheaper than this in the West End.

OTHER RESTAURANTS

BHAN THAI
21a Frith Street, Soho, W1V 5TS. Tel: 071-437 8504
Open: Mon-Sat 12.00-14.45, 18.00-23.15, Sun 12.30-14.30, 18.30-22.30
Tube: Leicester Square
Omnivorous. Thai. Average £5.00. Table and takeaway service. Good selection of vegetarian dishes highlighted on the menu with many

being vegan and much cheaper than the meat alternatives. Pudding menu includes coconut ice-cream and tapioca balls with lotus nuts, mmmm!

CHIANG MAI

48 Frith Street, Soho, W1V 5TE. Tel: 071-437 7444
Open: Mon-Sat 12.00-15.00, 16.00-23.00
Tube: Tottenham Court Road, Leicester Square
Omnivorous. Thai. Next door to Ronnie Scott's Jazz Club. A Time Out magazine best vegetarian meal finalist. Separate veggie menu with a choice of simple Thai dishes. Starters £3.75, main courses up to £4.95, Thai curry £4.95, yam hot and sour salads £4.95. Staff confirm whether or not any of the desserts are vegan.

EST

54 Frith Street, Soho, W1. Tel: 071-437 0666
Open: Restaurant Mon-Fri 12.15.00, 18.00-23.00, Sat 18.00-23.30. Bar Mon-Fri 12.00-23.00, Sat 12.00-23.30
Tube: Tottenham Court Road
Omnivorous. Italian. Bar/restaurant. Northern Italian cuisine run by a Frenchman and reflected in the menu. Some vegan choices. Spaghetti with fresh tomato and basil £4.50. Spaghetti with peppers, aubergine, zucchini, asparagus and porcini £5.25. Mixed leaves £2.25, tomato and basil salad £2.25. House wine £8.50 per bottle. Atmosphere generally casual and laid back. Trendy media and advertising professionals lunchtime, lively in the evenings.

MELATI

31 Peter Street, Soho, W1V 3RQ. Tel: 071-437 2011
Open: Mon-Sat 12.00-15.00, 18.00-24.00.
Tube: Leicester Square
Omnivorous. Indonesian. £5.00 minimum for supper. Standard Indonesian favourites with good veggie selection.

MELATI

21 Great Windmill Street, Soho, W1V 7PH. Tel: 071-437 2745
Open: Sun-Fri 12.00-23.30, Sat 12.00-00.30
Tube: Piccadilly Circus
Omnivorous. Indonesian. Average £7.00. Table service. Very busy restaurant with loads of Indonesian specialities, like fried bean curd with peanut sauce, for both vegans and vegetarians. Three course meal for under £12.50 right in the heart of town. Best to book in advance if going in the evening.

MILDRED'S

58 Greek Street, Soho, W1V 5LR. Tel: 071-494 1634.
Open: Mon-Sat 12.00-22.00
Tube: Piccadilly Circus, Tottenham Court Road

Vegetarian and fish. Modern. Often crowded. Average £6.00. Table and counter service. Very popular trendy cafe/restaurant with international menu that changes daily and always gets rave reviews. Vegan options are marked. Not the best place for a quiet chat as it's small and always busy and tables have to be shared.

NEW WORLD CHINESE RESTAURANT

1 Gerrard Place, Soho, W1V 7LL. Tel: 071-734 0396, 071-734 0677 Open: Every day 11.00-23.00.
Tube: Leicester Square, Piccadilly Circus
Omnivorous. Cantonese. Average £3.70. Table service. Usual range of Chinese veggie options.

POLLO

20 Old Compton Street, Soho, W1V 5RE. Tel: 071-734 5917
Open: Mon-Sat 11.30-23.30
Tube: Leicester Square, Tottenham Court Rd, Piccadilly Circus
Italian. Omnivorous. Average £7.00. Very popular, friendly and hectic Italian restaurant with a good choice of pasta for both vegetarians and vegans. Frequented by students, low budget travellers and those wanting a quick and filling cheap meal in the middle of town. No credit cards.

LA REASH COUS COUS HOUSE

23-24 Greek Street, Soho, W1V 5LG. Tel: 071-439 1063, 071-437 2366
Open: Every day 12.00-24.00
Tube: Leicester Square
Omnivorous. Moroccan/Lebanese. Most options from the large menu are vegetarian favourites from the Middle-East including hummus, tabouleh and cous-cous. Starters £3.00, main course £7.00.

SRI SIAM

14 Old Compton Street, Soho, W1V 5PE. Tel: 071-434 3544, 071-287 8775 Open: Mon-Sat 12.00-15.00, 18.00-23.15, Sun 18.00-22.30
Tube: Leicester Square, Tottenham Court Rd, Piccadilly Circus
Omnivorous. Thai. Average £15.00. Vegetarian Society approved menu. Table and takeaway service. More lively atmosphere than most Thai restaurants and with similar choices of vegetarian options, though slightly more expensive.

SHOPS

W.K. HEALTH FOOD

9 Wardour Street, W1V. Tel: 071-494 2088.
Open: 11.30-19.00.
Tube: Leicester Square, Piccadilly Circus.
Chinese health food store. Mainly cosmetics and supplements, very little to eat.

W1 PICCADILLY CIRCUS

North west of Trafalgar Square are Green Park and the ritzy hotels of Piccadilly, leading to bustling Piccadilly Circus. Here the statue of Eros is a favourite meeting place for the young, though once you've met you'll want to move on pretty quickly, probably for an all-you-can-eat vegetarian lunch at Country Life Restaurant. At the British Travel Centre, 12 Regent Street, you can pick up free information on anywhere in Britain and Ireland. Left handers head north two blocks for the shop Anything Left Handed in Brewer Street. You can find all the best records, record makers, and record breakers at:

ATTRACTIONS

TOWER RECORDS SUPERSTORE

1 Piccadilly Circus, W1. Tel: 071-439 2500
Open: Mon-Sat 09.00-24.00, Sun 11.00-22.00
Tube: Piccadilly Circus.
This store is open later than the pubs for those with a serious vinyl addiction.

ROCK CIRCUS

Top Floor, The London Pavillion, Piccadilly Circus, W1.
Tel: 071-734 8025
Open: Mon, Wed, Thur, Sun 11.00-21.00, Tue 12.00-21.00, Fri-Sat 11.00-22.00
Tube: Piccadilly Circus.
£6.95 adult, £5.95 students and senior citizens, £4.95 child, Family ticket for four (at least two must be children) £18.40.
Lots of fun for music fans as the exhibits move and sing via your headphones. Almost as expensive and less animated is:

GUINNESS WORLD OF RECORDS

The Trocadero Centre, Piccadilly Circus, W1. Tel: 071-439 7331.
Open: Mon-Sat 10.00-22.00, Sun 10.00-21.30
Tube: Piccadilly Circus.
£5.75 adults, £4.50 students and senior citizens, children £3.75, Families £15.00.
Tallest, shortest, daftest etc.

MUSEUM OF MANKIND

6 Burlington Gardens, W1. Tel: 071-437 2224 recorded information, 071-323 8599 information desk.
Open: Mon-Sat 10.00-17.00, Sun 14.30-18.00
Tube: Piccadilly Circus. Free.
Most museums are hectic at weekends and calmer on a Monday. But this one is very peaceful and is full of houses, artefacts and costumes showing how folk live all over the world. If you liked this then you

might also enjoy the Commonwealth Institute, W8. Coffee bar open till 16.00.

ROYAL ACADEMY OF ARTS

Burlington House, Piccadilly, W1. Tel: 071-439 7438, recorded information 071-439 4996
Open: Every day 10.00-18.00
Tube: Green Park, Piccadilly Circus

Oldest art institution in London. Entrance free but £5.00 adults per exhibition. Summer exhibition Jun-Aug. Crowded at weekends. Restaurant 071-287 0752 opens from 10.00-17.30, lunch 12.00-15.00. Good selection of vegetarian food and sometimes a vegan option.

VEGETARIAN RESTAURANTS

COUNTRY LIFE VEGETARIAN RESTAURANT

1 Heddon Street, W1R 7LE. Tel: 071-434 2922
Open: Sun-Fri 11.30-15.00
Tube: Oxford Circus, Piccadilly Circus

Vegan (though they use honey in some dishes). Wholefood. An absolute must. Stroll from Piccadilly up plush Regent Street and take the third left to herbivore heaven. It's through the fab foodstore and down the apples and pears to the self-service vegan one plate lunch for £3.75, or £4.50 with soup. Fill your platter from six hot dishes, 12 salads and four dressings. Jurassic sized tummies can even lay out a little extra for dessert. You're given a ticket and pay on your way out. The £4.50 option allows you to refill your plate. £5.25 gets you fruit salad as well. Other options are soup and salad £3.95, soup and fruit salad £3.95, soup with bread £2.00, fuit salad with bread £2.95, salad with bread £2.95. Puddings 95p, cakes £1.05 and £1.20. Various drinks. Vegan cheeses and spreads.

At evening classes, we lucky Londoners watch superchef Carol Marno concoct gourmet feasts, then we devour the lot. Country Life's vegan GP teaches true nutrition at these classes and is available for private consultations. Phone for details, or to make an appointment.

There's also a large wholefood shop with hundreds of delicious vegan foods, organic vegetables and books.

OTHER RESTAURANTS

DOWN MEXICO WAY

25 Swallow Street, Piccadilly, W1R 7HD. Tel: 071-437 9895
Open: Every day 12.00-24.00, bar till 03.00.
Tube: Piccadilly Circus

Omnivorous. Mexican. Average £15.00 for three course meal. Standard Mexican fare in this large and very lively restaurant with its own DJ.

Fajitas, tortillas and burritos are all vegetarian whilst vegan options include vegetable chilli, stuffed cabbage and stuffed peppers.

SMOLLENSKY'S BALLOON BAR & RESTAURANT
1 Dover Street, Piccadilly, W1X 3PJ. Tel: 071-491 1199
Open: Mon-Sat 12.00-24.00, Sun 11.00-22.30
Tube: Green Park
Omnivorous. American. Average £6.00. Table service. Very cheesy menu with vegetarian dishes like fried Camembert. With a little effort a number of the other dishes could easily be vegan. Live music every day.

SUSHI & SOZAI
In Piccadilly underground station, W1. Tel: 071-734 8746
Open: Mon-Sat 11.00-23.00
Japanese takeaway. Several vegan vegetable dishes with rice or noodles £3.50, £2.50 after 22.00. Miso soup contains fish stock. Other branches 51A Queen Victoria Street, EC4 (071 332 0108) and Moorgate.

VEERASWAMY'S
99-101 Regent Street, W1R 7HB. Tel: 071-734 1401, 071-437 1671
Open: Every day 12.00-14.30 and 18.00-23.00.
Tube: Piccadilly Circus
Omnivorous. North and South Indian. Average £15.00. 18 hole Doc Marten boots would look out of place in this up-market Indian restaurant which has a separate vegetarian menu. Food is excellent but prices are likely to be out of reach of the budget traveller.

SHOPS

ABSOLUTELY NUTS
Green Park Tube Station, Piccadilly, W1. Tel: 071-496 5299.
Open: Mon-Fri 07.3-20.00, Sat 11.00-19.00
Grab a snack and head for the park. In the underground station you'll find 32 kinds of nuts and vegetarian sweets to serve yourself. Crisps, vegetarian and vegan flapjacks, cereal bars, canned drinks.

ANYTHING LEFT HANDED
57 Brewer St, W1R 3FB. Tel: 071-437 3910.
Open: Mon-Fri 9.30-17.00. Sat 9.30-14.00, closed Sun.
Everything and anything for left-handers and those who buy presents for them. Left-handed cooks will love the corkscrews, can openers, potato peelers, knives, scissors, and other goodies like pens and address books. Send three stamps or international reply coupons for details of mail order and left-handers' club membership.

APHRODISIA

25 Shepherd Market, W1Y. Tel: 071-499 2901.
Open: Mon-Fri 10.30-17.30.
Tube: Green Park

A natural, healthy store nestling between Curzon St and Piccadilly, with foods, books including veganism, Japanese and personal growth, ginseng, chocolates.

THE BODY & FACE PLACE

59 Shaftesbury Ave, W1. Tel: 071-439 2092.
Open: Mon-Sat 10.30-18.30.
Tube: Piccadilly Circus.

Close to Piccadilly Circus is a super cosmetics shop. Comprehensive range of skin care products, based on plant oils and herbal extracts. No animal testing and manufactured in their own workshops in Scotland. All ingredients listed. Beautiful packaging. Personalised gift baskets made to order. Also dried flowers and bouquets.

THE BODY SHOP

Piccadilly Pavilion, The London Pavilion, Piccadilly Circus, W1V 9LA.
Open: Mon-Sat 11.00-17.45.

NUTSTOP

in Piccadilly tube station. Tel: 071-434 0069.
Open: Mon-Sat: 8.30-22.00, Sun 11.00-20.30.
All kinds of loose nuts, hot and cold drinks.

W1 OXFORD STREET

Oxford Street is a mile long shopping frenzy, crammed with famous department stores, all the clothing chainstores, postcard and souvenir shops, employment agencies, and a plethora of small shops. Why not pop into Selfridges and congratulate them on closing their fur department. Don't miss opulent Bond Street and Regent Street, with the six storey toy shop Hamleys at 188. Late night shopaholics can visit Oxford Street on Thursdays until about 20.00, and you can buy food from every continent at the all-night international grocers of Edgware Road.

The low numbers start at Tottenham Court Rd in the east, with Virgin Megastore at 14 Oxford Street, and run west to Marble Arch and Edgware Road. At the Virgin end you'll find fine veggie fare at Govinda's (see Soho) and Mandeer (see Tottenham Court Rd). Half way along at Oxford Circus, relax in Nuthouse or Cranks Marshall Street. Around number 350 is Bond Street, where you can tank up on cruelty-free munchies at Woodlands or another Cranks next to Selfridges. There's a Holland & Barrett health food shop in the Bond Street

underground station. And at Marble Arch you can flop out in Hyde
Park with a picnic.

VEGETARIAN RESTAURANTS

CRANKS MARSHALL STREET
8 Marshall Street, W1. Tel: 071-437 9431.
Open: Mon-Fri 08.00-20.00, Sat 9.00-20.00. Closed Sun.
Tube: Oxford Circus
Vegetarian. Health Food. Vegetarian counter service by day and table
service at night. Average £7.00. Health food shop open till 18.30 (17.30
Sat).

CRANKS ST CHRISTOPHER'S PLACE
23 Barrett Street, W1M 5HP. Tel: 071-495 1340.
Open: Mon-Fri 8.00-19.00, Sat 9.00-19.00. Closed Sun.
Tube: Bond Street
Vegetarian. Health food. Cracking wholefood for non-cranky (ie.
vegetarian) palettes. Average £3.50. (The wonderful Cranks shops in
London are not to be confused with the rather dull Cranks food section
on cross-channel ferries, where we could not find anything vegan apart
from a very small salad selection.)

NUTHOUSE VEGETARIAN RESTAURANT
26 Kingly Street, W1R 5LB. Tel: 071-437 9471.
Open: Mon-Fri 10.30-19.00, Sat 11.00-18.00. Closed Sun.
Tube: Oxford Circus
Vegetarian. Health food. Vegetarian eat in with counter service,
takeaway and shop. Average £5.00. Good cheap bolt hole when
shopping in Regent Street. Decor is spartan but food is good, there is a
wide menu and always vegan options.

RAW DEAL
65 York Street, Marylebone, W1H 1PQ. Tel: 071-262 4841
Open: Mon-Sat 10.00-22.00. Closed Sun.
Tube: Marylebone, Baker St.
Vegetarian. Health Food. Quiet and basic vegetarian cafe with
takeaway, away from the bustle of the Marylebone Road and handy for
Madame Tussaud's and Regents Park. Have not been that sympathetic
to vegans in the past but the times they are a changin' we've heard,
especially in the evenings. Average £3.60. Bring your own alcohol.

WOODLANDS RESTAURANT
77 Marylebone Lane, W1M 5GA. Tel: 071-486 3862
Open: Every day 12.00-14.30, 18.00-22.30
Tube: Bond Street
Vegetarian South Indian. Minimum Charge £4.40. Average £9.00.
Friendly and simple restaurant that seats 70. Serves South Indian

specialities including pancakes and steamed rice cakes. Vegetable
Thalis are £9.95 with loads for vegans.

NON VEGETARIAN RESTAURANTS

GAYLORD RESTAURANT

79-81 Mortimer Street, Fitzrovia, W1N 7TB.Tel: 071-636 0808,
071-580 3615
Open: Every day 12.00-15.00, 18.00-23.30
Tube: Oxford Circus
Omnivorous. Indian. Average £13.50 for three courses. Basic veg curry
£3.50, rice £2.50. Table service. Lots of vegetarian food. Uses vegetable
ghee.

SHOPS

BERWICK STREET MARKET

Open: Mon-Sat 09.00-17.00. Tube: Oxford Circus.
Food and clothing.

THE BODY SHOP

66 Oxford Street, W1N 9DD.
Open: Mon-Sat 09.30-19.30 (Tue & Thu 20.00, Sat 18.30),
Sun 12.00-18.00.
Beautiful presents for yourself or someone special.

THE BODY SHOP

268 Oxford Street, W1N 9DD.
Open: Mon-Fri 09.30-19.30 (Thu 20.30), Sat 09.30-18.30.

THE BODY SHOP

374 Oxford Street, W1N 9HB.
Open: Mon-Fri 09.30-19.15 (Thu 20.15), Sat 09.30-18.30.

THE BODY SHOP

32-34 Great Marlborough Street, W1V 1HA.
Open: Mon-Fri 10.30-19.00 (Thu 19.30), Sun 10.00-18.30.

CHURCH STREET MARKET

Off Edgware Road. Open: Tue-Sat 09.00-17.00.

HAMLEYS

188 Regent Street, W1. Tel: 071-734 3161.
Open: Mon-Wed 10.00-18.00, Thu 10.00-20.00, Fri 10.00-18.30, Sat
09.30-18.30, Sun 12.00-18.00. Tube: Oxford Circus.
World's biggest toy shop on six floors. Nearby is the Disney store. Both
have a baby changing room.

HMV

150 Oxford Street. Tel: 071-631 3423.
Open: Mon-Sat 9.30-19.00, Thur till 20.00. Tube: Oxford Circus.
Record superstore.

HOLLAND & BARRETT

123 Oxford Street, W1R. Tel: 071-287 3624.
Open: Mon-Sat 8.30-19.00 (20.00 Thu). Tube: Oxford Circus.
Health food shop. Takeaway food not vegan.

HOLLAND & BARRETT

In Bond Street underground station.
Open: Mon-Sat 8.30-19.00 (20.00 Thu).

HOLLAND & BARRETT

78 Baker Street. W1M 1DL. Tel: 071-935 3544.
Open: Mon-Sat 9.00-18.00 (17.30 Sat) Tube: Baker Street.
Health foods and non-vegan takeaway.

MUJI

26 Great Marlborough Street, West Soho, W1V 1HL. Tel: 071-494 1197.
Open: Mon-Sat 10.00-18.30 (19.00 Thu-Fri). Tube: Oxford Circus.
One of the two Muji shops selling a whole range of simply designed
stylish goods from Japan. They have every sort of container for
everything that you'd want to get organised, as well as clothes,
household wares and stationery.

NUTRI CENTRE LTD

7 Park Crescent, W1N. Tel: 071-436 5122.
Open: Mon-Fri 10.00-19.00, Sat 10.00-14.00.
Tube: Regents Park, Great Portland St.
Mainly cosmetics and supplements suitable for vegans and vegetar-
ians. Some snacks, such as gorgeous Plamil vegan chocolate bars for
90p.

NUTSTOP

In Baker Street underground station.
Open: Mon-Wed 9.00-21.00, Thu-Fri 9.00-22.30, Sat-Sun 11.00-19.30.
Self-service nuts and vegetarian snacks.

WHOLEFOOD

24 Paddington Street, W1M. Tel: 071-935 3924.
Open: Mon-Thu 8.45-18.00, Fri to 18.30, Sat to 13.00. Tube: Baker St.
Good selection of wholefoods, organic fruit and veg, books. Takeaway
pasties delivered Wed.

SOUTH WEST (INNER)

SW1	*Westminster, Victoria, Belgravia, Pimlico, St James's, Sloane Street*
SW3	*Knightsbridge, Chelsea, King's Road*
SW5	*Earls Court*
SW6	*Fulham, Parson's Green*
SW7	*South Kensington, Gloucester Road*
SW10	*West Brompton*

This chapter covers the south west postcodes sandwiched between the river Thames and Hyde Park from Fulham to Westminster. You're still very much in tourist London, with the emphasis on shopping and sightseeing.

Start at the government ministries and historic sights of Westminster, going through the residential terrace blocks of Victoria with its massive train and bus stations, the fashion stores of Chelsea, to the Australasian pubs and adventure travel agencies of Earls Court. There are some awesome and amazing museums in South Kensington. Shopping addicts can run up a huge credit card bill for high fashion in Knightsbridge and the King's Road, or have heaps of fun just browsing.

There's not as much to eat here as in the West End (W1), but with this guide in your pocket vegetarians and vegans won't be famished. Choose restaurants carefully as almost the same meal can cost you five times as much in a luxury place. And don't miss the new vegan cafe Ploughshares, tucked away in an antiques market in SW10.

SW1 WESTMINSTER & VICTORIA

Starting at Trafalgar Square, wander down Whitehall past Downing Street (John Major's is the grey house at no. 10) to Westminster Abbey, Parliament and Big Ben. Stroll through lovely St James's Park to Buckingham Palace.

The Victoria Coach (bus) and Train stations serve South East England, Europe and Gatwick airport. If you're heading for the coach station, it's a long 10 minutes walk with your luggage from the underground and trains to the coach, half way between Victoria and Sloane Square underground stations. Grab some grub from Victoria Kebab by the number 36 bus stop at Victoria station, where the menu features several vegetarian takeaways from £1.00. There's a snack shop in the underground station itself called Treats which sells vegan flapjacks and vegetarian pasties. Alternatively, we've included a few high-class (dead expensive) restaurants with veggie options for our numerous vegetarian movie and rock star readers. If you think this is serious money, check out the book 'London on £1000 a day (before dinner)', from better bookshops.

ATTRACTIONS

BUCKINGHAM PALACE

Tel: 071-930 4832 Tube: St James's Park, Victoria
Flag flies when the Queen is at home. Changing of the Guard takes place May-July 11.30 daily, Aug-Apr 11.30 alternate days. The Palace first opened its gates in the summer of 1993 to raise money to help restore fire damaged Windsor Castle. At least the occupants are better off than the animals they slaughter on their hunting trips. To see where they'll be tomorrow, check the court circular column in The Times, Daily Telegraph or Independent. Royal person spotters can visit certain parts of the palace. Queen's Gallery Tue-Sat 10.00-17.00, Sun 14.00-17.00. £2.00, £1.50 concessions.
State apartments open Aug-Sep 071-493 3175. Royal Mews, winter Wed 12.00-16.00, and Apr-Sep Tue-Thu. Entrance in Buckingham Palace Road.

HOUSES OF PARLIAMENT

Parliament Square, SW1. Tel: 071-219 4272 Tube: Westminster
House of Commons (the elected one) when in session Mon-Thur 14.30-20.30, Fri 9.30-15.00. House of Lords (the other one) Mon-Wed from 14.30, Thur from 15.00, Fri from 11.00. Get back to basics and watch democracy in action. It's free but best to book tickets in advance. It's easier to get in to see the Lords but an altogether more soporific experience. Magnificent building architecturally.

INSTITUTE OF CONTEMPORARY ART (ICA)

The Mall, SW1. Tel: 071-930 3647, recorded info 071-930 639
Tube: Charing Cross, Piccadilly Circus
Exciting contemporary art gallery £1.50, theatre, cinema £4.50, dance venue, bookshop, opposite St James's Park. This is the 'chillest' place to be seen in your non-leather black jacket. Cafe open 12.00-21.00, bar 12.00-15.00, 19.30-22.30.

ST JAMES'S PARK

The Mall, SW1. Open: Dawn to dusk daily. Tube: St James's Park
Drop out of the West End maelstrom for a picnic lunch in this tranquil park.

WESTMINSTER ABBEY

Dean's Yard, SW1. Tel: 071-222 5152
Open: Daily 8.00-18.00 (Wed till 19.45) Tube: St James's Park, Westminster
Free for nave but charges for other parts. Medieval Church of England church that acts as burial place and seat of coronation for English monarchs. Photos Wednesday evenings only. Cassette tour, guided tours, shop, wheelchair access.

WESTMINSTER CATHEDRAL
Victoria Street, SW1. Tel: 071-834 7452.
Open: Daily 07.00-20.00 (19.00 winter)
Tube: Victoria Free.
Spiritual home of the Catholic Church in England. Gift shop.

VEGETARIAN RESTAURANTS AND CAFES

ROSSANA'S RESTAURANT
17 Strutton Ground, off Victoria St, SW1P 2HY. Tel: 071-233 1701.
Open: Mon-Fri 12.00-23.00, women only evenings Wed-Fri.
Tube: St. James's Park
Vegetarian. Intimate, cosy, vegetarian restaurant, serving varied
menu which changes every month. Good atmosphere. Price per head
includes wine approx £9.00. Free parking outside after 18.30.

WILKINS NATURAL FOODS
61 Marsham Street, Westminster, SW1P 3DP. Tel: 071-222 4038 shop,
071-233 3402 restaurant.
Open: Mon-Fri shop 08.00-17.30.
Tube: St James's Park, Westminster
Vegetarian. Basic wholefood café, takeaway and shop. Half the food is
vegan. Homemade cakes and rolls, soup, savouries, salads, veg bake,
baked spuds. £2.50-£2.75.

THE WREN AT ST JAMES'S
35 Jermyn Street, SW1. Tel: 071-437 9419
Open: Mon-Sat 08.00-19.00, Sun 09.00-17.00
Tube: Green Park
Vegetarian. Wholefood. Noted for their soups, bakes of the day and
carrot cake. Vegan soup and chilli every day. Main courses are £3.95,
may be vegan, and include hot pots, bakes, lasagne, shepherdess pie,
broccoli mournay, quiches and salads. Unlicensed. Smoking outside.
95% baked on the premises. Set in attractive courtyard and very
popular with tourists, shoppers and people visiting the church next
door.

OTHER UP-MARKET RESTAURANTS

L'AUBERGE DE PROVENCE
St James's Court Hotel, Buckingham Gate, SW1. Tel: 071-834 6655
Open: Mon-Fri 12.30-14.30, 19.30-23.00, Sat 19.30-22.30
Tube: Victoria, St. James's Park
Omnivorous. French. Average Lunch £23.50, dinner £30.00 for three
courses. Vegetarian starters are provincial salad or mushroom ravioli.
Two main courses are a selection of vegetables in pastry with a creamy
garlic sauce, and another similar dish. There's nothing vegan, but it
could be arranged.

THE CONSERVATORY

Lanesborough Hotel, Hyde Park Corner, Victoria, SW1X 7TX.
Tel: 071-259 5599
Open: Every day 07.00-24.00
Tube: Hyde Park Corner

Omnivorous. Modern International. Worth a look for rich veggies. 7.00-
11.00 is time for breakfast, a snip at £11.50 for vegetarian fruit dishes,
granola, porridge, bakery, waffles, pancakes, juice, coffee. Three
course vegetarian lunch £18.75, dinner £24.50, changes weekly, eg
walnut and celery risotto followed by Mediterranean cassoulet with
mixed pulses and spices, then carrot and sultana spiced cake. Yummy.
A la carte menu includes wild mushroom risotto at £8.50 starter,
£12.00 main course, roasted artichoke salad starter £8.75, cannelloni,
basil lasagne.

THE INN OF HAPPINESS

St James's Court Hotel, Buckingham Gate, Victoria, SW1.
Tel: 071-834 6655
Open: Every day 12.30-15.00 (not Sat), 19.30-23.00.
Tube: St James's Park

Omnivorous. Chinese. Average £35.00-40.00 for two people. Starters
include fried bean curd and okra, vegetable spring rolls, several soups.
Main courses have lots of bean curd, noodles and veg. Desserts offer
fruit, sorbet, lychees.

OTHER BARGAIN RESTAURANTS

VICTORIA KEBAB

*Victoria bus station, by the 36 bus stop, other side of the bus stops from
the railway station.*
Open: Every day 11.00-05.00
Tube: Victoria

Turkish. Takeaway. Open almost all night. Before you board the night
train or coach to Europe, check out the several cheap vegetarian
choices. Salad or chips in pitta £1.00, hummus and salad in pitta £1.50,
falafel and salad £1.80, hummus salad roll £1.00. Extra salad 50p.

THE WELL

2 Eccleston Place, SW1. (main entrance Elizabeth St) Tel: 071-730 7303
Open: Mon-Sat 9.00 or 9.30-17.00 or 18.00. Lunch 11.30-15.30.
Tube: Victoria

Omnivorous. Coffee Bar with lunch counter service. Lots for veggies
like lentil dishes, pasta dishes, potatoes, cooked fresh each day. Stuffed
potato with salad £3.50. Veg soup £2.40. Sometimes vegan. They make
their own bread and scones.

SHOPS

THE BODY SHOP
Unit 9, Victoria Place, SW1W 9SA.
Open: Mon-Fri 08.00-20.00, Sat 09.00-18.00, Sun 12.00-18.00.

HEALTH PLACE AT VICTORIA
11 Strutton Ground, SW1P. Tel: 071-222 4588.
Open: Mon-Fri 7.00-18.00. Tube: St James's Park.
Health food shop, with vegan takeaways.

HOLLAND & BARRETT
Unit 5, 10 Warwick Way, SW1V 1RU. Tel: 071-834 4796.
Open: Mon-Sat 9.00-18.00 (from 9.30 Sat). Tube: Victoria.
Health foods and non-vegan sandwiches and pasties.

REVITAL HEALTH PLACE
3a The Colonnades, 123-151 Buckingham Palace Road, SW1W. Tel:
071-976 6615.
Open: Mon-Fri 08.30-19.00, Sat 09.00-17.00.
Health food shop with macrobiotic foods and a large range of sea
vegetables. Also vegan desserts, pasties, pizza and cakes - all freshly
made. Nutritionist based at shop. Sister shop in NW10.

SLOANE HEALTH SHOP
32 Sloane Square, SW1W 8AQ. Tel: 071-730 7046.
Open: Mon-Fri 8.30-19.00, Sat 9.00-18.00, Sun 10.00-17.00.
Tube: Sloane Square.
Health food, vitamins, BWC vegan cosmetics.

VICTORIA HEALTH FOOD & GROCERS
17 Elizabeth Street, SW1W. Tel: 071-730 7556.
Open: every day 8.30-18.30. Tube: Victoria.
Sunday grocer that no longer sells health food, just groceries and
flapjacks.

YHA ADVENTURE SHOP
In Campus Travel, 52 Grosvenor Gardens, SW1. Tel: 071-823 4739.
Open: Mon-Sat 9.00-18.00 (20.00 Thu).
Tube: Victoria.
Backpacking and camping gear and a bargain travel agent.

SW3 CHELSEA, KNIGHTSBRIDGE AND KING'S ROAD

In the King's Road and north to Brompton Road you'll find high
fashion and high prices. Check out the titanic, aristocratic Harrods,
which stocks absolutely everything for the well-heeled movie star from
tinned caterpillars to grand pianos. Down to earth clobber abounds in

Kensington Church Street and Kensington High Street (W8). Vegans won't find much to eat here unless they head for Ploughshares in SW10.

NON VEGETARIAN RESTAURANTS

HARRODS' HEALTH JUICE BAR

Harrods' basement, Brompton Road, Knightsbridge, SW3.
Tel: 071-730 1234.
Open: Mon-Sat 10.00-18.00 (Wed-Fri 19.00). Closed Sun.
Tube: Knightsbridge
Omnivorous. Cafe. Buffet. Freshly squeezed orange juice £1.25 small, £2.00 large. Coffee £1.60. Baked potato £2.55 plain, £3.50-£4.95 with filling. Pasta with veg £5.50. Not much vegan food.

PIZZA ON THE PARK

11-13 Knightsbridge, SW1X 7LY. Tel: 071-235 5550
Open: Every day 12.00-24.00 Tube: Knightsbridge
Omnivorous. Italian. Average £6.00. Veg chilli sin carne £6.00, pasta, salads. Can do vegan food. Jazz Music.

SYDNEY STREET CAFE

125 Sydney Street, SW3. Tel: 071-352 5600
Open: Every day 9.30-17.30, till 23.00 summer.
Tube: South Kensington
Omnivorous. Barbecue and international. Menu changes every two - three weeks. Always has veggie burgers, baked potatoes, many salads. £4.95 main course. Mostly outside seating. In the summer they have all-you-can-eat barbies for £10.00, which include a starter, then veggie-burgers, veggie sausages, corn on the cob, baked potatoes and salad.

ZEN CHINESE RESTAURANT

Chelsea Cloisters, Sloane Avenue, Chelsea, SW3 3DN.
Tel: 071-589 1781, 071-584 0596
Open: Mon-Fri 12.00-15.00, 18.00-23.00, Sat-Sun 12.00-23.30
Tube: South Kensington
Omnivorous. Chinese. Average £20.00. Lots of vegetarian food including bean curd.

SHOPS

THE BODY SHOP

54 King's Road, SW3 4DU.
Open: Mon-Sat 09.30-18.15, Sun 12.00.17.00.

THE BODY SHOP

15 Brompton Road, Knightsbridge, SW3 1ED.
Open: Mon-Tue, Sat 10.00-18.00, Wed-Fri 10.00-19.00, Sun 13.00-17.00.

CORNUCOPIA
51 Chelsea Manor Street, SW3. Tel: 071-352 7403.
Open: Mon-Fri 10.00-18.00. Tube: Sloane Square.
Sells curative herbs, homeopathy, flower remedies, aromatherapy.

HARRODS
Knightsbridge, SW3. Tel: 071-730 1234.
Open: Mon-Sat 10.00-18.00 (19.00 Wed-Fri) Tube: Knightsbridge.
London's most famous department store. Look out for Joan Collins.

HARVEY NICHOLS
109 Knightsbridge, SW3. Tel: 071-235 5000.
Open: Mon-Fri 10.00-19.00 (20.00 Wed), Sat 10.00-18.00.
Tube: Knightsbridge.
Here are all the clothes you can't possibly afford, under one roof.

SW5 EARLS COURT

Kangaroo valley, home of Aussies and Kiwis, and shops that sell Vegemite. And only one veggie-friendly restaurant we know of. So all you antipodean veggies, let us know where you forage please mates. See under Kensington (W8) for other nearby Lebanese restaurants, or head for the vegan restaurant Ploughshares in Lots Road, SW10.

NON VEGETARIAN RESTAURANTS

BAALBEK RESTAURANT
18 Hogarth Place, Earls Court, SW5 0QY. Tel: 071-373 7199
Open: Mon-Fri 18.30-22.30.
Tube: Earls Court
Omnivorous. Lebanese. The vegan menu has 20 starters for £2.35, and five main dishes £4.25, plus 10% service charge.

SHOPS

GO BICYCLE
9 Templeton Place, SW5. Tel: 071-373 3657
Open: Wed-Sat 09.30-18.00 and more days as they get busy in the summer.
Specialist bike hire and all accessories. Basic hybrid £10 per day, £20 weekend, £40 per week. Deposit of £150 required - Visa and Access will do nicely. They are in the car park of the Hotel George. Insurance available for £1.00 per day that reduces any liability for damage to the bike by 50%.

HEALTH CRAZE
115 Earls Court Road, SW5. Tel: 071-244 7784.
Open: Every day 9.00-24.00.

SW6 FULHAM

VEGETARIAN RESTAURANTS

MAMTA
692 Fulham Road, Fulham, SW6. Tel: 071-736 5914.
Open: Wed-Sun 12.30-15.00, Mon-Sat 18.00-22.30.
Tube: Parsons Green
Vegetarian. Indian. Average £11.00. Vegan or Jain (no onion or garlic) thali £7.25. Swish restaurant specialising in masala dosa, a giant stuffed pancake, served with coconut chutney and sambhar (dhal with vegetables). Use vegetable or butter ghee. Very popular. Excellent quality food. Booking advised.

WINDMILL WHOLEFOODS
486 Fulham Road, Fulham, SW6 5NH. Tel: 071-385 1570
Open: Every day restaurant 10.30-23.00 (Sun 12.00-23.00), shop 9.30-18.00, (Sun 10.00-15.00)
Tube: Fulham Broadway
Vegetarian. Health Food. Average £6.00. Good variety of wholefoods and salads with at least two dishes for vegans. Counter and takeaway service, table service evenings. Lunch main course £3.80 day, £4.80 Sun. Evening main course £4.20-5.50, starter £2.20. Very cosy, with jazz music evenings and classical by day. Organic wine, beer and cider. Also a wholefood shop.

SHOPS

HEALTH & DIET CENTRES
5 Jerdan Place SW6. Tel: 071 385 0015. Open: Mon-Sat 9.00-18.00.
Tube: Fulham Broadway.
Health foods and takeaway, which can order vegan food.

HEALTH FOODS
767 Fulham Road, SW6. Tel: 071-736 8848.
Open: Mon-Sat 9.00-18.00.
Tube: Parsons Green.
Health food, sandwiches (sometimes vegan).

SW7 SOUTH KENSINGTON

Here you'll find three of the biggest and most fascinating museums in the world.

ATTRACTIONS

NATURAL HISTORY MUSEUM
Cromwell Road, SW7. Tel: 071-938 9123.

Open: Mon 12.00-17.50, Tue-Sun 10.00-18.00, Sun 11.00-18.00.
Tube: South Kensington
£3.50 adult, £1.75 under 17's, under five's free, £8.00 family (two
adults, two children). Free Mon-Fri 16.30-18.00, Sat-Sun 17.00-18.00.
Enter for free late afternoon to see the massive environment gallery
and robotic dinosaurs. Next door is the:

VICTORIA AND ALBERT MUSEUM
Cromwell Road, SW7. Tel: 071-938 8500, recorded information 071-938
8441, exhibitions 071-938 8349
Open: Mon 12.00-17.50, Tue-Sun 12.00-17.50
Tube: South Kensington
Free, or pay the 'voluntary' donation £2.00 adult, 50p under 16's.
11 kilometres of quiet galleries oozing with stunning decorative
antiques. Restaurant open till 17.00. Shop. Wheelchairs available.

SCIENCE MUSEUM
Exhibition Road, SW7. Tel: 071-938 8000, 071 938 8080, recorded
information 071-938 8123.
Open: Mon-Sat 10.00-18.00, Sun 11.00-18.00
Tube: South Kensington.
£4.50 adults; £2.50 senior citizens, children, students; free after 16.30
and for under five's, disabled.
Full of all things scientific to play with, with more knobs than a space
shuttle. There is a new gallery on nutrition called Food for Thought -
which might give more thought to the cruelty-free diet if it wasn't
heavily influenced by you know McWho. Shop, bookstore, cafe.

NON VEGETARIAN RESTAURANTS

KWALITY TANDOORI
38 Thurloe Place, Brompton, SW7 2HP. Tel: 071-589 3663
Open: Every day 12.00-14.30, 18.00-24.00
Tube: South Kensington
Omnivorous. Indian. Vegetable curry £2.75, rice £1.50. Veg biryani
£4.55. Uses vegetable ghee.

SHOPS

HEALTH CRAZE
24 Old Brompton Road, SW7. Tel: 071-589 5870.
Open: Mon-Fri 8.45-19.30, Sat 9.30-18.30.
Tube: South Kensington.
Health foods, bread and takeaway with vegan snacks like samosas.

SW10 WEST BROMPTON

VEGAN RESTAURANTS

PLOUGHSHARES VEGAN RESTAURANT

The Auction Rooms, 71 Lots Road, Chelsea, SW10. Tel: 071-351 7771
Open: Fri, Sun 10.00-16.00, Sat 10.00-13.00, Mon 10.00-20.30
Tube: Fulham Broadway
Vegan. Cafe. The newest vegan place in London and sure to be a
winner as it's run by vegan food company Ploughshares of Glaston-
bury, who also train vegan chefs on the NVQ. Main meal changes
daily, such as spaghetti with asparagus, mushroom, red pepper and
almonds plus salad. Vegan pizza made in their own bakery. Large
selection of salads. Freshly made soup with organic ingredients £2.50
with bread. Sandwiches with home-made pate, vegan cream cheese,
hummus. Ploughshares cakes, gluten-free, sugar-free, from 80p.
Organic tea and coffee, and the house drink: hot apple with organic
lemon and ginger. Unlicensed. No smoking. It is planned to open a
high street restaurant in the future. The cafe is inside the auction
rooms where antiques are being sold, and it cannot be seen from the
street.

OTHER RESTAURANTS

KINGDOM RESTAURANT

457 Fulham Road, Fulham, SW10 9UZ. Tel: 071-352 0206
Open: Every day 12.00-14.30, 18.00-23.3.
Tube: Fulham Broadway
Omnivorous. Chinese. Average £8.00. Special set menu for vegetarians
£12.50. Set lunch menu £5.50. Main courses £3.30-5.30.

SHOPS

HOLLAND & BARRETT

220 Fulham Road, SW10 9NB. Tel: 071-352 9939.
Open: Mon-Sat 9.30-18.00 (17.30 Sat).
Tube: South Kensington.
Health foods plus takeaway sandwiches and pasties, which may not be
vegan.

Remember to say you saw it in the Cruelty-Free Guide

OUTER LONDON POSTCODES

EAST LONDON

E1	Docklands, Spitalfields, Whitechapel, St Katherine's Dock
E2	Bethnal Green
E3	Bow, Roman Road
E4	Chingford
E5	Clapton
E6	East Ham, Upton Park
E7	Forest Gate
E8	Hackney
E9	Homerton, Victoria Park
E10	Leyton, Lee Bridge Road
E11	Leytonstone
E12	Newham, Wanstead
E13	Plaistow
E14	Limehouse
E15	Stratford, West Ham
E16	Canning Town
E17	Walthamstow
E18	Woodford, Redbridge

NORTH LONDON

N1	Islington, King's Cross, Shoreditch
N2	East Finchley
N3	Finchley, Fortis Green
N4	Finsbury Park, Stroud Green
N5	Highbury
N6	Highgate
N7	Holloway
N8	Hornsey, Crouch End, Turnpike Lane
N9	Enfield, Edmonton
N10	Muswell Hill
N11	Friern Barnet
N12	North Finchley
N13	Palmer's Green
N14	Southgate, Oakwood
N15	Seven Sisters
N16	Stoke Newington, Stamford Hill
N17	Tottenham
N18	Upper Edmonton
N19	Archway, Upper Holloway, Tufnell Park
N20	Totteridge & Whetstone
N21	Winchmore Hill
N22	Wood Green

NORTH WEST LONDON

NW1	Camden Town, Chalk Farm, Regent's Park, Euston, Drummond Street,Marylebone
NW2	Neasden, Cricklewood
NW3	Hampstead, Belsize Park, Swiss Cottage
NW4	Hendon
NW5	Kentish Road
NW6	Kilburn, West Hampstead
NW7	Mill Hill
NW8	St John's Wood
NW9	Kingsbury
NW10	Willesden, Harlesden
NW11	Golders Green, Temple Fortune

SOUTH EAST LONDON

SE1	Borough, Waterloo, Old Kent Road, Elephant & Castle, London Bridge
SE2	Abbeywood
SE3	Blackheath
SE4	Brockley
SE5	Camberwell
SE6	Catford
SE7	Charlton
SE8	Deptford
SE9	Eltham
SE10	Greenwich
SE11	Oval, Kennington, Vauxhall
SE12	Lee, Grove Park
SE13	Lewisham
SE14	New Cross
SE15	Peckham, Nunhead
SE16	Rotherhithe
SE17	Walworth
SE18	Woolwich, Plumstead
SE19	Crystal Palace, Gypsy Hill
SE20	Penge
SE21	Dulwich
SE22	East Dulwich
SE23	Forest Hill, Honor Oak
SE24	Herne Hill
SE25	Norwood
SE26	Sydenham
SE27	West Norwood
SE28	Plumstead Marsh

SOUTH WEST LONDON

SW1	see Inner London
SW2	Brixton, Tulse Hill
SW3	see Inner London
SW4	Clapham
SW5	see Inner London
SW6	see Inner London
SW7	see Inner London
SW8	Vauxhall, South Lambeth
SW9	Stockwell, Brixton
SW10	see Inner London
SW11	Battersea, Clapham Junction
SW12	Balham
SW13	Barnes
SW14	Mortlake, Sheen
SW15	Putney
SW16	Streatham
SW17	Tooting
SW18	Wandsworth, Southfields
SW19	Wimbledon
SW20	Raynes Park, Merton

WEST

W1	see Inner London
W2	Paddington, Bayswater, Westbourne Grove
W3	Acton
W4	Chiswick
W5	Ealing
W6	Hammersmith
W7	Hanwell
W8	Kensington
W9	Maida Vale, Warwick Avenue
W10	Kensal, North Kensington, Ladbroke Grove
W11	Notting Hill, Holland Park, Portobello Road
W12	Shepherds Bush
W13	West Ealing, Drayton Green
W14	West Kensington, Olympia

OUTER LONDON

THE EAST END

EAST END & DOCKLANDS

The East End is the home of the London Cockney. A true Cockney is said to be someone born within the sound of the Bow Bells. Historically the economy of the East End relied heavily on the docks which have been in terminal decline since the 1950's as larger ships became unable to navigate the River Thames.

In the early eighties the government created a Quasi Autonomous Non-Governmental Organisation (QUANGO) called the London Docklands Development Corporation (LDDC) to revive the area from Tower Bridge, E1, through Wapping E14, Canning Town E16, to Barking Creek, E6, on the north bank of the Thames. And from London Bridge, SE1 to the South Dock of Surrey Quays, SE16 on the south bank.

Despite concerted local opposition, Docklands soon became Europe's largest building site with whole tracts of London being flattened and rebuilt before you could say 'gissa job'. The whole process became part of a massive property boom which spiralled out of control, leaving London with yet more empty office space, expensive private houses in an area crying out for affordable social housing, and some of the most controversial industrial architecture in the world.

The brutality of the process is perfectly encapsulated in the stark contrasts in landscape between the new and the old, which sit uncomfortably side by side. Ageing public sector estates nestle between up-market housing and dockside watersports facilities for the well off. However, for the visitor it is an unmissable opportunity to see the results of capitalism gone gaga and a permanent monument to the economic philosophy that will be forever associated with Margaret Thatcher.

A car is the most comfortable way to get around, but cycling offers the best opportunities for exploring. Forget bussing it unless you join a tour. The Docklands Light Railway gives you a taster but nothing more. Bear in mind that on weekdays this is an under-used commercial and residential district, at weekends it is positively dead.

E1 WHITECHAPEL

ATTRACTIONS

BRICK LANE MARKET
Open: Sun 05.00-14.00 Tube: Aldgate East
Massive range of all types of goods at rock bottom prices, new and second hand. Go early and combine your shopping with a bagel breakfast from the 24 hour Bagel Bakery and a cheap lunch in one of the many Indian cafes or inexpensive tandoori restaurants. Don't go home without visiting the Flower market, a short walk away in Columbia Road, E2.

PETTICOAT LANE MARKET
Middlesex Street, E1. Open: Sun 09.00-14.00.
Tube: Aldgate, Liverpool Street.
Feels like a market in decline, not helped by the bad publicity over dodgy dealing in the allocation of pitches by various councillors.

ST KATHERINE'S DOCK
St Katherines Way, E1. Tel: 071-488 2400
Open: 24 hours
Tube: Tower Hill, Tower Gateway (Docklands Light Railway). Free.
Shops for tourists, The Dickens Inn pub, mooring place for yachts. Small dockland development that has worked better than later 80's projects.

SPITALFIELDS ORGANIC MARKET
Commercial Street, E1.
Open: Sun: 09.00-14.00
Five minutes walk from Liverpool Street station. The market is inside a covered hall with lots of stalls, crafts and vegetarian takeaway food

stalls from around the world. Find the one selling Thai food. Quieter than the other markets nearby.

WHITECHAPEL GALLERY

Whitechapel High Street, E1. Tel: 071-377 0107, admin 071-377 5015.
Open: Thu-Sun & Tue 11.00-17.00.
Tube: Aldgate East. Free.

Good shows from contemporary artists. Bookshop. Licensed cafe (see below). Occasional talks. Wheelchair access.

NON VEGETARIAN CAFÉ

WHITECHAPEL CAFÉ

Whitechapel Art Gallery, 80 Whitechapel High Street, Whitechapel, E1 7QX. Tel: 071-377 6182.
Open: Mon 11.00-15.30, Wed 11.00-18.30, Tue & Thu-Sun 11.00-16.30
Tube: Aldgate East

Omnivorous. Wholefood. Almost entirely vegetarian. Counter service. Main dishes such as pasta bakes, moussaka bakes and vegetable curry are £4.00. Also do veggie sandwiches, salads and soups.

SHOPS

BRICK LANE BEIGEL BAKERY

159 Brick Lane, E1. Tel: 071-729 0616.
Open: daily 24 hours.

Mega-popular bagel bakery open 24 hours per day, seven days per week. Go early Sunday morning and fill up before taking on the market.

HOLLAND & BARRETT

25 Sedgwick Centre, Aldgate Barrs, E1. Tel: 071-481 3791.

E2 BETHNAL GREEN

ATTRACTIONS

COLUMBIA ROAD FLOWER MARKET

Open on Sundays and only a short stroll from Brick Lane.
Columbia Road looks like the traditional East End street that you'd expect to see on a film set. On Sundays the street is 'aglow' with a huge range of flowers and plants at rock bottom prices. The existence of the market has been under threat for some time from developers, so get there while you can.

THE GEFFRYE MUSEUM

140 Kingsland Rd, E2 8EA. Tel: 071-739 9896
Open: Tue-Sat 10.00-17.00, Sun and bank holidays 14.00-17.00
Tube: Old Street or Liverpool Street then bus 22A, 22B or 149. Free.

Furniture from 1600 to 1960 in period settings. Exhibitions. Saturday and holiday events. Close to Columbia Market and Brick Lane.

LONDON BUDDHIST CENTRE

51 Roman Road, E2. Tel: 081-981 1225
Open: Mon-Fri 10.00-17.00
Tube: Bethnal Green

Classes in Buddhism and meditation. Free lunchtime class in meditation and dharma study Mon-Fri 13.00-14.00. Wed intro class 19.00-21.00, first one free then £3-£5. Women only Thu eve. Also longer courses in Buddhism, meditation, study groups, retreats. There are whole communities of Buddhists living in the area and the centre is the focal point for a number of retail enterprises and community activities.

VEGETARIAN RESTAURANTS

CHERRY ORCHARD

241 Globe Road, Bethnal Green, E2 OJD. Tel: 081-980 6678
Open: Mon, Thur, Fri 11.00-16.00, lunch served 12.00-15.00.
Tue-Wed 11.00-19.00
Tube: Bethnal Green

Vegetarian. Average £12.50 for a three course meal for two people. Main meal £3.25-3.75, soups £1.45, salads £1.60-2.20, cakes from £0.75. Bring your own alcohol, corkage £1.00. Summer garden.

The Cherry Orchard is run by a team of Buddhist women and is affiliated to the London Buddhist Centre. They have been running for 12 years and have built up a considerable reputation and experience. They offer value for money, vegetarian and vegan food. Menu changes daily and includes fresh salads, soups, main courses, home made cakes and puddings. Also available for parties and functions with hot or cold food, table or buffet service.

NON VEGETARIAN

THAI GARDEN

249 Globe Rd, Bethnal Green, E2. Tel: 081-981 5748
Open: Mon-Fri 12.00-14.45, Mon-Sat 18.00-22.45. Tube: Bethnal Green

Vegetarian and fish. Thai. Average £15. Small restaurant on two floors. Great if you love curry, bean curd, peanut and coconut sauce, aubergine with black beans, mushrooms, basil and a contented tummy. They won the Time Out award for best vegetarian restaurant in 1991. There are 60 dishes on the menu, and most are vegan. Set meal £16.50 for 4 courses. Vegan desserts include fruit salad, banana in coconut milk, or rambutan, a fruit like lychees. Smoking area and busy space downstairs, quieter upstairs. This is a great restaurant with brilliant food that brightens up Bethnal Green.

SHOPS

FRIENDS FOOD

83 Roman Road, E2 0GN. Tel: 081-980 1843.
Open: Mon-Sat 9.30-18.00 (Thu 16.00, Fri 19.00).
Wholefood shop with excellent range of herb teas and soya milks,
cereals, dried fruits, frozen stuff. Takeaway snacks and sandwiches,
with vegan kebabs in pitta and pies. Co-op run by Buddhists. 10%
discount to Vegan Society members.

E3 BOW

NON VEGETARIAN RESTAURANTS

1789 FRENCH RESTAURANT

9a Fairfield Road, Bow, E3 2QA. Tel: 081-980 8233, 081-534 4164.
Open: Tue-Fri 12.00-14.00, Tue-Sat 19.00-22.30.
Tube: Bow Road
Omnivorous. French. Now run by an Irishman with an English chef.
Small restaurant only yards from the Bow Road but really secluded
and looks like an ordinary house during the day when it's not lit up.
Veg starters include pancakes or cous-cous. There are a number of veg
main courses on the menu and offered as dishes of the day. Vegans can
be catered for as they offer to cook any dish to order with prior notice.
Quiet bar to sit and drink before or after a meal. £15 for two courses.
Lunchtime special £12.50 for 3 courses.

E4 CHINGFORD

SHOPS

FOOD & FITNESS

43 Old Church Road, South Chingford, E4 6SJ. Tel: 081-524 0722.
Open: Mon-Sat 9.00-17.30.
Food supplements, dried fruits and pulses. Some takeawy food
including vegan. They have the locally developed 'Aquathin Pure
Water' purifier which is a reverse osmosis machine and better than
bottled water. £1.25 for 5 litres.

HERB HOUSE

Unit 5 Village Arcade Station Road, E4. Tel:081-524 3057.
Open: Mon-Sat 9.00-17.00.
Small shop specialising in herb teas, pre-packed herbs and vitamins.

E5 CLAPTON

ATTRACTIONS

KING'S HALL LEISURE CENTRE

39 Lower Clapton Rd, E5. Tel: 081-985 0961, 081-985 2158
Train: Hackney Downs BR
Run by Hackney Council and includes a swimming pool.

VEGETARIAN CAFÉ

PUMPKINS

76 Clarence Road, Hackney, E5 8HB. Tel: 081-533 1214
Open: Mon-Sat 11.30-21.30 Near to Pembury pub
Train: Hackney Central BR, Hackney Downs BR
Brilliant vegan and veggie coffee shop. Very affordable food. Large
selection of cakes, coffees, teas. Everyone welcome. Table service. Last
orders 21.30 sharp! If you want to linger for longer then try their other
cafe Pumpadelicks in E8. Children's play area. 95% vegan food, with
12 cakes, cookies, and tarts of which nine are vegan. The interior is
like a psychedelic trip, very homely with a painted wall and the Milky
Way on the ceiling. They try to cater for meat-eaters who are
detoxifying and hence have five pies with veg/salad or chips, of which
three are vegan. The two daily soups are vegan as are two out of five
main courses. Four vegan burgers, vegan milk shakes and capuccino.
Two courses for two people and a drink will set you back less than
£10.00. Corkage £0.50 beer, £1.00 wine per table. People come from
Leeds and the Isle of Wight to eat here.

NON VEGETARIAN RESTAURANTS

OASIS RESTAURANT & WINE BAR

113 Lower Clapton Road, Clapton, E5 0NP. Tel: 081-985 4140
Open: Mon-Sat 18.00-22.45.
Train: Hackney Downs, Hackney Central
Omnivorous. International exotic. Starters £2.75 include vegetable
soup, garlic bread, and for vegans, nacho chips and guacamole or salsa
sauce with salad. Main courses £7.25 can be esclivada, Mediterranean
roast vegetables with olive oil and garlic dressing, or Japanese stir-fry
with teriyaki sauce. Vegans can have rice instead of egg noodles, or a
vegan semolina dish with herbs and walnuts.

E6 EAST HAM, UPTON PARK

NON VEGETARIAN RESTAURANTS

THE BLUE GARDENIA

136 Barking Road, East Ham, E6 3BD Tel: 081-471 6685
Open: Mon-Thu 18.30-23.30, Fri-Sat 18.30-24.00, Sun bookings only.
Tube: East Ham, Upton Park
Omnivorous. Caribbean. Average £7.00. Table service & takeaway.
Vegan delights include main course stuffed cabbage, soya lentil cutlets,
spicy vegetables. Starters tend to be fruity for vegans. Dessert can be
sweet pot pudding made with coconut milk. Ring first and you can
have vegan ice-cream.

SHOPS

GHIR HEALTH FOODS & CHEMIST

426 Barking Road E6. Tel: 081-471 7576.
Open: Mon-Sat 9.00-19.00.
Lots of whole foods, some gluten free, soya products, vegetarian cheese,
bodybuilding supplements, pharmacy, BWC vegan cosmetics,
aromatherapy, diabetic food. Nickel-free jewellery, diagnostic
equipment, solar batteries, afro ranges. Acupuncture needles can be
ordered. Water purifiers, books, magazines. Snacks.

GRANARY HEALTH FOODS

165 High Street North, E6. Tel: 081-552 5988.
Open: Mon-Sat: 09.00-17.45.
General range includes organic food, vitamins & minerals, vegan ice-
cream and yoghurts. Takeaway food with pasties and cutlets for
vegans.

E7 UPTON

VEGETARIAN RESTAURANTS

RONAK RESTAURANT LTD

317 Romford Road, Forest Gate, E7 9HA
Tel: 081-534 2944, 081-519 2110.
Open: Tue-Sun 11.00-22.00.
Tube: Forest Gate, Wanstead Park
Vegetarian. Indian. Average £7.50. Thali De-Luxe £7.50, Masala Dosa
£4.00. Still going strong after 20 years. Small restaurant with 35 seats,
table service and takeaway.

SHOPS

HEALTH WORKS

148 Earlham Grove, E7. Tel: 081-519 0705.
Open: Mon-Sat 9.30-17.00.
Grains, nuts, dried fruit, herbal teas, TVP, multivitamins and
cosmetics. No takeaway.

E8 HACKNEY

There is a large mainland Turkish community here, hence the array
of takeaways with hummus and salad in pitta bread. Relax in the
friendly library in Mare Street. If you move here then don't be without
the excellent Hackney Green Guide, £2.00, published by Ecoprint, 95
Southgate Rd, London N1 3JS.

ATTRACTIONS

CENTREPRISE

136 Kingsland High Street, E8. Tel: 071-254 9632.
Open: Mon-Sat cafe 9.00-17.30, bookshop 10.30-17.30
Train: Dalston Kingsland BR,
Bookshop, cafe, advice centre and youth project. The omnivorous cafe
is fantastically cheap for a cuppa. Tea only 20p, coffee 35p, herb tea
35p, decaffeinated coffee 50p. Vegan soup £1.00. Quiche 90p. Chow
mein or vegan vegetables and rice £2.50. West Indian veg patties 90p.
The bookshop has lots of non-racist, non-sexist and vegetarian books.
There's exhibition space for local artists, meetings in the evenings, a
youth club on Wednesdays, and an adult literacy centre. This is a good
place to meet people and well worth popping in if you live locally. Free
legal and housing advice by appointment on Tuesdays in English, sign
and other languages.

VEGETARIAN RESTAURANTS

GREEN DOOR WHOLEFOOD CAFE

18 Ashwin Street, Hackney, E8 3DL. Tel: 071-249 6793
Open : Mon-Sat 9.00-16.00, 17.00 summer
Tube: Dalston Junction BR.
Vegetarian. Wholefood. Counter service and takeaway. Different food
daily from around the world, such as Mexican and Madras bakes,
curry dishes with rice and breads. £4.35 for a main course and salad.
Soup £1.60. Two vegan desserts like cheesecakes, fruit pies, apple
strudels, cake £1.00-£1.75. Everything made on the premises,
including fresh bread and rolls. Local artists' work on display.

PUMPADELICKS

191 Mare St, Hackney, E8 3QE. Tel: 081-985 5394.
Open: Coffee bar Mon-Fri 11.30-16.30. Shop Mon-Thur 10.00-17.30,
Fri 10.00-19.00, Sat 10.00-15.00.
Train: Hackney Central BR, Hackney Downs BR
Vegetarian and vegan cafe. Great organic vegetarian food shop with coffee bar downstairs, which also uses organic vegetables. The cafe is 90% vegan, painted like a spaceship and a good place to linger cheaply. Choose the size of your plate and take a selection of food for £1.50-£2.00. 13 dishes per day, pies, quiche, pumpkin specials, salads, stews. Desserts, cakes and tarts all vegan. Even vegan cheese. Also arts and crafts.

SHOPS

THE NUTHOUSE

6 Kingsland High Street, E8 2JP. Tel: 071-923 0887.
Open: Mon-Sat 9.00-17.00.
Wholesale fruit and nuts and West Indian produce.

OXFAM

570-572 Kingsland Rd, E8. Tel: 071-923 1532.
Open: Mon-Sat 9.30-16.45.
Tube: Highbury & Islington then bus 38 or 277, Dalston Kingsland BR.
The biggest Oxfam charity shop in London. Secondhand furniture, clothes, household goods, books. Will collect and deliver within four miles.

RIDLEY ROAD BAGEL BAKERY

13-15 Ridley Road, E8 2NP. Tel: 071-923 0666.
Open: 24 hours.
Bagel bakery with lots of delicious vegetarian treats. Great place to quell midnight munchies, though if you're vegan you'll have to take them home if you want animal free margarine on them.

RIDLEY ROAD MARKET

Ridley Road, E8. Train: Dalston, Kingsland BR.
Open: Mon-Wed 09.00-15.00, Thu 09.00-12.00, Fri-Sat 09.00-17.00.
Possibly the most cosmopolitan market in London. All nationalities mix here. If you've got some energy to burn you should join them - it's wild. Great fruit and veg, and just about everything else, though lots of dead carcasses to avoid.

E9 HOMERTON, VICTORIA PARK

ATTRACTIONS

SUTTON HOUSE

2-4 Homerton High St, E9 6JQ. Tel: 081-986 2264
Open: Wed-Sun 11.30-17.30
The oldest house in East London, built around 1535. Jacobean wall
paintings, National Trust shop. Cafe-bar with vegetarian dishes.
Exhibitions, concerts and talks.

SHOPS

THE WHOLEMEAL SHOP

190 Well Street, E9 6QT. Tel: 081- 985 1822.
Open: Mon-Sat 09.00-18.00.
Vegetarian shop with good range that includes organic bread, vitamins,
Weleda & Infinity body building products, all the usuals and takeaway
food.

E11 LEYTON

SHOPS

VITA HEALTH FOOD.

565 Lee Bridge Road, E10. Tel: 081-539 3245.
Open: Mon-Sat 9.00-18.00.
Wholefoods, diabetic, vegan ice-cream. No takeaway foods.

E11 LEYTONSTONE

SHOPS

ALCAN

703 High Rd, Leytonstone, E11. Tel: 081-532 8373.
Open: Mon-Sat 10.00-17.00.
Aluminium can recycling company which pays 40p per kilo (55 cans).
Will collect if you have 10 bin bags full. The cans should be clean, dry
and preferably crushed flat.

PEACHES HEALTH FOOD SHOP

143 High Street, Wanstead, E11 2RL. Tel: 081-530 3617.
Open: Mon-Fri 9.30-18.00, Sat 9.00-17.30.
Large range in a small shop including vegan takeaway food. English
fruit wines with no animal products except honey in the mead.

VANNS HEALTH STORE
28 Kirkdale Road, E11. Tel: 081-539 4196.
Open: Mon-Sat 9.00-18.30 (18.00 Sat).
Tube: Leytonstone.
Health food, organic bread, frozen food and magazines like Holiday
Vegetarian and Kindred Spirit.

E14 LIMEHOUSE

ATTRACTIONS

BILLINGSGATE FISH MARKET
87 West India Road, E14. Tel: 071-987 1118 Open Tue-Sat 05.00-09.30
Tube: West India Key (Docklands Light Railway)
Trading starts at 05.00. Huge variety of beautiful fish, all unfortunately, dead.

CANARY WHARF
Isle of Dogs, E14. Tel: 071-418 2000
Open: Mon-Sat 10.00-18.00
New development featuring Canary Wharf Tower. Not sure of the
exact address but then you can't miss Britain's tallest building, which
is visible from many parts of London. It hasn't been open to the public
since the Irish Republican Army (IRA) tried to redesign it with the use
of high explosives. A ground floor visitors centre is planned to open in
June 94.

LONDON DOCKLANDS VISITORS' CENTRE
3 Limeharbour, E14.
Tel: 071-512 1111 Open: Mon-Fri 09.00-18.00, Sat-Sun 09.30-17.00
Tube: Coldharbour (Docklands Light Railway)
Free entry, 10 minute history video of the Docklands, maps and
information. Guided tours. Shop.

MUSEUM IN DOCKLANDS
Unit C14, Poplar Business Park, 10 Preston Road, E14.
Tel: 071-515 1162.
Open by appointment with the librarian
Library and archives of the Port of London Authority. Tracing of
ancestors who worked on the river from the 1800's.

E15 STRATFORD, WEST HAM

You won't find Shakespeare here - he's at Stratford-upon-Avon.

VEGETARIAN FAST FOOD

HEALTHNUTS
39 Water Lane, Stratford, E15 4NL. Tel: 081-519 3228
Open: Mon-Fri 09.00-17.00, Sat 09.00-17.00 (in summer)
Train: Maryland, Stratford
Vegetarian though some chicken. Takeaway and small café. Healthy
sarnies with vegan margarine, made to order. Some vegan savouries.

SHOPS

APPLEJACKS
Unit 28, The Mall, The Stratford Centre, E15. Tel: 081-519 5809.
Open: Mon-Sat 9.00-18.00.
Excellent general healthfood shop. "If we don't have it, we'll get it
within a week." Most takeaway food is vegan such as Mexican flaps,
blackeye bean flaps, spinach and potato pakora, veg pasties, nut and
barley rolls, tofu pasties, and loads more. Vegetarian carrot cake and
pick and mix snacks.

THE BODY SHOP
9 East Mall, Stratford, E15 1XA.
Open: Mon-Sat 09.30-17.30.

E16 CANNING TOWN

ATTRACTIONS

LONDON CITY AIRPORT
King George V Dock, Silvertown, E16. Tel: 071-474 5555
The business traveller's airport to Europe that most Londoners have
only ever heard about.

E17 WALTHAMSTOW

ATTRACTIONS

WILLIAM MORRIS GALLERY AND MUSEUM
Lloyd Park, Forest Road, E17. Tel: 081-527 3782, 081-527 5544
Open: Tue-Sat 10.00-13.00, 14.00-17.00, first Sun of month 14.00-17.00.
Tube: Walthamstow, Walthamstow BR.
Free. Early home of the artistically gifted socialist. Displays of his
designs. Shop, mail order service. Tours by arrangement.

OTHER RESTAURANTS

FRIENDLY CHINESE RESTAURANT

235 Hoe Street, Walthamstow, E17 9PP.
Tel: 081-509 0875, 081-520 6536
Open: Tue-Sun 17.30-24.00
Tube: Walthamstow Central.
Omnivorous. Chinese restaurant with a vegetarian selection on the menu that is popular with the locals. Staff are very friendly and will adapt for vegetarians and vegans on request. A number of beancurd dishes done in different styles are available as well as mixed vegetables in numerous flavours. Food is excellent and moderately priced, and the beancurd in garlic and hot bean sauce is wonderful.

SHOPS

FOREST RECYCLING

2C Bakers Ave, Walthamstow, E17. Tel: 081-539 3856.
Sells recycled paper and collects paper for recycling, minimum 10 boxes sorted into white and coloured.

VENUS HEALTH FOOD

143 High Street Walthamstow E17. Tel: 081-520 3085.
Open: Mon-Sat 9.00-18.00.
Specialise in foodstuffs, teas, vitamins, with some vegan products. No takeaway.

NUTTERS OF WOODFORD

83 High Road, E18. Tel: 081-530 6136.
Open: Mon-Sat 9.00-17.30.
Tube: South Woodford.

NORTH LONDON

N1	*Islington , King's Cross, Shoreditch*
N2	*East Finchley*
N3	*Finchley, Fortis Green*
N4	*Finsbury Park, Stroud Green*
N5	*Highbury*
N6	*Highgate*
N7	*Holloway*
N8	*Hornsey, Crouch End, Turnpike Lane*
N9	*Enfield, Edmonton*
N10	*Muswell Hill*
N11	*Friern Barnet*
N12	*North Finchley, Woodside Park*
N13	*Palmers Green, Broomfield Park*
N14	*Southgate, Oakwood*
N15	*Seven Sisters*
N16	*Stoke Newington, Stamford Hill*
N17	*Tottenham*
N18	*Upper Edmonton*
N19	*Archway, Upper Holloway, Tufnell Park*
N20	*Totteridge & Whetstone*
N21	*Winchmore Hill*
N22	*Wood Green*

N1 ISLINGTON & KINGS CROSS

King's Cross station is not the most inviting place from which to surface from the underground. The area is dirty, very busy and always has a certain seedy feel about it. Drug dealing and prostitution are very public and it was here that the Director of Public Prosecutions was pulled for kerb-crawling by the Police. Coming out of Kings Cross station you'll see on your left a kebab shop on the closest corner of the triange at the top of Grays Inn Rd. This place sells falafels! Directly opposite the station is another takeaway that sells hummous and salad in pitta bread.

ATTRACTIONS

BRITANNIA LEISURE CENTRE
40 Hyde Rd, Hoxton, N1. Tel: 071-729 4485
Open: Daily 09.00-17.45, or till 22.00 (pool closes 21.00)
Sports centre with swimming pool run by Hackney Council. Pool £2.50 adult, £1.20 children.

VEGETARIAN RESTAURANTS

BENNETT & LUCK CAFÉ

54 Islington Park Street, N1 1PX. Tel: 071-226 3422.
Open: Mon-Fri 09.00-19.30, Sat 09.00-18.30.
Tube: Highbury & Islington
Vegetarian. Café with sandwiches, salads and a wholefood shop selling organic veg, wine, homeopathy, aromatherapy.

CANDID CAFE

3 Torrens Street, Islington N1. Tel: 071-278 9368
Open: Mon-Sat 12.00-22.00, Sun 12.00-18.00.
Tube: Angel
Vegetarian. International. Basic vegetarian food such as pasta, vegetable pie, cauliflower cheese, all with salad. Main course £3.50, soup £2.00. Some food is vegan, such as soup, but there is not always a vegan main course. Bring your own wine, corkage £1.00.

INDIAN VEGETARIAN BHELPOORI HOUSE

92-93 Chapel Market, N1 9EX. Tel: 071-837 4607
Open: Every day 12.00-15.00, 18.00-23.00
Tube: Angel
Vegetarian. Indian. Uses vegetable oil. Daily buffet lunch and dinner. Delicious Indian food at rock-bottom prices. Eat as much as you can for a fixed price lunch £3.25, dinner £3.50. Table and takeaway service. Great restaurant popular with London Vegans, with organic brown rice. Buffet includes mixed dried fruits for extra vitamins. Vegans watch out for a dish in the buffet which always has milk in it.

MILAN

52 Caledonian Road, Kings Cross, N1 9DP. Tel: 071-278 3812
Open: Mon-Fri 12.00-21.00, Sat 18.00-21.00.
Tube: Kings Cross
Vegetarian. Indian. All-you-can-eat lunch £3.95 Mon-Sat. Average £5.00. Veg biryani £3.20 takeaway or £3.50 eat in. Uses sunflower or corn oil. Table service and takeaway.

OTHER RESTAURANTS

ALMEIDA THEATRE WINE BAR

1a / 1b Almeida Street, Islington, N1 1TA. Tel: 071-226 0931 / 226 7432.
Open: Mon-Sat Food 12.00-14.30, 18.00-21.00, Wine 12.00-16.00, 17.00-23.00.
Tube: Angel
Omnivorous. Wine Bar. Two thirds of the menu is vegetarian, with a choice of 6-8 dishes. Vegans can have soup, and usually a vegan main course but not always. Average £4.00 for a main dish with salad.

ANGEL CURRY CENTRE

5 Chapel Market, Islington, N1 9EZ. Tel: 071-837 5727
Open: Every day 12.00-14.00, 18.00-23.00 (last order)
Tube: Angel
Omnivorous. Tandoori Indian. Average £10.00. Vegetarian dishes use
vegetable ghee. Licensed.

THE FINCA

96 Pentonville Road, N1 9JB. Tel: 071-837 5387.
Open: Mon-Fri 12.30-24.00, Sat-Sun 12.30-02.00
Tube: Angel, King's Cross
Liveliest tapas bar in London. Spanish dance classes weekday evenings
from 18.00 or 19.00, cost £5.00 for one hour, £7.00 two hours. Follow
this up by staying on for the nightclub from 21.00. It's Latin American
music every night except Wednesdays when the DJ changes. Entry
£3.00-£5.00.

LE MERCURY

140a Upper Street, Islington, N1 1QY. Tel: 071-354 4088.
Open: Mon-Sat 11.00-01.00, Sun 12.00-23.30.
Tube: Essex Rd, Highbury & Islington, Angel
Omnivorous. French. Wholefood & organic. Some French restaurants
are the last place a vegetarian would go, but here you'll find veg roulade
as a main course with another dish on the daily specials menu. Average
evening main course £5.45, starter £2.25, dessert £1.95.
3-course lunch £5.00. Licensed.

THE NEW CULTURE REVOLUTION

42 Duncan Street, Angel N1. Tel: 071-833 9083.
Open: Mon-Fri 12.00-14.30 & 18.00-23.00, Sat 13.00-15.00 &
18.00-23.00
Tube: Angel.
Chinese noodle bar with a number of good vegetarian dishes and at
least four vegan main course options. Holds about 65 people amid the
cool decor and black wood seating. Great food for under £10.00 makes
this one of the cheapest restaurants in the area.

SURUCHI

82 Mildmay Park, Kingsland, N1 4PR. Tel: 071-241 5213
Open: Every day 12.00-14.30, 18.00-23.30.
Tube: Highbury & Islington
Omnivorous. Indian. Average £10.00. Restaurant and takeaway. Lots of
vegetarian grub and they use vegetable ghee. Really nice food, yummy
chapattis. Reasonable price, cosy atmosphere. Licensed, but they
encourage you to bring your own alcohol and pay corkage.

SHOPS

BARNSBURY HEALTH FOODS

285 Caledonian Road, N1. Tel: 071-607 7344.
Open: Mon-Fri 09.00-18.30, Sat 09.00-17.45.
Tube: Caledonian Rd, King's Cross.
Wholefoods, health foods, cosmetics, supplements, takeaway with vegan pasties, books.

BUMBLEBEE

10 Caledonian Rd, Kings Cross N1 9DU. Tel: 071-837 5223.
Open: Mon-Sat 08.30-18.00.
Wholefoods, takeaway with vegan sandwiches, salads, hot foods.

THE BODY SHOP

7 Upper Street, Islington, N1.
Open: Mon-Fri 09.30-18.00, Sat 10.00-17.50.

HACKNEY WHOLEFOODS

95 Southgate Road, Islington, N1 3JS. Tel: 071-354 4923.
Open: Tue-Sat 10.00-19.00 (18.00 Sat).
Wholefoods, fresh organic fruit & veg, organic bread, takeaways (not vegan). Pick up a copy of the Green Guide to Hackney.

N2 EAST FINCHLEY

The UK headquarters of McDonald's is just one minute north of East Finchley tube station.

ATTRACTIONS

HAGGERSTON POOL

Wiston Rd, N2. Tel: 071-739 7166.
Open: Mon 08.00-19.30, Tue till 18.00, women 18.00-20.00, Wed 18.00-19.00 adults, 20.00-21.30, Thu/Fri 8.00-19.30, Sat till 18.00, Sun till 13.00.
Swimming pool run by Hackney Council. £1.30.

VEGETARIAN FAST FOOD

MAHAVIR SWEET MART

127a High Road, N2 8AJ. Tel: 081-883 4595
Open: Tue-Sat 11.30-20.30, Sun 10.30-18.30
Tube: East Finchley
Vegetarian. Indian. Nothing vegan, they use butter ghee. They will heat up samosas, batata vada, etc. Average price £2.00. Takeaway only.

N3 FINCHLEY

VEGETARIAN RESTAURANTS

RANI INDIAN VEGETARIAN RESTAURANT
3-5 Long Lane, Finchley, N3 2PR. Tel: 081-349 4386, 081-349 2636
Open: Every day 12.15-15.00 (last order, close 16.00), 18.00-22.30
(close 24.00)
Tube: Finchley Central
Vegetarian. Gujarati and South Indian. All-you-can-eat lunch buffet
£8.00 every day. Average dinner £15.00 for two courses, £15.00-20.00
with wine. Great veggie grub. Specialities change daily. For vegans
dairy-free munchies are marked, and no eggs are used. Wheat-free also
marked. Discount card for regular customers. Braille menu. The family
will give tips to charity.

SHOPS

B GREEN HEALTH FOOD PLUS
104/106 Ballards Lane, N3 2DN. Tel: 081-343 1002.
Open: Mon-Sat 9.30-17.30.
Tube: Finchley Central.
Takeaway section has pies, but not vegan.

N4 FINSBURY PARK, STROUD GREEN

VEGETARIAN RESTAURANTS

JAI KRISHNA
161 Stroud Green Road, Finsbury Park, N4 3PZ. Tel: 071-272 1680
Open: Mon-Sat 12.00-14.00, 17.30-23.00
Tube: Crouch Hill BR, Finsbury Park
Vegetarian. Indian. This is a good cheap place to eat, full of young
people. Set meal £5.95, a la carte £4-£5. Brown rice £1.75 plus curry
£2.00 makes a meal for £3.75. Of 83 dishes, 23 are vegetarian and 60
are vegan and marked on the menu. Check out the aloo jeera. Best to
book Fri and Sat night because it gets very busy. Not licensed but you
can bring your own. Corkage 20p can, 75p bottle of wine.

SUNDERBAN TANDOORI
50 Blackstock Rd, Finsbury Park, N4. Tel: 071-359 9243, 226 0215
Open: Every day 12.00-14.30, 18.00-24.00 (00.30 Fri/Sat)
Tube: Finsbury Park
Omnivorous. Indian. Average £7.00 if choosing individual vegetable
dishes, £8.50 for a veggie thali. A regular omnivorous Indian (in fact it
sells halal meat) but with great vegan dishes if you state your
preference, asking for dishes to be made with vegetable oil rather than

ghee. Especially delicious are these dishes: sag bhajee (spinach), tarka dhal (thick lentil soup with garlic) and stuffed paratha (bread). Friendly and accommodating staff. Of 126 menu items, 41 are vegan and 53 vegetarian, including breads, rices and desserts. Check out the vegan draught Kingfisher lager.

N5 HIGHBURY

ATTRACTIONS

THE HIGHBURY CENTRE
137 Grosvenor Ave, N5 2NH. Tel: 071-226 5805.
Natural health centre. Alexander technique, counselling, massage, singing, art therapy, pregnancy and birth classes, presentation skills.

SHOPS

HIGHBURY HEALTH FOODS
25 Highury Corner, Holloway Road, N5 1RA. Tel: 071-609 9471.
Open: Mon-Sat 09.30-18.30 (18.00 Sat).
Health foods and takeaway food, including vegan.

N6 HIGHGATE

ATTRACTIONS

HIGHGATE CEMETERY
Swain's Lane N6. Tel: 081-340 1834.
Open: Mon-Fri 10.00-15.45, Sat-Sun 11.00-16.00.
Tube: Archway.
Resting place of the famous such as Karl Marx. Times are for the Eastern side. Tours give the only access to the Western side. Weekdays at 12.00, 14.00, 16.00, weekend 11.00-16.00, till 17.00 Apr-Sep. It's better with fewer people on Sat or early Sun.

VEGETARIAN RESTAURANTS & CAFES

CAFÉ VERT
Jackson's Lane Centre, 269a Archway Road, N6 5AA. Tel: 081-348 7666
Open: Every day 11.00-15.30, Wed-Fri 19.00-22.00
Tube: Highgate
Gourmet vegetarian with a lot of dairy. Always have one or two vegan dishes, and if a group of vegans ring first they will have four dishes. Table and takeaway service. Never more than £3.50 for a main course such as lasagne, moussaka, curry, veg bake. Pies from £2.90. Stuffed veg £2.00-£2.50. Everything served with salad. Soup with garlic bread £2.50. Menu changes every day. 10% discount to Vegetarian and Vegan

Society members. Bar evenings and Sunday lunchtime. Free Jazz Sunday. Part of busy Arts & Community Centre close to the tube. Nightly classes include stand-up comedy, African drumming, dance, photography, counselling. For Centre events programme call 081-340 5226 or write to above address. You can book the 200 seat theatre for events and they do vegetarian outside catering.

N7 HOLLOWAY

VEGETARIAN RESTAURANTS & CAFES

BHELPURI HOUSE
149 Holloway Road, N7 8LX. Tel: 071-700 6840
Open: Mon-Sat 12.00-14.30, 18.00-22.00, Sun 12.00-22.00.
Tube: Holloway Road, Highbury & Islington
Vegetarian. South Indian. Eat as much as you like lunch buffet for £3.55. Average price £6.00. Also does takeaway. Fully licensed.

SHOPS

ALARA WHOLEFOODS
58 Seven Sisters Road, N7. Tel: 071-609 6875.
Open: Mon 10.00-18.00, Tue-Thu 09.30-18.00, Fri-Sat 09.00-18.00 (18.30 Fri).
Tube: Finsbury Park.
Every kind of wholefood plus takeaway with vegan filled pitta bread, pastries, cakes. There is a market nearby.

AVENUE HEALTH FOODS
113 Turnpike Lane, N8. Tel: 081-348 5000.
Open: Mon-Sat 09.00-18.30 (18.00 Sat).
Tube: Turnpike Lane.
Health foods and takeaway food with one or two vegan items.

BUMBLEBEE WHOLEFOOD CO-OP
30, 32 and 33 Brecknock Road, Tufnell Park, N7 0DD. Tel: 071-607 1936 shop, 284 1314 admin.
Open: Mon-Sat 09.30-18.30.
Tube: Camden Town, Kentish Town.
Three shops with an excellent choice of wholefoods, health foods, organic produce, macrobiotic foods and bakery. Even Neal's Yard seems understocked by comparison.

ECOLOGY SHOP - FOOD MATTERS
12a Brecknock Rd, N7. Tel: 071-700 2638.
Open: Mon-Sat 09.30-17.45 (from 10.00 Sat).
Tube: Camden Town.
Recycled goods, natural paint, low energy bulbs, books, gifts.

HAELAN CENTRE
41 The Broadway, Crouch End, N8 8DT. Tel: 081-340 4258.
Open: Mon-at 09.00-18.00 (18.30 Fri).
Tube: Finsbury Park then bus W7 or W2.
Wholefoods, herbs, teas, shampoo, takeaway with vegan food.

HOLLAND & BARRETT
452 Holloway Road, N7 6QA. Tel: 071-607 3933.
Open: Mon-Sat 09.00-17.30. Tube: Holloway Road.

NATURAL REMEDIES
35 Brecknock Road, N7 0BT. Tel: 071-267 3884.
Open: Mon-Sat 09.30-18.30.
Tube: Camden Town, Kentish Town.
Cruelty-free beauty products galore, plus gemstones, books on
alternative therapies and nutritional supplements. Also a natural
health clinic. Next to Bumblebee.

N8 HORNSEY, CROUCH END, TURNPIKE LANE

NON-VEGETARIAN RESTAURANTS

BARBELLA
1 Park Road, Crouch End, N8 8TE. Tel: 081-348 5609
Open: Sun-Thur 11.00-24.00, Fri-Sat 10.00-01.00
Tube: Hornsey, Crouch Hill, Highgate
Vegetarian & Fish. African-Caribbean. Lots of vegetarian food. Vegans
can have tortilla chips and soup or salads or try Pizza Bella opposite.
Average £4.50. Licensed.

FARHEENAH TAKEAWAY
69 Turnpike Lane, N8. Tel: 081-340 2453
Open: Every day 12.00-23.00
Tube: Turnpike Lane
Omnivorous. Indian. Lots of cheap Indian food made with vegetable
ghee. Mixed veg and rice £2.50 takeaway, add 10% for eat in.

PIZZA BELLA
4-6 Park Road, Crouch End, N8. Tel: 081-342 8541
Open: Sun-Thur 11.00-24.00, Fri-Sat 10.00-01.00
Omnivorous. Italian. Eight vegetarian pizzas from £3.40, seven pastas
from £3.95. Can do vegan pizza or salad. 30 items on the salad bar
which is £2.25 per helping. Opposite Barbella with same owner.

SHOPS

GOODLIFE

7 Broadway Parade, N8. Tel: 081-340 0601.
Open: Mon-Sat 09.00-18.00. Tube: Turnpike Lane.
Wholefoods, supplements, takeaway with vegan food.

N9 ENFIELD, EDMONTON

TAKEAWAYS

CURRY HOTLINE

596 Hertford Road, Edmonton, N9 8AH. Tel: 081-804 1352,
081-805-3101
Open: Sun-Thu 17.00-23.30, Fri-Sat 17.00-24.00.
Tube: Lower Edmonton BR
Omnivorous takeaway with five vegetarian starters, 12 curries and 20
side dishes offering a free delivery service. Very cheap and tasty, try
the vegetable Ceylon cooked in coconut sauce or the green peppers and
onions dupiaza. All dishes can be made hotter or milder as you prefer
and delivered to your door.

SHOPS

HOLLAND & BARRETT

7 North Mall, Edmonton, N9 0EQ. Tel: 081-807 6711.
Open: Mon-Thu 09.00-17.00, Fri-Sat 9.00-17.30

N10 MUSWELL HILL

VEGETARIAN CAFÉS

OSHOBASHO CAFÉ

Highgate Wood, Muswell Hill Road, N10 3JN. Tel: 081-444 1505
Open: Tue-Sun 08.30-1/2 hour before sunset (dusk)
Tube: Highgate
Vegetarian. International. Average £4.00. Jazz on Wednesday evening.
A warm and friendly atmosphere in the cold months, and al fresco
dining in a rose-filled garden surrounded by cherry blossoms and
rhododendrons in the spring and summer. An oasis in the middle of a
beautiful wood.

SHOPS

FLEUR AROMATHERAPY

Pembroke Studios, Pembroke Rd, N10. Tel: 081-444 7424.
Essential oils and aromatherapy products. Certified organic range

available.

HOLLAND & BARRETT

121 Muswell Road, N10 3HS. Tel: 081-883 1154.
Open: Mon-Sat 09.00-17.30. Tube: Highgate then bus 134 or 43.

HEALTH & DIET

243 Broadway, N10. Tel: 081-444 7717. Open: Mon-Sat 09.00-18.00.
Tube: Highgate.
Wholefoods, vitamins, takeaway with vegan food Mon-Fri like tofu
pies, pasties and flans.

N12 NORTH FINCHLEY, WOODSIDE PARK

SHOPS

FINCHLEY HEALTH FOOD CENTRE

745 High Road, N12 0BP. Tel: 081-445 8743.
Open: Mon-Sat 08.00-18.00. Tube: Finchley Central.

NATURAL HEALTH

339 Ballard's Lane N12. Tel: 081-445 4397.
Open: Mon-Sat 09.15-17.30.
Tube: Woodside Park.
Wholefoods, no takeaway.

N13 PALMERS GREEN, BROOMFIELD PARK

SHOPS

COUNTRYSIDE WHOLEFOODS

90 Aldermans Hill, Palmers Green, N13. Tel: 081-882 2799.
Open: Mon, Wed, Fri, 07.00-19.00. Tue, Thu 10.00-19.00. Sat 08.00-
18.00.
Wholefood store. 5% discount to Vegan Society members, not applica-
ble to delivery service customers

HOLLAND & BARRETT

332 Green Lanes, Palmers Green, N13 5TW. Tel: 081-886 6769.
Open: Mon-Sat 09.00-17.30.
Tube: Turnpike Lane.
Health foods, takeaway pies, pizzas, cakes (not vegan).

N14 SOUTHGATE, OAKWOOD

SHOPS

PURE HEALTH

56 Chaseside, N14. Tel: 081-447 8071.
Open: Mon-Sat 09.00-17.30.
Tube: Southgate.
Wholefoods, cosmetics, vitamins. Some takeaway but it goes quickly,
including vegan pasties.

N16 STOKE NEWINGTON, STAMFORD HILL

The vegetarian Republic of Stoke Newington is a great area for
vegetarians to set up home or forage from adjoining N1 or E8. It
doesn't have a tube station but is well worth a visit, if only for the
overrun and atmospheric Salvation Army cemetery full of stone angels
and magnificent tombs. Trendy shops sell crafts, jewellery, New Age
things and second-hand period clothes.

ATTRACTIONS

ABNEY PARK CEMETERY

Stoke Newington High St and Stoke Newington Church St, N16.
Open: 08.00-dusk.
32 acres of varied woodland where you can see birds, squirrels, foxes
and feral cats. Woodland, wildlife and monument walks Sunday at
12.00 and 14.00 by Friends of Abney Park Cemetery, 12 Kinburn
House, Lewisham, SE16 1DN. They aim to save the cemetery from
dereliction.

Volunteers needed for light work first Sunday of the month at noon.
Meet at South Lodge with stout boots and heavy workwear. Contact:
Cemetery Conservationist and Administrator, South Lodge, Stoke
Newington High Street, N16. Tel: 071-275 7557.

CLISSOLD PARK

Stoke Newington Church St, N16.
Birds, wildfowl, deer and rabbits in Hackney's best park. The Mansion
House has a cafe with vegetarian snacks.

CLISSOLD PARK NATURAL HEALTH CENTRE

154 Stoke Newington Church St, N16. Tel: 071-249 2990.
Open: Mon-Fri 10.00-19.00, some weekends.
Acupuncture, Alexander technique, aromatherapy, counselling,
herbalism, homoeopathy, massage, osteopathy, reflexology, shiatsu,
therapy. Average £20.00 by appointment. Reception open 9.30-13.00,
14.00-17.00.

CLISSOLD POOL
Clissold Rd, N16. Tel: 071-254 4272.
Open: Mon-Fri 7.30-21.30, closed Wed. Sat 12.00-17.30, Sun 10.00-17.30.
Swimming pool run by Hackney Council. There could be classes at any time so call in for a programme.

N16 FITNESS CENTRE
46 Milton Grove, N16 8QY. Tel: 071-249 0631
Open: Mon-Fri 10.00-21.30, Sat-Sun 10.00-17.00
Sauna, body and circuit training, aerobics, karate, massage. Cafe with health food. £5.00 per class. Annual membership £385 then all classes free.

SPRINGFIELD PARK
Between Upper Clapton Rd and the River Lea.
Steep gradients ensure great views to the East. Brilliant lake with birds, wildfowl, and an island.

VEGETARIAN RESTAURANTS & CAFES

MILLWARDS VEGETARIAN RESTAURANT
97 Stoke Newington Church Street, N16 0UD. Tel: 071-254 1025
Open: Mon-Thu 12.00-22.30, Fri-Sat 12.00-23.00, Sun 12.30-22.30.
Train: Stoke Newington BR
Fish and vegetarian. International. Main course £3.75-£5.50, starters £3.00, desserts £2.50. Small and informal. New owner introduced fish to the menu in May 1994. Usually a starter and main course for vegans but best to ring first.

RASA
55 Stoke Newington Church Street, N16 0AR. Tel: 071-249 0344
Open: daily 12.00-14.30 & Mon-Thu 18.00-24.00, Fri-Sat 18.00-23.00
Train: Stoke Newington BR
Locals will know the owner, Mr Dass, who used to manage Spices before it closed down. Rasa is a south Indian restaurant that caters well for vegans and has some unusual dishes on the menu. Starters are under £2.00, try the hot and spicy rasam soup or the cashew nut pakora. Main courses are under £4.50, for a bit of a change get stuck into the idi appam (rice noodles) that come with a vegetable and coconut sauce. Anyone not wanting to go to bed on an empty stomach should finish off with the vegan kesari, a semolina dish with cashew nuts and sultanas. Very peaceful place with the colours of the food reflected in the decor. Cultural activities planned for the future.

OTHER RESTAURANTS

AMINA TANDOORI BALTI HOUSE

15 Stoke Newington Church Stree, N16.Tel: 071-275 0366/0166
Open: Sat-Thu 12.00-14.30, & Fri-Sat 17.30-24.00, Sun-Mon to 17.30-
23.30
Train: Stoke Newington BR.
Omnivorous. Balti House (see Ethnic section 'Pakistani'). The first Balti
House in London. Main meal vegetable dishes made with vegetable
ghee available in most well known flavours such as bhuna, korma,
rogan, biryani. 14 vegetarian starters at £1.75 and a good range of
flatbreads and rice. Take-away available with main meals between
£2.95-£3.40. Sunday lunch family buffet, eight items for £5.25,
Children £2.95.

ANGLO ANATOLIAN RESTAURANT

123 Stoke Newington Church Street, N16. Tel: 071-923 4349
Open: Daily 12.00-late.
Train: Stoke Newington BR
Omnivorous. Turkish. Meat dominated menu but many Mediterranean
vegetarian specialities available from amongst the starters and salad
side dishes. Haricot beans in olive oil, stuffed aubergines or aubergines
with a tomato sauce, stuffed peppers with rice and pine kernels, green
beans in olive oil are all cheap. Take-away sevice and deliveries if you
order more than 10 items.

KARNAPHULI

20 Stoke Newington Church Street, N16 0LU. Tel: 071-254 0661
Open: every day 12.00-14.00, 18.00-24.00
Train: Stoke Newington BR
Omnivorous. Indian. Average £6.00 for a vegetarian curry. Thali £6.90.
Uses vegetable oil.

LE CARIBE

20 Northwold Road, N16. Tel: 071-241 0011
Open: Mon-Sat 19.00-24.00.
Train: Stoke Newington BR
Caribbean cuisine with take-away service. Music on Sundays, stylish
feel but a lot of meat and fish. £12.00 for three vegetarian courses such
as red bean stew or curried vegetables. They are not really able to cater
for vegans.

SHAMSUDEEN'S

35 & 119 Stoke Newington Church Street, N16.
Tel: 071-241 4171/254-5696. Free local delivery: 071-241 4171
Open: Daily 11.45-15.15 & 18.00-24.00.
Train: Stoke Newington BR
Omnivorous. Singapore, Malaysian and South Indian cuisine. No 35 is

licensed, at no 119 you can take your own wine. Large menu, with one vegan dish from each cuisine though most vegetarian options come chiefly from the south Indian dishes.

SPICE OF ASIA

56 Stoke Newington Church Street, N16 0NB. Tel: 071-923 4285
Open: Daily 12.00-14.30, Sun-Thu 18.00-24.00, Fri-Sat 18.00-01.00
Train: Stoke Newington BR
Omnivorous. Tandoori & Vegetarian. Average £8.00. Restaurant, takeaway and delivery. Vegetarian thali £6.90 eat in, £5.95 takeaway, £7.25 delivered. Butter ghee, if used is stated on the menu, otherwise it's vegetable ghee or corn oil.

YUM YUM

26 Stoke Newington Church St, N16 0LU. Tel: 071-254 6751.
Open: Every day 12.00-14.30, 18.00-23.00
Train: Stoke Newington BR
Omnivorous. Thai. Average £12.00. The menu includes two pages of vegetarian dishes. Yum Yum has now expanded and taken over Spices which was next door. Huge menu and huge place.

SHOPS

FOOD FOR ALL

3a Cazenova Road, N16 6PA. Tel: 081-806 4138.
Open: Mon-Sat 09.00-18.00, (17.00 Sat), Sun 10.00-14.00.
Train: Stoke Newington BR.
Vegan wholefood shop with complementary medicine, herbs and spices. Takeaway including vegan.

GREEN EARTH WHOLEFOODS

49 Stoke Newington Church Street, N16 0AR. Tel: 071-923 1477.
Open: Mon-Fri 09.30-18.00 (19.00 Fri), Sat 10.00-19.00.
Tube: Angel then bus 73.
Organic wholefood shop with fruit, veg, green products and literature.

SHARON'S BAKERY

154 Stamford Hill, N16. Tel: 081-800 9769,
Stoke Newington BR.
24 hours a day, seven days per week bakery selling bagels.

N17 TOTTENHAM

ATTRACTIONS

WALTHAMSTOW RESERVOIRS

Ferry Lane N17. Tel: 081-808 1527.
Open: 07.30-dusk
Train: Blackhorse Road BR, Tottehham Hale BR.
A protected site because of the huge amount of wildlife.

N19 ARCHWAY, UPPER HOLLOWAY, TUFNELL PARK

NON VEGETARIAN TAKEAWAY

DELICIOUS DELICATESSEN

167 Junction Road, Upper Archway, N19 9JJ. Tel: 071-281 5684
Open: Mon-Fri 09.30-18.30. Closed weekends.
Tube: Tufnell Park, Archway
70% Vegetarian. Takeaway. Also sells some pulses. 10% Vegetarian or
Vegan Society members' discount. One vegan main course every day.
Patties and hummus are vegan. Also do outside catering.

N20 TOTTERIDGE & WHETSTONE

SHOPS

ALTERNATIVES HEALTH SHOP

1369 High Road, N20. Tel: 081-445 2675.
Open: Mon-Sat 8.30-17.45.
Tube: Totteridge & Whetstone.
5% Vegetarian Society discount on all vitamins, supplements and
cosmetics. Also sells homeopathy supplies.

N22 ALEXANDRA PALACE

ATTRACTIONS

ALEXANDRA PARK

Muswell Hill, N22. Tel: 081 365 2121, 081-444 7696.
BR Open: 24 hours daily Tube: Wood Green, Alexandra Palace
Alexandra Palace is a conference and festival venue on top of a hill
surrounded by a huge park. Venue for a number of events, lake with
boating, cafe, pitch & putt, dry ski-slope, animal sanctuary with deer,
ponies and a llama.

VEGAN CAFÉS

POPCORN IN THE PARK

... in the Grove, Alexandra Palace Park, near Garden Centre, N22 4AY.
Open: Every day except Tue 10.30-17.30. Closed Tue.
Train Wood Green (zone 3), Alexandra Palace BR + bus W3
Vegan. International. Set meal and drink is only £3.45. Seating outside. Counter service. All voluntary staff. Proceeds to Haringay MENCAP. No cheques, no capuccino, no cards, no cola, no crisps, no candy, no junk! Just excellent vegan eats and Cafe-direct. In the Grove car park, by the bandstand.

SHOPS

THE BODY SHOP

85 High Road, Wood Green, N22 6BB.
Open: Mon-Sat 09.00-18.00 (Thu 19.30).

THE GREENHOUSE

Units 65-68 Market Hall Wood Green Shopping Centre, High Road, N22. Tel: 081-881 1471.
Open: Mon-Wed 9.00-17.30, Thu-Sat 9.00-18.00.
Tube: Wood Green.
Wholefoods, healthfoods, nuts, takeaway with microwave and at least two vegan choices.

NORTH WEST LONDON

outer london

NW1	Camden Town and Chalk Farm, Regent's Park, Euston, Drummond Street, Marylebone
NW2	Neasden, Cricklewood
NW3	Hampstead, Belsize Park, Swiss Cottage
NW4	Hendon
NW5	Kentish Town
NW6	Kilburn, West Hampstead
NW7	Mill Hill
NW8	St John's Wood
NW9	Kingsbury
NW10	Willesden, Harlesden
NW11	Golders Green, Temple Fortune

NW1 CAMDEN

Drummond Street, on the west side of Euston Station, is full of popular, value for money south Indian vegetarian restaurants and grocers.

ATTRACTIONS

CAMDEN MARKET
Camden High Street, NW1
Open: Sat & Sun 08.00-18.00 Tube: Camden Town.
A number of markets converge to give you the best choice of hip new and secondhand clothes in town. Some good food stalls and takeaways. The arty bit around the lock is more expensive but has an interesting range of stalls. You can buy all your presents here in one go. Throbbin' in summer.

LONDON PLANETARIUM
Marylebone Road, NW1. Tel: 071-486 1121.
Open: Mon-Sat 09.30-17.30, Sun 10.20-17.00 Tube: Baker Street
£4.20 adults, £2.60 children, £3.25 senior citizens, no under fives.
Flop out in a comfy chair as the universe is explained above you for 30 minutes. Touch sensitive computer screens give information about the planets. A video about astronauts and space travel means you can extend your visit to one hour. Cafe serves cheesey veggie snacks.

MADAME TUSSAUD'S
Marylebone Road, NW1. Tel: 071-935 6861
Open: Daily May-Sep 09.00-17.30, Oct-Jun 10.00-17.30.
Tube: Baker Street
£5.95 adults, £3.95 children, £4.45 senior citizens.
Wax dummies museum. Bring plenty of colour film (or black and white

if you're John Major) to snap yourself with your favourite wax dummies. Big queues at peak times. Disabled toilets, wheelchairs by arrangement. An extra £1.50 gets you into the Planetarium too.

REGENT'S PARK

Off Marylebone Road, NW1. Tel: 071-486 7905 Regent's Park, St John's Wood, Camden Town.
Open: Daily 05.00-dusk Tube: Baker Street,
Attractive gardens, tennis courts, animal prison (zoo), canal at northern end, lake with boating, open-air theatre in summer, restaurant and running track. The restaurant is the Rose Garden Buffet, open daily 10.00-15.30. Tel: 071-935 5729. They always have one vegetarian hot dish though it's unlikely to be vegan.

REGENT'S CANAL INFORMATION CENTRE

289 Camden High Street, NW1. Tel: 071-482 0523
Open: Apr-Oct Mon-Fri 10.00-16.00, Sat-Sun 10.00-17.00
Tube: Camden Town
The canal links Little Venice and Limehouse on the Thames and is an ideal place for walking and jogging.

LONDON WATERBUS COMPANY

Camden Lock Place, Camden, NW1. Tel: 071-482 2550, 071-482 2660
Offer trips and private bookings on converted traditional working narrowboats. Day trips to Limehouse and the River Lea and shorter trips to Little Venice and London Zoo. The shorter trips leave from Camden Lock and Little Venice, Warwick Crescent, W2, daily between April and September. First sailing at 10.00 and then hourly until 17.00. Adult fares are £3.00 one way £4.00 return, children and senior citizens £1.85 and £2.35. Weekends only in the winter. From Camden Lock at 11.15, 12.45, 14.15, 15.45, from Little Venice 45 minutes earlier. Buy your ticket on the boat.

VEGETARIAN RESTAURANTS AND CAFES

CHUTNEYS

124 Drummond Street, Euston, NW1 2PA. Tel: 071-387 6077
Open: Every day 12.00-14.45, 18.00-23.30
Tube: Euston, Euston Square
Vegetarian. Indian. Average dinner £10.00, buffet lunch £5.00. Very friendly with food from all over India, and a favourite haunt of London Vegans. The Sunday buffet is particularly good. Vegans can get alternatives to dairy produce in the Thalis.

DIWANA BHELPOORI HOUSE

121-123 Drummond Street, Euston, NW1 2HL. Tel: 071-387 5556, 071-380 0730 Open: Every day 12.00-23.45
Tube: Euston, Euston Square

Vegetarian. South Indian. Average £5.00. Table and takeaway. Unlicensed, bring your own booze (free corkage). Very busy and lively restaurant offering a different buffet lunch every day for £3.95 between 12.00-14.30.

HUFFS

28 Chalk Farm Road, Camden Town, NW1 8AG. Tel: 071-267 5751, 071-284 1240
Open: Mon-Fri 10.00-18.00, Sat-Sun 09.00-18.00
Tube: Camden Town, Camden Road BR
Vegetarian. English wholefood. Lasagne, potato pies, crepes, salads, cakes and pastries. Free-range eggs but little for vegans. Main course £4.50. Everything homemade. Counter and takeaway service. Jazz band Saturday lunchtime. See also Huffs (Café in the Lock) below and Huffs, NW3.

HUFFS (CAFÉ IN THE LOCK)

Camden Lock, Camden Town, NW1. Tel: 071-267 9656
Open: Sat-Sun 08.30-18.00
Tube: Camden Town
Similar menu to HUFFS above. Buy your food downstairs and then find a seat in the café above.

MANNA WHOLEFOOD VEGETARIAN RESTAURANT

4 Erskine Road, Chalk Farm, NW1 3AJ. Tel: 071-722 8028
Open: Every day 18.30-24.00
Tube: Primrose Hill, Chalk Farm
Vegetarian. International wholefood menu changes daily. Always one vegan main dish, such as leek, red pepper and nut bake or cauliflower and potato curry, that comes with vegetables or salad for £5.50-£6.00. Also several salads. Wide range of starters and desserts range from £1.90-£2.30. They are known for their apple crumble made with vegan margarine. Set in a picturesque street near Primrose Hill. Reputed to be the oldest vegetarian restaurant in London and still going strong after 25 years. The decor reflects the era in which it opened. Taped music. No smoking section

RAJ BHELPOORI

19 Camden High Street, Camden Town, NW1 7JE. Tel: 071-388 6663
Open: Mon-Sat 12.00-15.00 & 18.00-23.30, Sun 12.00-22.30
Tube: Camden Town
Vegetarian. South Indian. Excellent value for money, possibly the cheapest Indian restaurant in this part of town. £3.25 eat as much as you like lunchtime buffet, £3.50 evening. The buffet includes salads and puddings and is freshly prepared each day. Table, buffet and takeaway service. Free corkage.

RAVI SHANKAR

133-135 Drummond Street, Euston, NW1 2HL. Tel: 071-388 6458
Open: Every day 12.00-23.30
Tube: Euston, Euston Square
Vegetarian. Indian. Starters £1.50-£2.50, main courses £2.75. Three course set meal £5.95. Always a special dish of the day with plenty of choice for vegans including cashew nut pillau, pancakes and loads of veg. Saturday special includes rice, batura, chickpea curry and desert £2.95. Table service. Recently refurbished. Gets very busy but only parties can book. Popular with local office workers from Capital Radio, the BBC and bank staff who haven't yet been made redundant.

ST MARYLEBONE CAFÉ

St Marylebone Crypt, 17 Marylebone Road, NW1 5LT. Tel: 071-935 6374
Open: Monday-Friday 8.30-14.30
Tube: Baker Street, Regents Park
Vegetarian. International. Average £5.00. Menu changes every day in this basement restaurant that serves soups, casseroles with rice, quiche, sandwiches, puddings, though not much for vegans. Counter and takeaway service. Free corkage. Disabled access and toilet.

OTHER RESTAURANTS

FLUKES CRADLE

173/5 Camden High Street, Camden Town, NW1 7BX.
Tel: 071-284 4499 Open: Mon-Sat 12.00-23.00, Sun 12.00-22.30
Tube: Camden Town, Camden Road BR
Omnivorous. Nigerian, French and English food which is 80% veggie and usually has three vegan dishes. Delicacies include blackeye bean stew and plantain. The bad news for everyone who loves Flukes Cradle is that it is to become part of the Cafe Toto chain during 1994. The menu will 'die a bit of a death' with much more emphasis on Mexican meat cuisine.

THE JAZZ CAFÉ

5 Parkway, Camden Town, NW1 7PG. Tel: 071-916 6000 box office,
071-916 6060 admin Open: Sun-Thu 19.00-24.00, Fri-Sat 19.00-02.00
Tube: Camden Town, Camden Road BR
Omnivorous. International. Modern British bistro inside the trendiest jazz venue in London. Admission £6.00-£12.00 depending on the artist. Average meal £10.00 with a choice of two vegetarian dishes. They will accommodate vegans with prior notice.

THANH BINH

14 Chalk Farm Road, Camden, NW1 5LT. Tel: 071-267 9820
Open: Tue-Sat 12.00-14.30 & 18.00-23.30, Sun 12.00-17.00
Tube: Chalk Farm, Primrose Hill
Omnivorous. Vietnamese. Good selection of bean curd, stir-fried

vegetables, noodles and rice dishes. Look out for the stir-fried
vegetables in coconut milk with onions and peanuts. Simply decorated
restaurant near Camden Market. Table service.

VICEROY OF INDIA

3-5 Glentworth Street, Marylebone, NW1 5PG. Tel: 071-486 3401,
071-486 3515 Open: Every day 12.00-15.00, 18.00-23.30
Tube: Baker Street, Marylebone
Omnivorous. North Indian. Table service. Vegetarian Thalis for £14.95.
Starters at £3.25 include mixed pakoras, bhelpoori and a sweet and
sour onion and garlic rice dish straight from the beaches of Bombay.
Main meals are £3.25-£4.35. They offer three types of dhal - black,
yellow and masala which is thin and hot.

SHOPS

HOLLAND & BARRETT

Unit 5 The Plaza, 191 Camden High Street, NW1 7BT.
Tel: 071-485 9477.

HOUSE OF MISTRY

129 Kentish Town Road, NW1. Tel: 071-485 7493.
Open: Mon-Sat 10.30-18.30.
Wholefood shop but with no takeaway food.

SESAME HEALTH FOODS

128 Regents Park Road, NW1. 071-586 3779.
Open: Mon-Fri 10.00-18.30, Sat 10.00-18.00, Sun 12.00-17.00.
Wholefoods and freshfoods, 50% vegan. Takeaway items include soups,
salads, rice and vegetables, quiche, hot-pots, snacks, cakes and fruit
and vegetables. Bread comes from several different bakers. Everything
you could want for a picnic on Primrose Hill.

NW2 NEASDEN, CRICKLEWOOD

If you're hungry then head west for the Indian vegetarian takeaways
in NW10, or try NW6.

MISTRY HEALTH FOOD SHOP AND PHARMACY

16 Station Parade, Willesden Green, NW2. Tel: 081-450 7002
Open: Mon-Sat 9.00-17.00 Tube: Willesden Green
Very friendly and helpful health food shop, with a pharmacy next door
where there are two homeopaths.

NW3 HAMPSTEAD, SWISS COTTAGE, BELSIZE PARK

Famous dog walking area for elderly socialists and the well off. Don't miss the fantastic Vegetarian Cottage Chinese restaurant.

ATTRACTIONS

HAMPSTEAD HEATH

Hampstead, NW3. Tel: 081-340 5303
Tube: Hampstead
Real heathland in the middle of the city. Cafe in Kenwood House, outdoor classical music concerts opposite Kenwood Lake on Saturday nights in summer. Men only, women only and mixed bathing ponds. Athletics track.

PARLIAMENT HILL

Parliament Hill, NW3. Tel: 071-485 4491. Open: Daily 24 hours.
Tube: Belsize Park, Gospel Oak BR, Hampstead Heath BR.
Great views looking south across the city. Good kite flying terrain. Excellent tobogganing if the snow falls when you're here. Tennis courts.

VEGETARIAN RESTAURANTS

FRIENDLY FALAFELS

South End Green, Hampstead, NW3.
Open: Wed-Sun 19.45-24.00, closed Mon-Tue
Tube: Hampstead Heath BR, Belsize Park
Vegan, plus vegetarian cake. Middle Eastern. Takeaway only. Falafals in pitta bread with hummous £2.20, £2.70 with salad too.

VEGETARIAN COTTAGE

91 Haverstock Hill, NW3 4RL.Tel: 071-586 1257
Open: Mon-Sat 18.00-23.30, Sun 12.00-15.30, 18.00-23.30
Tube: Belsize Park
Vegetarian and fish. Chinese. 80% vegan. Massive eight course set dinner for only £11.80. A la carte average £14.00. Sunday lunch £8.00. The first Chinese vegetarian restaurant we know in London, and winner of Time Out's best Chinese restaurant in 1993. Tasty selection of desserts with Tofutti vegan ice cream!! Booking advisable. Takeaway service as well. Last orders 23.15. Chinese beer, soya and coconut milk. You can try a Buddha's Cushion — mixed vegetables with black moss.

OTHER RESTAURANTS

ATTO'S TAKEAWAY

75 Heath Street, Hampstead, NW3. Tel: 071-435 7861
Open: Daily 12.00-22.00
Tube: Hampstead
Omnivorous. Indian. Not what you'd expect to find in one of the most expensive high streets in London. Choose from the plentiful home-cooked vegetarian dishes at only £3.20 per pound weight, bread and snacks. The foil containers will keep everything warm until you climb the hill to the heath — perfect for a picnic.

BAWARCHI

235 Finchley Road, Swiss Cottage, NW3. Tel: 071-794 9207
Open: Daily 11.00-12.00
Tube: Finchley Rd, Finchley Rd / Frognal BR
Omnivorous. North Indian. Vegetarian main dishes included in a separate section of menu in this small takeaway. Average £2.00 per dish.

FALAFEL HOUSE

95 Haverstock Hill, Hampstead, NW3 4RL. Tel: 071-722 6187
Open: Mon-Sat 18.00-23.30
Tube: Chalk Farm, Belsize Park
Omnivorous. Middle Eastern. Wide range of Middle Eastern food. Starters are £1.95-£2.25. They include a hot spicy tomato dish called

Shakshouka which can be made vegan, falafel, fresh artichokes in a vinaigrette dressing and Salat Hatzilim a delicious aubergine puree. Main portions come in a standard or large size and cost £4.95 and £5.55. They offer vegan options like the cous-cous, rice and beans, Guvetch - a ratatouille style dish - and an oriental salad. Always six to seven salads. Desserts around £1.45. 25 years on this site and one of the first falafel houses in London. Atmosphere is casual with candles on the table and background music.

HUFF'S FOODSTUFF
55 South End Road, Hampstead, NW3 2QB. Tel: 071-794 8144, 071-794 8145
Open: Mon-Sun 10.00-18.00
Tube: Hampstead
Omnivorous. Predominantly vegetarian restaurant though they do serve bacon! Average £4.00. Table, counter and takeaway service. Menu is similar to restaurant of the same name in NW1 - basically lacto-vegetarian with little for vegans. All food homemade on the premises. No smoking. Licensed.

SHOPS

THE BODY SHOP
7 High Street, Hampstead, NW3 1TU.
Open: Mon-Sat 09.30-18.00 (Thu from 10.00), Sun 11.00-18.00.

FERNS TEA AND COFFEE WAREHOUSE
2 Flash Walk, NW3. Tel: 071- 435 0959.
Coffee and tea specialists.

HAMPSTEAD HEALTH FOOD SHOP
57 Hampstead High Street, Hampstead Village, NW3 1QH. Tel: 071-435 6418. Open: Mon-Sat 10.00-18.30, Sun 12.00-18.30. Tube: Hampstead.
Healthfoods and wide selection of takeaway food with lots of vegan options including cottage pies, veggie sausages, rice and curry, cakes and flapjacks.

HOLLAND & BARRETT
14 Northways Parade, NW3 5EN. Tel: 071-722 5920.

HOUSE OF MISTRY
15-17 South End Road, Hampstead Heath, NW3. Tel: 071-794 0848, 071-794 4954. Fax: 071-431 5695. Open: Mon-Fri 09.00-19.00, Sat 09.00-18.00.
Owned by Mr Mistry, who is a chemist and nutritonist, this shop has a clinic attached for advice on diet and healing. There is a cold takeaway section as well as cruelty-free cosmetics, body products, oils and toiletries which are not tested on animals.

PEPPERCORN'S NATURAL FOOD MARKET

2 Heath Street, NW3. Tel: 071-431 1251. Open: Mon-Sat 10.00-18.30, Sun 11.00-18.00.

Health food shop selling organic vegetables, bread, vitamin supplements, organic beer and wine and Neal's Yard products. The takeaway food includes salads, soups, lasagne, stir-fried vegetables and snacks.

NW4 HENDON

NON VEGETARIAN RESTAURANTS

JUAN PEKING CUISINE

12 Sutton Parade, Church Road, Hendon, NW4 1RR. Tel: 081-203 4064
Open: Mon-Fri 12.00-14.30, 18.00-23.30, Sat-Sun 13.00-23.30
Tube: Hendon Central

Chinese. Omnivorous. £14.50. Very small restaurant and takeaway. Vegetarian set meal with eight courses including braised vegetables in garlic, mixed vegetables and bean curd, bamboo shoots and fried rice costs £14.50. Minimum charge £7.50.

KADIRIS OF HENDON

2 Park Road, Hendon, NW4 3PQ. Tel: 081-202 2929, 081-202 9851
Open: Daily 12.00-10.30
Tube: Hendon Central, Hendon BR

Omnivorous. Indian. Small restaurant and takeaway offering free home delivery service. Dial-a-meal hotline 081-202 9851. Average £2.50 per dish.

WINDOW ON THE WORLD RESTAURANT

Fenwick's, Brent Cross Shopping Centre, Hendon, NW4 3FN.
Tel: 081-202 8200
Open: Mon-Fri 10.00-19.15, Sat 9.00-17.15
Tube: Brent Cross

Omnivorous. English. Restaurant with a view in a big department store. Traditional English cuisine means lots of chips. Veggie options include nut cutlets, vegetable curry, mushroom stroganoff and others. Vegan dishes with advance notice. Average £4.00. Table service. Licensed.

SHOPS

THE BODY SHOP

Unit 25 Brent Cross Shopping Centre, NW4 3FT. Open: Mon-Fri 10.00-20.00, Sat 09.00-18.00.

HENDON HEALTH FOOD CENTRE

125 Brent Street, NW4. Tel: 081-202 9165. Open: Mon-Sat 09.00-18.00. Stocks heavy organic bread from the South London Bakery Co.

Takeaway food includes a number of savouries, carrot cake, flapjacks, vegan Eccles cakes and mince pies.

HOLLAND & BARRETT

Brent Cross Shopping Centre, NW4 3FP. Tel: 081-202 8669.

NW6 KILBURN AND WEST HAMPSTEAD

NON VEGETARIAN RESTAURANTS

GEETA

59 Willesden Lane, NW6. Tel: 071-624 1713
Open: Mon-Sat 11.30-15.00, Mon-Thu 17.30-22.45, Fri-Sat 17.30-22.45
Tube: Kilburn

Omnivorous. South Indian. Lots of good vegetarian food from Tamil Nadu and Kerala at low prices. Three courses will only set you back about £8.00. A long-established South Indian restaurant that has received a lot of media coverage for the quality and value of its food.

THE LANTERN

23a Malvern Road, Kilburn, NW6 5PS. Tel: 071-624 1796
Open: Every day 12.00-15.00, 19.00-23.30.
Tube: Queens Park, Kilburn Park

Omnivorous. International and French. A couple of interesting veggie dishes on the menu here including tomato and mushroom pate, pancakes with vegetables and tomato sauce, and a mixed vegetable bowl with kidney beans. Prices range from £2.50 for a starter, £3.95 main course, £2.25 dessert. Three course special menu for £8.90. Good use of garlic and herbs. Taped jazz in the background, can get lively.

VIJAY INDIAN RESTAURANT

49 Willesden Lane, Willesden, NW6 7RF. Tel: 071-328 1982,
071-328 1087
Open: Mon-Thu 18.00-23.00, Fri-Sat 18.00-23.45, Sun 12.00-14.45
Tube: Willesden Green

Omnivorous. South Indian. All the vegetarian favourites like dosa, vada, iddli and a wide range of desserts including kulfi, gulabjam, carrot halva (with butter unfortunately), mango and lychees. Average £6.00. Table and takeaway service. Been in business for 28 years and reckoned by the owner to be the first South Indian restaurant in London. Booking advisable at weekends.

SHOPS

ABUNDANCE NATURAL FOODS

246 Belsize Road, NW6. Tel: 071-328 4781. Open: Mon-Sat 09.30-18.30,
Sun 11.00-16.00.

Organic and wholefood shop selling a good range of vegan products and cruelty-free cosmetics including Sogood vegan yoghurt and soya cheese. Good prices on beans, rice and grains.

B GREEN

260 West End Lane, NW6. Tel: 071-433 1664. Open: Mon-Fri 10.00-18.30, Sat 10.00-17.30, Sun 11.00-14.00.
1200 lines in stock at this healthfood shop.

FOODWORLD

244 Kilburn High Road, NW6 2BS. Tel: 071 328 1709. Open: Mon-Sat 09.00-20.00, Sun 10.30-18.30.
Loads of vegan food and toiletries, soap at only 45p, three kinds of cruelty-free toothpaste, bulk legumes, lavah bread, nuts, seeds, organic vegetables and other exotica.

HUMAN NATURE

25 Malvern Road, NW6. Tel: 071-328 5452.
Two deliveries of takeaways every week include bhajias, spring rolls, vegetarian cheese pizzas and other snacks. Distributor of Japanese tonics such as the drink Energy Bomb, Relax chewing gum (featured on the Big Breakfast TV programme) and Pass, the smokers chewing gum. Take away a feeling of well being by letting Nari give you an Indian head massage (£15.00 for 15 minutes) or a deep massage (£50.00 for 90 minutes). As featured in Elle, Girl About Town, Forum and other magazines.

OLIVE TREE

84 Willesden Lane, NW6. Tel: 071-328 9078.
Open: Mon-Sat 10.00-18.30.
Assorted wholefoods, loose herbs, flower remedies, multi-vitamins, cosmetics, homeopathy, dried fruit and nuts, vegan ice-cream, yoghurts and pasta sauces. Takeaway food includes pitta, salads, hummus and bean burgers. All displayed in an old worldy style wooden interior.

PEPPERCORN'S NATURAL FOOD MARKET

193-195 West End Lane, NW6. Tel: 071-328 6874. Open: Mon-Sat 10.00-19.00, Sun 10.00-18.00.
Whopping selection of takeaway food and macrobiotic specialities from around the world, suitable even for those awkward vegan types. Sandwiches, tortillas, Mexican bean slices, vegetarian scotch eggs, rotis, latis, country pies, vegetarian sushi, spinach filo pastries, tofu parcels, rice rolls, etc. Also in stock are vitamin supplements, organic vegetables, breads, yeast and wheat free cakes. And how about this - the only place we know that does organic hummus (£2.68 per lb). All this on top of the usual toiletries, cosmetics etc.

NW8 ST JOHN'S WOOD

ATTRACTIONS

SAATCHI GALLERY
98a Boundary Road, NW8. Tel: 071-624 8299
Open: Daily 12.00-18.00 Tube: St John's Wood
Art gallery housing the massive Saatchi collection. Shows change every six months. £2.00 adults, under 12 free. Free on Friday.

LONDON CENTRAL MOSQUE
146 Park Road, NW8. Tel: 071-724 3363
Open: Daily 03.00-24.00 for worship Tube: Baker Street
Best time for visitors is 09.00-20.00. On Saturdays the Islamic Circle chaired by Cat Stevens (ex pop star) has talks about Islam. All visitors should dress modestly, women should cover arms and legs and have a scarf or other hair covering. Free literature.

VEGAN TAKEAWAY

MANNA FALAFEL CENTRE
Church Street Market, off Edgware Road, NW8.
Tube: Edgware Road
Vegan. Falafels. Vehicle trailer in outdoor market. Not there every day.

SHOPS

HOLLAND & BARRETT
55 St Johns Wood High Street, NW8 7NL. Tel: 071-586 5494.

NW9 KINGSBURY

Kingsbury is one of the areas of north and west London with a large Gujurati population so you'll find plenty of tasty ingredients in the grocers.

VEGETARIAN RESTAURANTS AND TAKEAWAY

CHANDNI SWEET MART
141 The Broadway, West Hendon, NW9 7DY. Tel: 081-202 9625
Open: Tue-Sat 10.00-19.00, Sun 10.00-17.00
Tube: Hendon BR, Hendon Central
Vegetarian. Indian. Takeaway only. Mostly Indian sweets such as jalabi, barfi, ladu and a few for vegans. £2.50 per lb. All made with vegetable ghee.

GAYATRI SWEET MART
467 Kingsbury Road, Kingsbury, NW9 9DY. Tel: 081-206 1677
Open: Mon-Fri 10.30-18.30, Sat 10.00-19.00, Sun 9.00-16.30
Tube: Kingsbury
Vegetarian. Indian. Takeaway only. Mostly Indian sweets but with
some savouries such as samosas, Bombay mix and gathia.

KRISHNA BHAJIA HOUSE
198 The Broadway, West Hendon, NW9. Tel: 081-202 4590
Open: Mon-Fri 11.30-21.00, Sat-Sun 10.30-21.00
Tube: Hendon, Hendon Central
Vegetarian. Indian. Full meal of rice, curry and chapatti for only £2.75.
Weekend special £3.50. Plenty of vegan options with a range of special
sweets cooked on the premises by the owner. Mainly a takeaway, 20
seats inside. Unlicensed. Able to cater for parties, weddings and other
functions.

NW10 WILLESDEN, HARLESDEN

The library in Willesden High Road is open till 8.00pm. A great place
to relax, read and write for a day and totally free. In the complex are
free toilets, telephone, cafe, bookshop and a cinema, and opposite are a
post office and stationery store.

VEGETARIAN RESTAURANTS AND CAFES

BHAVNA SWEET MART
237 High Road, Willesden, NW10. Tel: 081-459 2516
Open: Daily 10.00-21.00
Tube: Dollis Hill or Willesden Green
Vegetarian. Indian. Takeaway with six seats inside. Large variety of
savouries including vegetarian curries and rice, bhajias, samosas. Rice
and curry is £1.65 large, £1.30 small. Nan or paratha 50p. No eggs
used.

SABRAS INDIAN VEGETARIAN RESTAURANT
263 High Road, Willesden, NW10 2RX. Tel: 081-459 0340
Open: Tue-Sun 11.30-15.30 & 18.30-22.30
Tube: Dollis Hill
Vegetarian. South Indian. Mysore Cafe menu at lunchtime, with dishes
like dosa (large stuffed pancake) for £2.35, all drinks including mango
or coconut joice £65p, beer and lassi £1.25, sweets £1.25. Sabras
Restaurant menu in the evenings with a three course meal for £12.00.
Extremely friendly and helpful to vegans, using groundnut oil in dosas
and for frying. They have just introduced a new range of sweets made
from pistachio and cashew nuts that are decorated to give them the
appearance of mangos, watermelons and other fruit. Finalist in 1991

Time Out Restaurant of the Year. 12.5% service charge in the evenings is waived if you join the Sabras Club for £12.50 per year. The new Tycoon Club for £1 gives 10% discount on 30 beers and 25 vegetarian wines for a year. 18.30-19.30 is happy hour with a glass of wine, beer and starters all costing just £1.00.

WILLESDEN SWEET MART

265 High Road, Willesden, NW10 2RX. Tel: 081-451 1276
Open: Wed-Mon 10.00-20.00, Tue closed
Tube: Dollis Hill
Vegetarian. Indian. Sweets, savoury snacks and meals. Curry and rice £1.10-£2.60 depending on size. Paratha 40p. Uses butter ghee and milk, but some dishes are vegan, and all are made on the premises. Takeaway and counter service with a small number of seats.

SHOPS

MEERAS HEALTH FOOD CENTRE

2 High Street, Harlesden, NW10 4LX. Tel: 081-965 7610.
Open: Mon-Sat 09.30-18.00.
Healthfood shop with organic bread and vegetables, and Tofutti vegan dairy ice-cream. They have a herbalist, nutritionist and acupuncturist on site to give free advice on the products stocked.

RAINBOW HEALTH FOOD STORE

71 Chamberlayne Road, NW10. Tel: 081-960 2686.
Open: Mon-Sat 10.00-17.30.
Takeaway foods including samosas and aduki pies.

REVITAL HEALTH SHOP

35 High Road, Willesden NW10. Tel: 081-459 3382.
Open: Mon-Sat 09.30-19.00.
Nutritionist on site to give free advice on supplements. Macrobiotic foods also stocked. Sister shop is near Victoria station, see SW1.

NW11 GOLDERS GREEN

VEGETARIAN RESTAURANTS

THE GREENERY

853-855 Finchley Road, Golders Green, NW11 8LX. Tel: 081-455 0692
Open: Sun-Thu 10.00-22.00, Fri 10.00-15.00 Tube: Golders Green
Vegetarian. Wholefood. For vegans there is always one vegan soup at £2.20, at least one main meal such as nut roat and many savouries like spring rolls, hummus and a selection of salads. Also a vegan dessert and a couple of cakes, which can be washed down with a wide range of herb teas. Based in the Jewish Vegetarian Society building with no indication it is a restaurant from the outside. Friendly, simple, earthy

decor. Counter and table service. 30 seats. Free corkage.

TABOON BAKERY

17 Russell Parade, Golders Green Road, Golders Green, NW11.
Tel: 081-455 7451
Open: 20.00-24.00
Tube: Brent Cross
Kosher vegetarian takeaway with falafel, hummus and salad for only
£1.75.

SHOPS

HOLLAND & BARRETT

81 Golders Green Road, NW11 8EN. Tel: 081-455 5811. Health foods.

TEMPLE HEALTH FOODS

Temple Fortune Parade, NW11. Tel: 081-209 0059. Open: Mon-Fri
08.45-18.00, Sun 10.00-14.00.
Lots of non-dairy goods including two brands of vegan ice-cream, ice-
cream bars and yoghurts. Large stock of vitamins and minerals and
will order anything requested.

SOUTH EAST LONDON

SE1	Borough, Waterloo, Old Kent Road, Elephant & Castle, London Bridge
SE2	Abbey Wood
SE3	Blackheath
SE4	Brockley
SE5	Camberwell
SE6	Catford
SE7	Charlton
SE8	Deptford
SE9	Eltham
SE10	Greenwich
SE11	Vauxhall, Kennington, Oval
SE12	Lee, Grove Park
SE13	Lewisham
SE14	New Cross
SE15	Peckham, Nunhead
SE16	Rotherhithe
SE17	Walworth
SE18	Woolwich, Plumstead
SE19	Crystal Palace, Gypsy Hill
SE20	Penge
SE21	Dulwich
SE22	East Dulwich
SE23	Forest Hill, Honor Oak
SE24	Herne Hill, Brixton
SE25	Norwood
SE26	Sydenham
SE27	West Norwood
SE28	Plumstead Marsh

SE1 THE SOUTH BANK

South London spreads out from SE1, historically a commercial area that developed because of its proximity to the City, which is just the other side of any one of the bridges in the area. There are some major tourist sights including the South Bank complex, the capital's largest arts venue.

ATTRACTIONS

BERMONDSEY ANTIQUES MARKET

Corner of Long Lane and Bermondsey Street, SE1.
Open: Fri 05.00-12.00 Tube: London Bridge
Loads of antiques and artefacts to choose from.

DESIGN MUSEUM
Butlers Wharf, Shad Street, SE1. Tel: 071-403 6933, 071-407 6261
recorded information.
Open: Mon-Sun 10.30-17.30 Tube: London Bridge
£3.50 adults, £2.50 concessions, under sixes free.
Evolution of household items. Bar, cafe, restaurant, shop.

HMS BELFAST
Morgan's Lane, Tooley Street, SE1. Tel: 071-407 6434
Open: Daily Mar-Oct 10.00-18.00, Nov-Feb 10.00-15.00
Tube: London Bridge. £4.00 adults, £3.00 concessions, £2.00 children.
Ex second world war battleship, now a floating museum.

IMPERIAL WAR MUSEUM
Lambeth Road, SE1. Tel: 071-416 5000, recorded info 071-820 1683.
Open: Daily 10.00-18.00 Tube: Lambeth North, Elephant & Castle
£3.70 adults, £2.65 concessions, £1.85 children. Free after 16.30.
Experience the horror of an air raid or the trenches without getting
hurt or dirty. Enough to turn anyone pacifist. Many London museums
close on bank holidays so phone ahead. Wheelchair access. Shop, cafe,
films.

LONDON DUNGEON
28-34 Tooley Street, SE1. Tel: Admin 071-403 7221,
recorded information 071-403 0606 Open: Daily 10.00-17.30
Tube: London Bridge £6.00 adults, £5.00 concessions, £4.00 children.
Gruesomely evil medieval torture museum. Entrance includes audio
shows about the guillotine and Jack the Ripper.

MUSEUM OF THE MOVING IMAGE (MOMI)
South Bank, SE1. Tel: Box office 071-928 3232, recorded information
071-401 2636. Open: Daily 10.00-18.00 Tube: Waterloo
£5.50 adults, £4.75 concessions, £4.00 children, family ticket £16.00.
Interactive fun seeing the story of film and television.

SHAKESPEARE GLOBE MUSEUM
Bear Gardens, Bankside, SE1. Tel: 071-928 6342.Open: Mon-Sat 10.00-
17.00, Sun 14.00-17.30. Tube: London Bridge
£3.00 adults, £2.00 concessions £2.00 children. Cafe.

SOUTH BANK ARTS CENTRE
Belvedere Road, Albert Embankment, SE1. Tel: Box office 071-928 8800,
information 071-928 3003, recorded information 071-633 0932
Open: Daily 10.00-23.00. Tube: Waterloo
Standby tickets from 17.00 on day of performances. Free exhibitions
and lunchtime musical performances, cafes, book and music shops, or
splash out on a big name classical concert in the evening. The South
Bank is a major centre for arts, theatre, drama, dance and classical and
operatic music. The complex includes the Royal Festival Hall (largest

concert hall), Queen Elizabeth Hall (small concert hall), Purcell Room (recital hall), Hayward Gallery, National Film Theatre, National Theatre. Love it or hate it this concrete riverside venue offers fine productions and is a great place to hang out and have a coffee. Substantial reductions on concert tickets for students. Free music Sunday lunchtimes.

TOWER BRIDGE

Tel: 071-407 0922 Open: Apr-Oct daily 10.00-14.30, Nov-Mar daily 10.00-18.30. Museum £3.50, concessions £2.50.

The bridge the Americans thought they were buying and the one that raises to allow large ships through, with excellent views over the Thames. There are various shows on the different levels and you end up in the engine room. The tour last about 90 minutes (see also EC3).

NON-VEGETARIAN RESTAURANTS

CAFÉ CLUB

62 Union Street, Southwark, SE1 1TD. Tel: 071-378 1988
Open: Mon-Fri 12.00-14.30 cafe, 21.00-02.00 Jazz Club and restaurant
Tube: Borough/London Bridge

Traditional British home cooking with an international flavour. Waiter service in the evening and counter service at lunchtime in this bombed out 50's dive where nothing matches — that's how the manager describes it. Unpretentious and full of character you can eat, drink and listen to jazz until the early hours. Good selection of vegetarian food and always one vegan option as they do a number of hotpots, ratatouilles and ragouts. Cover charge is £3.00 midweek, £4.00-£5.00 at the weekend.

CAFÉ ROUGE

Hays Galleria, 3 Counter Street, Tooley Street, London Bridge, SE1.
Tel: 071-378 0097/6 Open: Mon-Fri 10.00-22.00, Sat-Sun 10.00-18.00
Tube: London Bridge

Omnivorous. French. Average £5.50-£9.50 for a main course. Menu changes regularly. The soup is usually vegan, but best to ring in advance to book a main course as most veggie options are cheesey. Coffee bar too. Based in an expensive 80's shopping development.

CAESARS AMERICAN RESTAURANT

103-107 Waterloo Road, Waterloo, SE1 8UL. Tel: 071-928 5707
Open: Mon-Sat 11.30-23.30, Sun 11.30-20.00.
Tube: Waterloo

Omnivorous. American in size of portions which all come with potatoes or chips and salad. Vegetarian section and separate menu with starters such as garlic mushrooms or potato skins at £2.60. Main courses, usually two of which are vegan are approximately £5.50 and include lasagne, a veggie burger, vegetable pancake roll, cashew pillau, veg chilli and mushroom stroganoff. Taped music and fast service amid romanesque decor.

DOWNTOWN SULEMANS
1 Cathedral Street, SE1 9DE. Tel: 071-928 6374
Open: Mon-Fri 12.00-14.45, 18.30-22.30.
Tube: Waterloo
Omnivorous. Continental restaurant with a jazz club in the evenings and £4.00 entrance Friday. Menu changes monthly. Light meal for two £11.00. Three vegetarian dishes with rice. There are usually vegan options but it's best to ring first. No vegetarian wines. Very modern, set in a historic area opposite the Cathedral and Borough fruit and veg market.

FESTIVAL HALL SALAD BAR
Festival Hall Foyer, South Bank, SE1 8XX.Tel: 071-921 0800
Open: Daily till 22.00
Tube: Waterloo
Omnivorous. Mediterranean. Average £4.50 for a salad. Buffet style salad bar in the Festival Hall near the bar, record shop and bookshop. Good place to chill out and enjoy occassional live music, even for Philistines.

MESON DON FELIPE
53A The Cut, SE1 8LF. Tel: 071-928 3237
Open: Mon-Sat 12.00-23.00.
Tube: Waterloo
Omnivorous. Spanish tapas bar with stools and tables. A number of vegetarian tapas in this lively bar. Gets crowded prior to performances at either of the two Vic (Young and Old) theatres nearby.

MUTIARA
14 Walworth Road, Newington, SE1. Tel: 071-277 0425
Open: Mon-Fri 12.00-14.30, daily 18.00-23.15.
Tube: Elephant & Castle
Omnivorous. Indonesian/Malay. Vegans sidestep the eggs in some dishes. Vegetarian or vegan lunch £2.95. The Elephant is not the sort of place you'd travel to even for Indonesian food, unless of course you're going to the Ministry of Sound nightclub - though by the time most Ministry merrymakers are hungry the restaurant will have been closed for six hours.

PIZZERIA CASTELLO
20 Walworth Road, Newington, SE1 6SP. Tel: 071-703 2556
Open: Mon-Fri 12.00-23.00, Sat 17.00-23.00
Tube: Elephant & Castle
Omnivorous. Pizzas. Average £8.00. Table service and takeaway. Chill

out at the downstairs bar with some Italian bottled beer. You can have pasta and pizza without the cheese which all has animal rennet.

SHOPS

ABSOLUTELY STARVING

Unit 14, Hay's Galleria, Tooley Street, SE1 2HD. Tel: 071-407 7417.
Open: Mon-Fri 07.00-20.00, Sat-Sun 10.00-21.00.
Sandwiches in many forms are a speciality at this delicatessen, though there are anly about 10 varieties for vegetarians with a few savouries that are vegan. Vegetarian cheese is used, Some interesting food with specialities from Thailand and Italy. Surplus food donated to the local churches.

COOPERS

17 Lower Marsh, SE1. Tel: 071-261 9314.
Open: Mon-Fri 8.30-17.30, Sat 9.30-13.30.
Takeaway pies and pasties for vegans, vitamin supplements, wholefoods.

HAY'S GALLERIA

Tooley Street, SE1. Tel: 071-357 7770. Open: Mon-Sun 06.00-23.30.
Tube: London Bridge / London Bridge BR.
Very 80's up-market shopping and eating covered arcade created from the remains of old warehouses. Serving mostly local office workers so busy at lunchtime and after work.

NUTSTOP

Waterloo railway station by platform 8.
Open: Mon-Fri 8.30-23.30, Sat 9.00-20.30, Sun 10.00-20.30.
Self-service nuts and vegetarian snack foods.

ON YER BIKE

52-54 Tooley Street, SE1. Tel: 071-357 6958
Open: Mon-Fri 09.99-18.00, Sat 09.30-17.30
Bike hire available, racers and three-speeds £8.00 first day, £6.00 subsequent day, £15.00 per weekend, £25.00 per week. £50.00 deposit. Mountain bikes are £14.00 for the first day, £10.00 for the subsequent day, £25.00 weekends and £50.00 per week. They require a deposit of £200. Identification with proof of address required for all hire.

SE3 BLACKHEATH

ATTRACTIONS

BLACKHEATH COMMON
Shooters Hill Road, SE3.
Large open space on the south side of Greenwich Park. One of the best
kite flying venues in London especially on Sundays. Blackheath
Village and Greenwich are both a pleasant stroll away.

OXLEAS WOOD
Shooters Hill Road, SE3.
The only ancient woodland remaining in London, though it wouldn't be
if the Department of Transport had had its wicked way and turned
part of it into the East London River Crossing.

VEGETARIAN RESTAURANTS

WELL BEAN VEGETARIAN RESTAURANT
10 Old Dover Road, SE3. Tel: 081-858 1319
Open: Mon-Fri 09.00-18.30, Sat 09.00-17.30
Train: Blackheath BR
Vegetarian. Wholefood. Everything cooked on the premises. Soup of
the day £1.35 always vegan and usually other alternatives too such as
chickpea pasties. Special dish of the day £3.25. Other items include
four types of quiche £1.95, curried vegetable pie, vegetable tikka
masala and rice, sausage rolls, cheese and potato pie, vegetarian scotch
eggs and potato pie. All made with vegetable rennet cheese.

SHOPS

HEALTH & DIET CENTRE
31 Tranquil Vale, Blackheath, SE3. Tel: 081-318 0448.
Open: Mon-Sat 09.00-18.00.
A healthfood shop with vegan manager. Changing range of takeaways
for you to get to grips with including Mexican bean slices, pasties,
bhajias, pakoras. Chilled foods include vegan 'rashers', tofu, vegan
hard and soft cheeses, Toffutti ice-cream. There is a great variety of
specialist bread. All with a 10% discount to Vegan Society members -
off you go.

WELL BEAN HEALTH FOOD SHOP
9 Old Dover Road, SE3. Tel: 081-858 6854.
Opposite the restaurant of the same name. Vegetarian Society
discount.

SE5 CAMBERWELL

NON VEGETARIAN RESTAURANTS

SECRET GARDEN

Behind Franklin's Antique Market, 161 Camberwell Road, SE5.
Tel: 071-703 8089.
Open: Mon-Sat 12.00-16.00, Sun 13.00-17.00
Train: Denmark Hill BR, Oval, Elephant & Castle
Omnivorous. International. Menu includes sweet potato, pie, and curry. Starter £1.75, main £2.50, dessert £1.75. Children's portions. Corkage 75p. Vegetarian proprietor. Not always a lot for vegans but give them a ring first. The secret, secluded ramshackle walled garden is a world away from the Walworth Road, sit out in summer and dream on.

SEYMOUR BROTHERS

2 Grove Lane, Camberwell SE5. Tel: 071-701 4944
Open: Mon-Sat 09.00-19.00, Sun 09.00-18.00.
Train: Denmark Hill BR
Omnivorous. Camberwell won't be on many tourist itineraries but for locals there is more in the area than at first meets the visitor's eye. This converted Victorian building is a relaxing cafe, especially in summer when the walled garden traps the sun and you can imagine you're somewhere really exotic before queuing for the 36 bus. The food is omnivorous with a lot of cheese but the coffee and atmosphere are conducive to sustained newspaper reading.

SOPAR THAI RESTAURANT

105 Southampton Way, Peckham, SE5 7SX. Tel: 071-703 8983
Open: Mon-Sat 18.30-23.00.
Train: Peckham Rye BR, Elephant & Castle
Omnivorous. Thai. Takeaway service available. The tragedy of the Sopar is that only locals are likely to visit because of its location in north Peckham. Originally a cafe in a converted terraced house, the Sopar offers a great menu with 16 vegetarian main dishes, many vegan, ranging from £3.00-£4.50, two vegan starters at £2.00, desserts at £1.50 and Singha Thai beer at £1.80 a bottle. It is entirely staffed by women. All food is prepared on the premises and is better than you'll find in many Thai restaurants in town charging twice the price. The curries are excuisitely flavoured and the banana cooked in sweet coconut cream is a dream to finish off with. This is Thailand if you're drinking Bacardi.

SHOPS

HEALTH FARM SHOP

6 Camberwell Church Street, SE5. Tel: 071-703 7130.
Open: Mon-Sat 08.00-18.00.
Small shop but strategically very important for those in SE5. Some takeaway food though mostly pre-packed and wholefoods.

SE6 CATFORD

VEGETARIAN RESTAURANT

VEGETARIA RESTAURANT

275 Brownhill Road, Catford, SE6 1AE. Tel: 081-461 5550
Open: Every day 18.00-23.30.
Train: Catford Bridge
Vegetarian. South Indian. Thali £4.75. Starters £2.75 dosa and samba. No eggs used. Sweets are not vegan. The only vegetarian restaurant in the Catford area nowadays. 1992 Vegetarian Living magazine award winner. Takeaway too. Book at weekends.

SHOPS

HOLLAND & BARRETT

Catford Centre, 33 Winslade Way, SE6 4JU. Tel: 081-690 3903.

SE8 DEPTFORD

VEGETARIAN RESTAURANT

HEATHER'S CAFÉ-BISTRO

190 Trundleys Rd, Deptford, SE8. Tel: 081-691 6665. Open: Wed-Sat 19.00-22.30, Sun 12.30-18.00.
Tube: Surrey Quays, New Cross Gate, New Cross. Train: New Cross Gate, South Bermondsey BR
Vegan/Vegetarian. Wholefood. All you can eat homemade buffet £7.50 includes bread, soup, hot and cold dishes and sticky puddings and changes every day. No smoking on Wed, Fri, Sun. Corkage £0.30. Heather's has absolutely taken SE8 by storm since opening in late '93 and getting rave reviews for the atmosphere and quality of the food in all the London press - even that part of it not usually sympathetic to the cruelty-free cause. So popular at the weekend we couldn't even get a reservation when we wanted to go and had to send a posse to check it out. They caught the monthly women-only night with live music which they tell was great and late. There are also exhibitions and various competitions to add to the fun. Unmissable though not the easiest

outer london

place to get to. A regular café during the day. Walled garden at back.

SE9 ELTHAM

SHOPS

COURT FARM GRANARIES
89 Mottingham Road, Eltham, SE9 4TJ. Tel: 081-857 0857.
Open: Mon-Sat 09.00-18.00.
Wholefoods. Daily changing selection of takeaway vegetable pasties, flans, shepherds pies. Fresh bread. Some organic goods. Lots of vitamin tablets.

HOLLAND & BARRETT
198 Eltham High Street, SE9 1BJ. Tel: 081-859 7075.

ONLY **£7.50** BUYS YOU **ALL YOU CAN EAT**

BRING YOUR OWN DRINK AND AN EMPTY STOMACH!

30p per head corkage

INDULGE YOURSELF FROM OUR HOME COOKED **VEGAN+VEGETARIAN BUFFET**

(£4.00 children)

AT **HEATHER'S CAFÉ-BISTRO**

190 TRUNDLEYS ROAD DEPTFORD SE 8
RESERVATIONS 081-691-6665

PRICE INCLUDES: HOMEMADE BREAD AND SOUP, SELECTION OF HOT AND COLD DISHES, SALADS AND DESSERTS.

OPEN FROM 7PM WED - SAT
12.30-6PM SUN. (Evening by arrangement only)

NO SMOKING ON WEDNESDAYS, FRIDAYS OR SUNDAYS.

Remember to say you saw it in the Cruelty-Free Guide

SE10 GREENWICH

ATTRACTIONS

GREENWICH CRAFTS MARKET

Off College Approach, SE10. Open: Sat-Sun 10.00-17.00
Train: Greenwich BR or foot tunnel from Island Gardens (Docklands Light Railway)
Undercover market selling a range of quality crafts and handmade goods. Covent Garden Piazza with a smaller range but smaller mark up.

GREENWICH OPEN AIR MARKET

Town Centre end of Greenwich High Road, SE10.
Open: Sat-Sun 10.00-17.00. Train: Greenwich BR or foot tunnel from Island Gardens (Docklands Light Railway)
Good quality secondhand clothes, bric-a-brac, antiques. Some cheap book shops nearby.

GREENWICH PARK

Charlton Way, SE10. Tel: 081-858 2608. Open: 06.00 pedestrians, 07.00 traffic, till dusk. Train: Greenwich, Maze Hill BR
Pleasant park that extends up the hill to Blackheath. Borders the National Maritime Museum, houses the Observatory and gives one of the best views of London. Cafe. Tel: 081-858 9695.

NATIONAL MARITIME MUSEUM

Romney Road, SE10. Tel: 081-858 4422. Open: Mon-Sat 10.00-17.00, Sun 14.00-17.00. Train: Greenwich, Maze Hill BR
Museum of all things nautical. Linked administratively with the Old Royal Observatory and the Cutty Sark. A ticket to all three sites is £7.45 adult, £14.50 family and would keep you going for most of the day. Entrance to one site is £3.75.

ROYAL OBSERVATORY

Greenwich Park, SE10. Tel: 081-858 4422.
Train: Greenwich, Maze Hill BR
The centre of the universe as far as time goes. Optical instrument museum.

ROYAL NAVAL COLLEGE

King William Walk. Open: Wed-Fri 14.30-17.00. Train: Greenwich, Maze Hill BR. Free.
Designed by Sir Christpher Wren.

VEGETARIAN RESTAURANTS AND CAFES

ESCAPED BISTRO

141 Greenwich South Street, Greenwich, SE10 8NX. Tel: 081-692 5826

Open: Mon-Sat 10.00-22.30, Sun 11.00-20.00.
Train: Lewisham, Greenwich BR
Vegetarian. International. 30 special dishes that rotate with five on at any one time such as Woodland Casserole with chestnuts and a herb sauce, Thai stir-fry with noodles in lemon grass and coconut milk. 40% vegan and some gluten-free dishes. Three course meal for around £10.00, corkage 60p. Also art gallery, gifts, postcards and posters, free chess and board games to use. This has always been a great place to while away the time, write letters and postcards. It's now branching out with free children's entertainment on Sundays and Shiatsu massage classes. A little way from the centre of Greenwich but bus stop right outside. And one day there will be vegan desserts.

ROYAL TEAS

76 Royal Hill, Greenwich SE10 9BY. Tel: 081-691 7240
Open: Mon-Sat 10.30-18.00, Sun 10.30-18.30.
Tube: Greenwich BR.
Vegetarian. Café. Revive yourself after a sightseeing tour of Greenwich and a haggle in the market in this vegetarian wholefood cafe-restaurant just off the beaten track. It serves savouries and cakes but offers few vegan options. Herbal teas and coffee are a speciality and corkage is free.

GOOGIES

19 Greenwich South Street, Greenwich, SE10 8NW. Tel: 081-305 0626
Open: Mon-Fri 9.00-20.00, Sat 10.00-17.30, Sun 11.00-17.00
Train: Greenwich BR
Vegetarian and fish. Wholefood. Café and shop. Snacks and desserts £1.25, main meal £3.25. Vegan food includes stir-fries, salads, bean and sausage casserole, veg and lentil curries, soya mince shepherds pie (no need to peel any shepherds), veg chilli, rice and seaweed balls. Menu changes daily. Everything made on the premises and they sell their own frozen foods in the shop.

SHOPS

HEALTH-WISE

86 Royal Hill, SE10. Tel: 081-692 0305.
Open: Mon-Sat 9.00-17.30, Sun 10.00-13.30.
Small health food shop with no hot takeaways.

STEPPING STONES

97 Trafalgar Road, SE10. Tel: 081-853 2733. Open: Mon-Thu 10.00-18.00, Fri-Sun 10.00-17.00.
New Age shop with everything for the old hippy. Books, tarot, astrology, aroma oils, stones and crystals, candles, music, incense, flower remedies. Therapy room soon. Tarot readings and classes, and healing workshops.

SE11 KENNINGTON

THE FINCA
185 Kennington Lane, SE11 4EZ. Tel: 071-735 1061
Open: Mon-Sat 12.00-24.00, Sun 12.00-23.00
Tube: Kennington.
Omnivorous. Spanish tapas and wine bar. 11 vegetarian tapas on the menu. Has a sister branch in N1 with the same name.

SE13 LEWISHAM

NON-VEGETARIAN RESTAURANTS

THE COFFEE SHAK
39 Lee High Road, Lewisham, SE13 5NS. Tel: 081-297 9058
Open: Mon-Sat 10.00-17.30, Sun 11.00-18.00
Train: Lewisham BR, Ladywell BR
Omnivorous. European and Indian. Ex-vegetarian restaurant. Table and counter service. Main meals include vegetable curries, lasagne, salads, pasta, macaroni and various bakes as well as vegan cakes and pastries. Mango lassi is very popular as well as the fresh lemonade and lemon juice. Also have a takeaway service and patisserie. Display work by local artists.

SHOPS

THE BODY SHOP
Unit 40a, The Lewisham Centre, Lewisham High Street, SE13 5JX.
Open: Mon-Thu 09.30-17.30 (Tue fm10.00), Fri 9.30-18.00, Sat 9-18.00.

SE14 NEW CROSS

VEGETARIAN RESTAURANTS

THE CAFFE
304 New Cross Road, New Cross, SE14 6AF. Tel: 081-602 1290
Open: Mon-Fri 9.30-16.30, Sat 11.00-15.00.
Tube: New Cross, New Cross Gate
Vegetarian. Wholefood counter service. Easy to meet people here as you can end up sharing a table with all sorts of interesting folk, often with business at Goldsmiths Art College just around the corner. A real oasis for those looking for a healthy lunch or drink in the area. Good selection of more unusual pastries and snacks, many of which are vegan, as well as hot dishes and salads. Crowded between 1-2pm in term time. Has the added bonus of being next door to Cross Currants where you can pick up your wholefoods.

SHOPS

CROSS CURRANTS WHOLEFOOD STORE
302 New Cross Road, SE14. Tel: 081-692 1290.
Next door to The Caffe with really helpful and knowledgeable staff who even mark up Nestle products. (Nestle ignore UN resolutions by giving away powdered milk in developing world hospitals. Which is why more and more people are saying Nescafe no thanks.)

SE15 PECKHAM, NUNHEAD

ORIGIN CAFÉ
Asylum Road, Peckham, SE15. Tel: 071-277 8914.
Open: Mon-Fri 10.00-18.00
Train: Queens Road BR.
Omnivorous. Small cafe that has recently started serving an interesting vegetarian menu in the most unlikely of locations. It's not going to attract tourist traffic being 100 yards from the Old Kent Road but is great for locals and students at the college next door, who can now choose from dishes like corn, peanut and dry potato curry, chilli con soya with spinach, mushroom and ginger cream. Seats about 16.

SE17 WALWORTH

SHOPS

BALDWINS HEALTH FOOD SHOP
171 Walworth Road, Elephant & Castle, SE17 1RW. Tel: 071-701 4892.
Open: Mon-Sat 9.00-17.30. Tube: Elephant & Castle.
Takeaway and shop. Hot and and cold snacks, with vegan bhajias and samosas. Organic vegetables.

BALDWINS HEALTH FOOD CENTRE
171 Walworth Road, SE17. Tel: 071-703 5550. Open: Tue-Sat 09.00-17.30.
Herbalist. Herbs, oils, candles, incense, books etc.

EAST STREET MARKET
East Street, SE17. Open: Tue-Thu & Sun 08.00-15.00, Fri-Sat 08.00-17.00. Tube: Elephant & Castle
Cheap market for food, household goods and secondhand goods on a Sunday morning. Authentic working-class South London.

FARESHARES FOOD COOP
56 Crampton St, Pullens Estate, SE17. No phone. Open: Thu, 14.00-20.00, Fri-Mon 15.00-1900
All vegan - get your totally cruelty-free household goods, dried foods,

fruit and veg, preserves, spreads, toiletries, cleaning products and groceries for much less than you'd pay in the high street.

SE18 WOOLWICH

So what can we say about Woolwich apart from, 'We're not with them. We're with the Ecology Building Society, Co-op Bank, and Ethical Investors'.

ATTRACTIONS

THAMES BARRIER

Unity Way, Woolwich SE18. Tel: 081-854 1373
Visitor's Centre open Mon-Fri 10.30-17.00, Sat-Sun 10.30-17.30
Train: Charlton BR. £2.50 adults, £1.55 senior citizens and children.
Cafe which always has vegetarian soup, quiche, potatoes. Vegans can be cooked for in a group if they ring first 081-316 4438. Wheelchair access.

SHOPS

THE BODY SHOP

80 Powys Street, Woolwich, SE18 6LQ. Open: Mon-Sat 09.00-17.30.

SE19 CRYSTAL PALACE, GYPSY HILL

ATTRACTIONS

CRYSTAL PALACE NATIONAL SPORTS CENTRE

Ledrington Road, SE19. Tel: 081-778 0131
Box office open: Mon-Fri 09.30-17.00
Open: Wed-Sat 19.00-22.30, Sun 12.30-18.00. Train: Crystal Palace BR
Britain's national sports centre. Major athletics and swimming venue. Concerts in the large park on Sundays in the summer. Camp site in the grounds.

SE20 PENGE

SHOPS

BEANBAGS

152 Maple Road, SE20. Tel: 081-659 1242. Open: Tue, Thu-Sat 9.00-17.00, Mon 10.00-13.00. Closed Wed, Sun.
Whole foods, loose spices and herbs. 40% organic fruit and veg, free-range and organic eggs. No takeaway. Owner's sister is vegan. Oko and Second Skin t-shirts.

SE22 EAST DULWICH

SHOPS

LORDSHIP LANE DELICATESSEN

9 Lordship Lane, East Dulwich, SE22 8EN. Tel: 081-299 3181. Open: Mon-Sat 9.00-20.00, Sun 10.00-19.00.
75% health and wholefood, TVP, nuts, pulses, veg, frozen food, general groceries. Sandwiches and rolls but little for vegans.

SE24 HERNE HILL

VEGETARIAN CAFES

121 CAFÉ

121 Railton Road, Brixton, SE24 0LR. Tel: 071-274 6655.
Open: First and third Thursday of the month from 20.00.
Tube: Brixton
Vegetarian. Cheap vegetarian and vegan meals. Featuring experimental live music. The café is based at the anarchist centre bookshop which opens Wed-Sat 13.00-17.00.

SHOPS

VEGETARIA

25 Half Moon Lane, Herne Hill, SE24. No phone.
Small wholefood shop. Grab a bite and walk across to Brockwell Park to test your fitness. The perimeter road is exactly two miles round. If you can run it in under 8 minutes you are one fit veggie - award yourself a carrot.

SE26 SYDENHAM

SHOPS

WELL BEING HEALTH FOODS

19 Sydenham Road, SE26. Tel: 081-659 2003. Open: 09.00-18.00
Organic food, beers and wines, herbal medicines. Chinese acupuncturist, homeopathic and iridology consultant. Bakery.

SOUTH WEST (OUTER)

SW 1, 3, 5, 6, 7, 10 - see south west London (inner)
SW2   Brixton, Tulse Hill
SW4   Clapham
SW8   Vauxhall, South Lambeth
SW9   Stockwell, Brixton
SW11   Battersea, Clapham Junction
SW12   Balham
SW13   Barnes
SW14   Mortlake, Sheen
SW15   Putney
SW16   Streatham
SW17   Tooting
SW18   Wandsworth, Southfields
SW19   Wimbledon
SW20   Rayners Park, Merton

SW2 BRIXTON, TULSE HILL

NON VEGETARIAN RESTAURANTS

INDORASA
53a Streatham Hill, SW2 4TS. Tel: 081-671 5919
Open: Wed-Thu, Mon & Sun 18.30-23.00, Fri-Sat 18.30-23.30
Train: Streatham Hill BR
Omnivorous. Indonesian/Dutch. Rijstaffel cuisine with some great
vegetarian food. Small, comfortable and intimate restaurant with very
helpful staff. Vegetarian set meal has 11 dishes and can be adapted for
vegans. It is £13.00 and is a real blow out. Main courses are rotated
fom a list of 200 recipes. There is also a selection of spicy salads to
choose from. Indorasa would be packed out all the time but for its
location, stuck half way between Brixton and Streatham.

SHOPS

AQUARIUS HEALTH FOODS
60 Morrish Road SW2. Tel: 081-674 8727. Open: Mon-Sat 10.00-22.30,
Sun 12.00-15.00, 19.00-22.00.
Organic wine, vegetables and beer. Takeaway food with some vegan
items. Can deliver if over £15.00.

Tea Rooms des Artistes

697 Wandsworth Road. London SW8
telephone 071 652 6526

**Extensive vegetarian and vegan menu served in
accordance with the Vegetarian Society's
Restaurant Charter**

*Herbed vegetarian sausages in potato bread with puy lentils and
casserole of side vegetables 5.50*
*Tofu, mushroom and courgette satay with saffron rice, coconut
sambal and garnish of vegetables 5.75*
*Mexican tortillas Tea Rooms style, filled with spicy chilli beans and
served with guacamole and corn cobs 5.95*

**party bookings and buffets a speciality
open every evening and all day at weekends
LATE NIGHT LICENCED BAR**
*Take a walk on the wild side and savour exquisite vegetarian or
vegan meals in this mediaeval barn on the edge of Clapham Old
Town. Described as rustic grunge, the decor is positively dripping
with candlelit chandeliers, stained glass, original exposed beams
and other artifacts and you can dine al fresco in the garden during
the summer months. Self service with a smile and always a warm
friendly welcome but the faint hearted should avoid weekends
when the Tea Rooms takes on a warehouse party mode.*

Remember to say you saw it in the Cruelty-Free Guide

SW4 CLAPHAM

OTHER RESTAURANTS

CAFÉ WANDA
153 Clapham High Street, SW4. Tel: 071-738 8760
Open: Daily 09.00-24.00.
Tube: Clapham Common
Café, restaurant and wine bar. It does have some veggie food, though
you may have to leave the vegan in the wine bar unless s/he likes
salad. Meals include pancakes, risotto and pasta. There is a vegan
dessert, torto de noche, a pastry with ground hazel nuts.

ECO
162 Clapham High Street, Clapham, SW4. Tel: 071-978 1108
Open: Mon-Sat 11.30-16.00, 18.30-23.30. Sun 12.00-17.00, 18.30-22.30.
Closed Wed lunch.
Tube: Clapham Common
Omnivorous. Pizza. Lots of vegetarian and even vegan pizzas. "The
best pizzas are vegetarian", says the manager, piling on double tomato,
olive oil, spinach, aubergine, mushroom and leek to make a vegan one.
Pizza £4.50-£5.00, starter such as avocado vinaigrette £2.10. Possibly
the best pizzas you can buy in this always busy, very modern looking
place with lots of steel, wood and sand walls. This is a pizza place with
panache.

SHOPS

TODAY'S LIVING
*92 Clapham High Street, SW4. Tel: 071-622 1772. Mon-Sat 09.30-
18.00.*
Supplements, oils, frozen foods, remedies, organic, gluten-free and
bodybuilding products.

SW8 VAUXHALL, SOUTH LAMBETH

VEGETARIAN RESTAURANTS

BONNINGTON SQUARE CAFÉ
Vauxhall Grove, Vauxhall, SW8. Tel: see below.
Open: Mon-Fri 19.00-23.00, Fri & Sun 17.30-late, Sat 19.00-late
Tube: Vauxhall and Vauxhall BR.
Vegetarian. Café/restaurant. Unique café in an old London square that
has an eclectic mix of residents. Historically a large squatter
community thrived here and the cafe caters well for those on a low
budget. Different people open up on different nights. The atmosphere

is very laid back and you get a three course meal for only £5.00, though the portions could be just a little larger. Sunday is an all vegan night for which you can book (071-498 6412). Corkage is free and there is sometimes piano music at the weekends.

TEA ROOM DES ARTISTES
697 Wandsworth Road, Clapham, SW8 3JF Tel: 071-652 6526
Open: Mon-Fri 18.00-24.00, Sat 17.00-24.00, Sun 19.00-23.30.
Train: Wandsworth Road, Clapham Common
Vegetarian. Wine Bar. Wholefood and international cuisine. Starters £1.95-£3.50, main courses £5.95, desserts £1.90-£2.50. Counter service. Vegetarian Society approved and always something for vegans. Medieval building, decorated in arty, grungie style with live music. Great menu in great venue with plenty of room to mingle. The owners are vegetarian and vegan and make a big effort to provide interesting dishes. Each main course is like two meals and the menu changes regularly. Ethiopian lentil stew with spiced swede kibbeh and sesame pitta is stunning, as was the beetroot and celeriac rosti with mushroom stroganoff with braised red cabbage.

SW9 STOCKWELL, BRIXTON

ATTRACTIONS

BRIXTON MARKET
Brixton Station Road / Electric Avenue, SW9. Open: Mon-Sat 8.30-17.30 (not Wed afternoon). Tube: Brixton.
A lively open-air fruit and veg market with adjoining shops and covered market. They are good for secondhand clothes, books, exotic and cheap fruit and veg, with some great cafes nearby, see below.

VEGETARIAN CAFÉS

CAFÉ PUSHKAR
16c Market Row, Brixton, SW9 8LD. Tel: 071-738 6161
Open: Daily 9.00-17.00 except Sun, Wed.
Tube: Brixton
Vegetarian. International. Relax after shopping in the covered market with a delicious vegetarian or vegan hot meal, salad, tea, vegan cake, coffee or herb tea. Soya cappuccino. 10% discount for Vegan Society members. Special offer 2.00-5.00pm UB40 and students. Average £5.00. Recession breakfast £2.00, midweek main meal and drink £2.80. More seating upstairs. Takeaway service too. Relaxed atmosphere and live guitar music on Saturday afternoon.

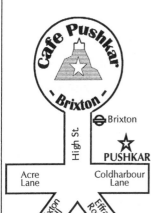
outer london

COOLTAN ARTS CENTRE

The Old Dole Office, 372 Coldharbour Lane, Brixton SW9 8LN.
Tel: 071-737 2745. Open: Tue & Thu 10.00-late, Wed-Fri & Sat-Sun
12.00-late Tube: Brixton.

If some people had their way this is what would happen to every
unemployment benefit office. Now squatted as an arts centre the
Cooltan has the Vegan Café: Tue 12.00-18.00, the Vegan Thought
Police Café: Thu 12.00-18.00, the Acoustic Vegan Café: Thu 20.00-late
and Oisin's Table Vegan Café: 20.00-01.00 with storytelling and poetry.
There are a range of events, classes and workshops on at the Cooltan
usually from about 12.00 every day, except Monday when you can help
out with building maintenance as a volunteer. You can even book
rehearsal space. The food, admission and fees for classes are low, low,
low. A three course meal won't cost you more than £3.30. As the
brochure says 'Don't just sit there ... do something.' Don't expect to
meet many city types here. Check before going as it's often under
threat of redevelopment.

OTHER RESTAURANTS

BRIXTONIAN RESTAURANT

11 Dorrell Place, off Nursery Road, SW9. Tel: 071-978 8870
Open: Bar Mon-Sun 17.30-24.00. Restaurant Tue-Wed 12.00-24.00,
Thu-Sat 12.00-01.00, Sun 17.30-23.00.
Tube: Brixton

Trendy and expensive downstairs café/bar with cocktails (try a Brixton
Riot in a Glass, made with three types of rum), with restaurant above.
African/Caribbean cuisine with French influence, £20.00 for three
courses. Dishes from a different Caribbean island each day. Vegetarian
selection but vegans should check in advance.

JACARANDA GARDEN RESTAURANT

11-13 Brixton Station Road, Brixton, SW9. Tel: 071-274 8383
Open: Mon-Sat 06.00-20.00, Sun 12.00-17.00.
Tube: Brixton

Omnivorous. International Jamaican. Lots of veggie main meals £2.95-
£4.95. Snacks are veggie and so is the soup. Quiche £2.70, starters
£2.60. Good savoury food for vegans like Gobi dhal and pitta, carrot
and mushroom bake and sesame seeds. Cakes are always made with
vegetable oil. Natural wooden floors and plants make this place very
relaxing. Open to children and groups.

SATAY GALLERY RESTAURANT

393 Coldharbour Lane, Brixton, SW9 8LQ. Tel: 071-731 2042
Open: Mon-Thur 19.00-23.00, Fri-Sat 19.00-24.00.
Tube: Brixton

Omnivorous. Indonesian and Malaysian. Big selection of veggie dishes at £3.95. Really popular small restaurant with students atmosphere, and music that helps give a very casual feel to the place. You'll need to book at the weekends.

TWENTY TRINITY GARDENS

20 Trinity Gardens, Brixton, SW9 2UG. Tel: 071-733 8838
Open: Mon-Thu 19.00-22.30, Fri-Sat 19.00-23.00, Sun 11.30-12.30
brunch, 12.30-15.30 lunch.
Tube: Brixton
Omnivorous French cuisine. £9.95 two courses, £13.50-£16.50 three courses. Plush French restaurant in secluded street near the Trinity pub, offering gourmet dishes for omnivores and vegetarians. Starters include Leek tartlet with red wine sauce, and pears and Stilton. Main dishes include offerings like vegetable pancakes with carrot, tahini and orange and layered cheese pudding. Cheese contains animal rennet. Vegans should notify them in advance.

SHOPS

THE BODY SHOP

Brixton Enterprise Centre, 464 Brixton Road, SW9 7RD. Open: Mon-Sat
09.30-18.00 (Thu from 10.00), Sun 11.00-1600.

BRIXTON HEALTH FOODS

419 Coldharbour Lane, SW9. Tel: 071-274 6675.
Open: Mon-Sat 9.00-17.30 (16.30 Wed).
Vegetarian food, herbal teas and vitamins. No takeaway.

BRIXTON WHOLE FOODS

56-58 Atlantic Road, SW9. Tel: 071-737 2210.
Open: Tue-Thu and Sat-Sun 09.30-17.30, Mon & Fri 09.30-18.00.
Wide range of health and wholefood products with the emphasis on low prices. Lots of vegan takeaways including cakes, flapjacks, apple strudels, burgers, tofu and seaweed pasties and rolls and pies, pitta with falafel and more.

THOMPSON'S BAKERY BREAD SHOP

Market Row, Brixton, SW9 8LD. Tel: 071-737 1325.
Open: Mon-Sat 09.00-17.30.
Bread shop selling the whole range of Thompson's products which include animal free breads, patties, and buns. See Thompson's Bakery, SW12 for more details and don't go home without your bulla cakes.

SW11 BATTERSEA, CLAPHAM JUNCTION

ATTRACTIONS

BATTERSEA PARK

Albert Bridge Road and Queenstown Road, SW11. Tel: 081-871 7530
Open: 07.30-dusk summer, 08.30-dusk winter
Tube: Battersea Park BR, Sloane Square.
Buddhist Pagoda, children's zoo in summer, play facilities, boating lake, cafe, tennis courts, garden for disabled, festivals and holiday events, athletics track, Sri Chinmoy Peace Mile. The new Pumphouse Art Gallery is open winter 11.00-15.00, Apr-mid Oct 11.00-16.00, closed Mon. There is a cafe (071-498 2557) open every day 9.00-19.00 and serving spaghetti for £3.00, vegetarian pasty, quiche, or cauliflower cheese.

VEGETARIAN RESTAURANTS

FUNGUS MUNGUS

264 Battersea Park Road, SW11. Tel: 071-924 5578
Open: Mon-Fri 12.00-15.00, 18.00-24.00, Sat 12.00-24.00, Sun 12.00-23.00. Train: Battersea Park BR
Vegetarian. International. £12.00 for three courses. Busy, popular and deservedly so, with music some nights. Good vegan options. Try Thai veg curry or the aptly titled Fungus Flying Saucers - mushrooms with tomato and herb sauce with toast. Menu changes weekly. Outrageous futuristic hippy decor. Outdoor patio. High chairs available. 10% discount for Vegan Society members. Bar at the front where you can work up an appetite just lounging around. Music with DJ's and, hopefully, bands on Sunday soon.

OTHER RESTAURANTS

THE GREEN ROOM

62 Lavender Hill, Battersea, SW11 5RQ. Tel: 071-223 4618
Open: Mon-Sun 19.00-23.30.
Train: Clapham Junction, Wandsworth Rd BR
Omnivorous. International. Top quality wholefood with emphasis on organic produce. Vegetarian Living magazine award winner in 1992 for best restaurant serving vegetarian meals and recommended by the Egon Ronay Good Food Guide. Excellent wine list including some suitable for vegans. Vegan dishes all the time. Live music on Fridays. Average £15.00.

SHOPS

DANDELION NATURAL FOODS

120 Northcote Road, SW11. Tel: 071-350 0902.
Open: Mon-Sat 09.30-18.00.
Lots of vegan takeaways which are their speciality. Soups are always vegan, with soya cream, stuffed peppers and gluten-free takeaways. Always a vegan cake and pasties, made with soya milk.

HOLLAND & BARRETT

51 St. Johns Hill, SW11 1TT. Tel: 071-228 6071.
Open: Mon-Sat 09.00-18.00. Tube: Clapham Common.
Healthfood store with takeaway, including vegan food.

NATURAL FACT

30-40 Elcho St, SW11 4AV. Tel: 071-228 9652.
Pure cotton clothes and underwear made without dyes or bleaches.

SW12 BALHAM

ATTRACTIONS

SUNRA YOGA & NATURAL HEALTH CENTRE

26 Balham Hill, Clapham, SW12 9EB. Tel: 081-675 9224
Open Mon-Fri 12.00-22.00, Sat-Sun 10.00-18.00.Tube: Clapham South
Health centre providing a wide range of treatments and therapies. Also run classes in yoga, reflexology, massage, tai-chi, meditation, dance and body awareness, homeopathy etc. Has a floatation tank, sauna and jacuzzi

VEGETARIAN CAFÉ

SUNRA VEGETARIAN CAFÉ

26 Balham Hill, Clapham, SW12 9EB. Tel: 081-675 8274
Open: Daily 11.00-16.00. Tube: Clapham South
Teas and freshly brewed coffee, soups, main meals, sandwiches, filled rolls, baked potatoes, salads and home-made cakes. Eat in or take away. Small café that seats about 12. A good little place to know about as such places are thin on the ground in this area. It closed in March 1994, only temporarily we hope, so you should check before going.

SHOPS

BALHAM WHOLEFOOD & HEALTH STORE

8 Bedford Hill SW12. Tel: 081-673 4842.
Open: Mon-Sat 9.30-13.30, 14.30-18.00 (Tue/Thu 19.00).
Friendly, helpful service in this old-fashioned store with Classic FM and oils burning. Books, and lots of aromatherapy oils.

BELLE-DONNA
Westbury Parade, SW12. Tel: 081-673 3121. Open: Mon-Sat 09.00-19.00 (13.00 Thu, 18.00 Sat). Tube: Clapham South.
Health foods. No takeaway.

HEALTH & BEAUTY
156 Balham High Road, SW12. Tel: 081-675 3586.
Open: Mon-Sat 9.00-18.00.
Health food.

THOMPSON'S BAKERY
Unit 12 Zennor Road Industrial Estate, Balham SW12 0PP. Tel: 081-673 2249. Open: from Mon midday continuously until Friday 22.00.
Thompson's Bakery produce a range of savoury foods, sweet cakes, buns and bread. Their vegetable patties are vegan. So are their breads, buns and bulla cakes. Their products can be bought all over London but particularly where there is a large African or Caribbean population. Don't miss the fruit bun which is a bit like fruit malt but heavier and flavoured with mixed spice cinnamon and nutmeg. The bulla cakes come in packs of three, are lighter in colour and are exquisitely flavoured with ginger nutmeg and cinnamon. They have a shop opposite the Cafe Pushkar in Brixton SW9 if you're in that area.

SW13 BARNES

ATTRACTIONS

BARN ELM RESERVOIRS
Merthyr Terrace, SW13. Tel: 081-748 3423
Open: Mar-Nov 07.30-dusk. Tube: Hammersmith
One of the best places to see unusual birds who are only outnumbered by the hoards of fishermen.

SHOPS

BARNES HEALTH FOODS
60 Barnes High Street, SW13. Tel: 081-876 5476. Open: Mon-Sat 09.30-17.30. Tube: Hammersmith. No takeaways.

SW14 MORTLAKE, SHEEN

SHOPS

THE BODY SHOP
407 Upper Richmond Road, East Sheen, SW14 7NX. Open: Mon-Sat 10.00-17.30.

CERES HEALTH FOOD
*427a Upper Richmond Road West, East Sheen SW14. Tel: 081-878
7403. Open: Mon-Sat 09.00-17.30. Tube: Mortlake.*

HEALTH & DIET
*194 Upper Richmond Rd, SW14. Tel: 081-788 0944. Open: Mon-Sat
09.00-18.00 (19.00 Thu).*
Wholefoods, with vegan takeaways. Vegetarian Society discount.

SW15 PUTNEY

SHOPS

THE BODY SHOP
*77 Putney High Street, SW15 1SR. Open: Mon-Fri 10.00-18.00, Sat
09.00-17.30.*

HEALTH & DIET
*151 Putney High Street, SW15. Tel: 081-788 0944. Open: Mon-Sat
09.00-18.00 (19.00 Thu). Tube: Putney Bridge, Putney BR.*
Wholefoods. Takeaway with at least two vegan dishes. Vegetarian
Society discount.

PUTNEY HEALTH FOODS
*28 Upper Richmond Road, SW15. Tel: 081-877 0041. Open: Mon-Sat
10.00-19.30. Tube: East Putney.*
Organic everything like fruit and veg, dairy, pasties, pies. Also a clinic
with aromatherapy, shiatsu, remedial massage, homeopathy. Free
homeopathic advice Mon 10.00-12.00. Sells Vegetarian Society
magazine, Kindred Spirit, Ark, and has leaflets. Homeopathic first-aid
course and yoga classes.

SW16 STREATHAM

VEGETARIAN RESTAURANTS

SHAHEE BHEL-POORI VEGETARIAN RESTAURANT
*1547 London Road, Norbury, SW16 4AD. Tel: 081-679 6275
Open: Every day 12.00-14.30, 18.00-23.00.
Train: Norbury*
Vegetarian. Indian. Large vegan clientele and no wonder. Most dishes
are non-dairy and all menu items are marked. Vegetable oil is used
rather than ghee and there's even vegan ice-cream for afters. There are
two starter menus, one hot and one cold. They include many popular
South Indian dishes as well as vegetable kebabs and cutlets, pani
poori, pakora and many more. Four of the 10 Thalis are vegan and are
all under £4.00. Prices are low, starters come in at under £2.00 and you

can't pay more than £4.10 for a main course dosa. This restaurant has been mentioned in the Evening Standard, various good food guides and Time Out. Large, light and airy the restaurant is air-conditioned and seats 80. Milder dishes are available for children. Simply decorated with a very relaxed feel. See you there!

WHOLEMEAL VEGETARIAN CAFÉ
1 Shrubbery Road, Streatham, SW16 2AS. Tel: 081-769 2423
Open: Every day 12.00-22.00.
Train: Streatham, Streatham Hill BR
Vegetarian. Wholefood. For vegans there is always soup £1.60, at least one starter £2.10 such as garlic mushrooms, one main dish £3.90-£4.20 such as Thai casserole, or one of the bakes. They make the mashed potato for the shepherds pie with soya marge and soya milk and, guess what, no one notices. They also have loads of cakes and desserts for £1.60 which are a bit of a speciality here, as well as fruit crumble and other sweets like flapjacks. Fully licensed and everything prepared on site. Organic beer and wine.

OTHER RESTAURANTS

BRITISH RAJ

1534 London Road, Norbury, SW16 4EU. Tel: 081-679 7700, 081-764 3033. Open: Every day 12.00-14.30, 18.00-24.00.
Train: Norbury
Omnivorous. Indian. Average £12.00. Table, counter and takeaway service. Uses oil not ghee, with plenty for vegans from a standard menu, and they can prepare special dishes to order.

SHOPS

HOLLAND & BARRETT

110 Streatham High Road, SW16 1BW. Tel: 081-769 1418. Open: Mon-Sat 09.00-17.30. Train: Streatham Vale.
Health food, plus non-vegan pasties, sandwiches and cakes.

NATURAL WAY

252 Streatham High Road, SW16. Tel: 081-769 0065. Mon-Sat 09.30-18.00.
Very large range of foodstuffs, supplements, remedies, oils, green products and stationery. Staff are very interested and spend time with customers and give expert advice on bodybuilding products. There's plenty for vegans. They stock the whole Plamil range and people come from a long way to shop here. Takeaway products include carrot cutlets, eccles cakes and other goodies.

SW17 TOOTING

VEGETARIAN RESTAURANTS

AMBALA SWEETS

48 Upper Tooting Road, Tooting, SW17 7PD. Tel: 081-767 1747
Open: Mon-Sat 10.00-20.00, Sun 10.00-19.00
Tube: Tooting Bec, Tooting Broadway
Vegetarian. Indian. Takeaway only. Average £2.25. Three curries per day, four specials at weekend.

KASTOORI

188 Upper Tooting Road, Tooting, SW17 7EJ. Tel: 081-767 7027
Open: Mon-Sat 12.30-14.30, 18.00-22.00 (23.00 Sat)
Tube: Tooting Broadway, Tooting Bec
Vegetarian. Indian and East African. Vegan items are marked on the menu and there's stacks of choice. Both North and South Indian food, and now they've started East African main dishes for £3.50-£3.75. There's only one per day but they are worth a tasting. Salivate over the sweetcorn cassodi or green banana if you're a vegetarian or the Karela

bharela (a sort of bitter courgette) or chilli banana if you're vegan. Try the millet loaf, a sort of thick chapatti, with the aubergine curry if you go for Sunday lunch.

MILAN SWEET MART
158 Upper Tooting Road, Tooting, SW17 7ER. Tel: 081-767 4347
Open: Every day 9.30-20.00 (Wed to 14.30).
Tube: Tooting Bec
Vegetarian. Gujarati Indian cuisine. Uses butter ghee. Maximum £4.00. Table, counter and takeaway service. Unlicensed.

TUMBLEWEEDS
32 Tooting Bec Road, SW17 8BD. Tel: 081-767 9395.
Open: Tue-Fri 12.00-15.00 & 18.30-22.30, Sat-Sun 12.00-23.30
Tube: Tooting Bec.
Vegetarian. Wholefood. Usually four to five dishes on the menu which changes every day and repeats monthly. Always vegan options. Soup £1.90. Vegan starters might include gado-gado, broccoli filo parcels, peanut butter croquettes with tahini sauce. Main dishes, £4.90, include baked peppers with chickpea and lemon stuffing, tofu and tahini casserole. Half price children's portions. All food prepared on site. Counter service with table service in the evenings. Corkage £1.00. It's easy to spot the large glass frontage with painted flowers. Inside the furniture is ex-church pews and chairs, with lighting custom-made from recyled kitchen utensils. Very mixed clientele.

OTHER RESTAURANTS

SREE KRISHNA
192-194 Tooting High Street, SW17. Tel.: 081-672 4250, 081-672 6903
Tube: Tooting Broadway. Open: Daily 12.00-15.00 & Mon-Thu & Sun 18.00-23.00, Fri-Sat 18.00-24.00
Omnivorous. South Indian. Predominantly vegetarian menu though it has quite a bit of meat too. The food has a good reputation and the restaurant is very popular. Only vegetable ghee is used. Takeaway too.

SW18 WANDSWORTH, SOUTHFIELDS

SHOPS

HOLLAND & BARRETT
29 The Arndale Centre, Wandsworth, SW18. Tel: 081-871 3706.
Open: Mon-Sat 09.00-17.30.
Health foods. Takeaway normally has something vegan like pasties.

SW19 WIMBLEDON

SHOPS

THE BODY SHOP
Unit 205 Centre Court Shopping Centre, Queens Road, Wimbledon, SW19 8YA. Open: Mon-Fri 09.00-19.00 (Thu 20.00), Sat till 18.00.

HOLLAND & BARRETT
68 The Broadway, Wimbledon, SW19 1RQ. Tel: 081-542 7486. Open: Mon-Sat 9.00-17.30. Tube: Wimbledon.
Health foods. Takeaway drinks, flapjacks, cakes, and pasties may not be vegan.

SW20 RAYNES PARK, MERTON

SHOPS

FAB FOODS
1 Wimbledon Chase Station, Kingston Road, SW20. Tel: 081-540 5923. Open: Mon-Sat 09.30-17.00. Train: Wimbledon Chase BR.
Health foods.

WEST LONDON

W1	*(West End: see under Central London)*
W2	*Paddington, Bayswater, Westbourne Grove*
W3	*Acton*
W4	*Chiswick*
W5	*Ealing*
W6	*Hammersmith*
W7	*Hanwell*
W8	*Kensington High Street*
W9	*Maida Vale, Warwick Avenue*
W10	*Kensal, Latimer Road, North Kensington, Ladbroke Grove*
W11	*Notting Hill, Holland Park, Portobello Road*
W12	*Shepherds Bush*
W13	*West Ealing, Drayton Green*
W14	*West Kensington, Olympia*

W2 PADDINGTON AND BAYSWATER

Trains to the West Country (from Bristol to Cornwall) and Wales leave hourly from Paddington station. There are lots of hotels and some late night grocers. Chess addicts can visit the Kings Head Pub on Moscow Road (Tube: Queensway or Bayswater) on any evening.

ATTRACTIONS

HYDE PARK

Tube: Queensway (NW), Lancaster Gate (N), Marble Arch (NE), Hyde Park Corner (SE), Knightsbridge (S) Open: daily 05.00-24.00
Largest park in London. Serpentine Gallery, lake, bands, horse-riding area and cafes. On Sundays, 'Speakers Corner' in the north east corner by Marble Arch, is the spot for vociferous politicos to stand on their soap boxes and tell everyone how to set the world to rights. In the south east corner is a fenced off wood full of squirrels, who sunbathe on the branches and emerge to take brazil and hazel nuts from your hand. If it seems deserted, just stand quietly and wait for a few minutes.

VEGETARIAN RESTAURANTS & CAFES

DIWANA VEGETARIAN RESTAURANT

50 Westbourne Grove, Bayswater, W2 5SH. Tel: 071-221 0721
Open: Tue-Sun 12.00-15.00. Sat-Sun 18.00-22.45. Closed Mon.
Tube: Bayswater, Queensway, Royal Oak
Vegetarian. Indian. Great value with lots of vegan food. Uses vegetable ghee. £5.80 for 3 course set thali with dessert. Don't eat breakfast

before going to this great value place because all-you-can-eat lunch buffet with 16 items is £3.95. Bring your own alcohol, free corkage.

OTHER RESTAURANTS

BRASSERIE RESTAURANT

Park Court Hotel, 75 Lancaster Gate, W2 3NN. Tel: 071-402 4272 ext 2370. Open: Every day 12.00-23.00. Tube: Lancaster Gate

Omnivorous. Average £5.25. For cruelty-free diners they have vegetable moussaka, mushroom and cashew nut Wellington, and stir fried veg which can be without the egg noodles for vegans.

KALAMARAS

66 Inverness Mews, Bayswater, W2.
Tel: 071-727 5082 (small restaurant), 071-727 9122 (large restaurant)
Open: Mon-Sat 19.00-24.00. Tube: Bayswater, Queensway

Omnivorous. Greek. Two restaurants, same kitchen. Family run. Average £10.00. Table service. Vegetarians can try lots of starters for £2.20-£3.00, such as aubergine or garlic dip, or okra in tomato sauce. It's not so good for vegans as the Greeks like to use yoghurt. Last orders at 23.00 in the small restaurant, 24.00 in the large one. The small restaurant lets you bring your own wine but not beer, or you can buy it in the large one.

SHOPS

WHITELEY'S

Queensway, W2. Tel: 071-229 8844. Open: Mon-Sat 10.00-20.00, Sun 12.00-19.00. Tube: Queensway.

Old department store converted for retail use, with a Body Shop, bars, cafes serving some veggie food, and eight cinema screens. Wheelchair accessible.

THE BODY SHOP

Unit 10, Whiteleys Shopping Centre, Queensway, W2. Open: Mon-Sat 10.00-20.00 (21.00 Fri), Sun 12.00-19.00.

W3 ACTON

SHOPS

MARKET PLACE HEALTH FOODS

8 Market Place, Acton W3 6QS. Tel: 081-993 3848.
Open: Mon-Sat 9.00-18.00.
Health foods, cosmetics, soya cheese and cream, aromatherapy supplies.

RAINBOW EXPRESS
4 Maldon Road, W3. Tel: 081 992 5987.

W4 CHISWICK

Good hitch-hiking to the West Country from the flyover at the Chiswick roundabout (Gunnersbury underground).

NON VEGETARIAN RESTAURANTS

HELENKA BRASSERIE
156 Chiswick High Road, W4. Tel: 081-995 1656
Open: Mon-Fri 18.00-23.00, Sat-Sun 12.00-23.00.
Tube: Turnham Green
Omnivorous. Polish. Average £10.00 for three courses. Traditional Polish fare with plenty for veggies like potato dumplings, vegetarian borsch, buckwheat pancakes, apple fritters and even pasta. Polish beer.

SHOPS

CINAGRO
189 Acton Lane, W4. Tel: 081-994 5442. Open: Tue-Fri 11.00-17.30, Sat 11.00-15.00.
All organic vegetables. Also dried fruit, nuts, oats, muesli.

CORNUCOPIA
1 Devonshire Road, W4. Tel: 081-995 0588. Open: Mon-Sat 09.30-18.00.
Health foods. Takeaway sandwiches, samosa, spring rolls, pasties, many of them vegan. Caters for special diets. Free local delivery.

HOLLAND & BARRETT
416 Chiswick High Road, London W4 5TF. Tel: 081-994 1683. Open: Mon-Sat 9.00-17.30.

W5 EALING

SHOPS

THE BODY SHOP
56 The Broadway, Ealing, W5 5JN. Open: Mon, Wed, Fri 09.30-18.30, Tue 10.00-18.30, Thu 09.30-19.00, Sat 09.00-18.00.

CORNUCOPIA
64 St Marys Road, W5. Tel: 081-579 9431. Open: Mon-Sat 09.30-18.00.
Health foods. Takeaway sandwiches, samosa, spring rolls, pasties, many of them vegan. Caters for special diets. Free local delivery.

HOLLAND & BARRETT

6 Ealing Broadway, near Station, W5 2NU. Tel: 081-840 1070.
Health food shop with takeaway food, mostly vegan. Like all H&B,
they give 10% discount to card-carrying Vegetarian Society and Vegan
Society members on orders over £5.00.

VICTORIA HEALTH FOODS

*Unit 12b Ealing Broadway Centre, The Broadway W5. Tel: 081-840
6949. Open: Mon-Sat 9.00-18.00.*
All the usual foods, vitamins, BWC vegan cosmetics. 10% discount to
Vegetarian or Vegan Society members.

W6 HAMMERSMITH

VEGETARIAN RESTAURANTS & CAFES

THE GATE

*51 Queen Caroline Street, Hammersmith, W6 9QL. Tel: 081-748 6932
Open: Mon, Sat 18.00-23.00, Tue-Fri 12.00-15.00, 18.00-23.00
Tube: Hammersmith*
Vegetarian. International. Three courses £12.50, £15.00 with wine.
Head chef Vicky Beever and Sous-chef Howie Milham produce some of
London's most elegant French, Greek, Japanese, Thai and other
vegetarian cuisine, and the Gate has a high reputation in the
gastronomic press. For vegans there are always at least two starters,
one main course and a dessert. With advance notice big vegan groups
will be well taken care of. Using quality ingredients means that
portions can be small, so don't come here if you haven't eaten for 24
hours, or else have an extra starter.

OTHER RESTAURANTS

ROOF GARDEN CAFÉ

*Lyric Theatre, King Street, Hammersmith, W6 02L. Tel: 081-741 0824
Open: Mon-Sat 10.30-21.00.
Tube: Hammersmith*
Omnivorous. Plentiful veggie food includes the usual salad, quiche and
main meals like cous-cous. Prices range from £1.75 for soup to £3.85
for a main course. Usually a vegan option but if nothing grabs you
there's a small takeaway selection at Bushwackers not far away- see
below.

SHOPS

THE BODY SHOP

*Unit 6, Kings Mall, Kings Street, W6 9PH. Open: Mon-Fri 10.00-18.00,
Sat 09.30-1800.*

BUSHWACKER WHOLEFOODS
132 King Street, Hammersmith, W6. Tel: 081-748 2061. Open: Mon-Sat 09.30-18.30.
Wholefood supplies, vegetarian and vegan takeaways.

HOLLAND & BARRETT
5 Kings Mall, King Street, Hammersmith, W6 0PZ. Tel: 081-748 9792. Open: Mon-Sat 9.00-17.30.
Health foods and takeaway. 10% discount to Vegetarian and Vegan Society members spending over £3.00.

W7 HANWELL

NON VEGETARIAN RESTAURANTS

ARCHES WINE BAR & RESTAURANT
7 Boston Parade, Boston Road, Hanwell, W7 2DG. Tel: 081-567 9708
Open: Mon-Fri 12.00-15.00, 17.30-23.00.
Tube: Boston Manor
Omnivorous. Average £10.00-15.00. Veggies can try pasta, quiche, dips. Can prepare vegan food.

W8 KENSINGTON

Kensington, next door to the Earls Court Australasian community, is home to several adventure travel agencies. If you fancy organizing your own round-the-world jaunt, start by checking out the cultures of the ex-British Empire at the brilliant and free Commonwealth Institute. Then call into Trailfinders for a free travel magazine and maybe a guidebook. Grab some vegan ice-cream at Holland & Barrett, plonk yourself down amidst the flowers of Kensington Gardens, and plan your dream holiday. For luscious and luxurious Mediterranean vegetarian food, you can't beat Kensington's Lebanese restaurants.

ATTRACTIONS

COMMONWEALTH INSTITUTE
Kensington High St at junction with Earls Court Rd, W8.
Tel: 071-603 4535. Open: Mon-Sat 10.00-17.00, Sun 14.00-17.00. Free.
Tube: High St Kensington. Next to Holland Park.
Exhibition of lifestyles from 40 countries. Amazing split level building with displays on Commonwealth countries. Performance space. Interactive displays. Imperial beginnings but now more of a celebration of other cultures. Shop and festivals arranged to celebrate national days of other countries. International cafe with some veggie fare £1.50-£4.50. There is always a vegetarian meal for lunch, such as quiche, and they'll try to cater for vegans. Cafe open till 16.00, with lunch 12.00-

15.00. Fresh coffee 70p, herb teas 75p.

HOLLAND PARK
Kensington High Street, W8. Open: daily 07.30-dusk.
Tube: High Street Kensington, Holland Park.
Open air theatre, youth hostel, adventure playground, tennis courts.
Near Commonwealth Institute. Nice place to sunbathe, stroll, or relax
after a hectic shopping session along Kensington High Street.

KENSINGTON GARDENS
West side of Hyde Park, W8. Open: 05.00-dusk. Free.
Tube: High Street Kensington
Beautiful flower filled gardens and park adjoining Hyde Park. It
contains the London home of Charles and Di before the split. State
apartments for royalty junkies in Kensington Palace, £3.75, Mon-Sat
09.00-17.00, Sun 11.00-17.00.

NON-VEGETARIAN RESTAURANTS

AL BASHA
222 Kensington High Street, W8 7RG. Tel: 071-938 1794
Open: Every day 12.00-24.00.
Tube: High Street Kensington
Omnivorous. Lebanese. The vegetarian menu is £16.00 per head for a
minimum of two people, which gets you seven or eight dishes with
hummus, aubergine dip, falafel, green beans, lentil puree, tabouleh,
pitta, pastries and coffee. Music in the evenings and belly dancer Fri-
Sat when the price goes up to £30.00 plus service and drinks. Next to
Holland Park, with a terrace. Book at weekends.

BYBLOS RESTAURANT
262 Kensington High Street, W8 6ND. Tel: 071-603 4422
Open: Every day 12.00-24.00.
Tube: High Street Kensington
Omnivorous. Lebanese. Small homely restaurant with great veggie/
vegan menu for £7.85 which contains a whole range of Meze - small
Lebanese dishes. 10% discount to Vegan or Vegetarian Society
members with card or magazine containing their ad. Also does
takeaway.

PHOENICIA
11-13 Abingdon Road, W8 6AH. Tel: 071-937 0120
Open: Daily 12.15-23.45 (last orders).
Tube: High Street Kensington
Omnivorous. Lebanese. Average £12.00. Buffet lunch including dessert
and coffee Mon-Sat 12.15-14.30 for £9.95 has 40 meze dishes, 80% of
them vegetarian. Dinner or Sunday lunch from £15.30 up to a
sumptuous £28.30.

SAILING JUNK

59 Marloes Road, Kensington, W8 6LE. Tel: 071-937 2589
Open: Every day 18.00-23.30.
Tube: High St Kensington, Earls Court
Omnivorous. Chinese. £15.00 vegetarian set meal including sweet and coffee. A la carte £4.00-£6.00 per dish.

SHOPS

THE BODY SHOP

137 High Street Kensington, W8 6BA. Open: Mon-Fri 10.00-18.30 (Thu 19.00), Sat 09.30-18.00.

HOLLAND & BARRETT

139 Kensington Church Street, W8 7LP. Tel: 071-727 9011. Open: Mon-Sat 9.00-17.30 (from 09.30 Wed). Tube: Notting Hill Gate.
Health foods and flapjacks but no takeaway.

HOLLAND & BARRETT

260 Kensington High Street, W8 6ND. Tel: 071-603 2751. Open: Mon-Sat 9.00-17.30. Tube: High Street Kensington.
Health foods and lots of takeaways, including vegan Mexican bean slice and pasties which may sell out by Saturday. Vegan choc ices and Tofutti, the dairy-free ice-cream that is taking Britain by storm.

KENSINGTON MARKET

49-53 Kensington High Street, W8. Open: Mon-Sat 10.00-18.00.
Tube: High Street Kensington.
Indoor market selling a range of cheap, fashionable and unusual clothes.

TRAILFINDERS TRAVEL AGENCY

42-48 Earls Court Road, W8 6EJ. Tel: Europe and Atlantic 071-937 5400, long haul 071-938 3366. Open: Mon-Sat 9.00-18.00, Sunday telesales only 10.00-16.00. Tube: Earls Court.

TRAILFINDERS TRAVEL AGENCY

194 Kensington High Street, W8 7RG. Open same hours as Earls Court Rd branch and also Sun. Tube: High Street Kensington.
Most employees are experienced world backpackers and from memory they can put together bargain round-the-world airfares using the cheapest company on each leg. You'll search long and hard to find this kind of service elsewhere. They also sell Lonely Planet guidebooks and some travel goods. Tel: First and Business Class 071-938 3444, Europe and North Atlantic 071-938 3366, long haul 071-938 3939.

WATERSTONES

193 Kensington High St, W8. Tel: 071-937 8432. Open: Mon-Fri 9.30-21.00, Sat 9.30-19.00, Sun 11.00-18.00. Tube: High Street Kensington.
Late night big bookstore with a section on vegetarian cooking.

YHA ADVENTURE SHOP
174 Kensington High St, W8. Tel: 071-938 2948.
Everything for backpacking and camping.

W9 WESTBOURNE PARK

W9 also includes Maida Vale, Warwick Avenue, and at least two omnivorous eateries with vegetarian dishes.

NON VEGETARIAN RESTAURANTS

PIZZA PLACE
5 Lanark Place, Little Venice, W9 1BT. Tel: 071-289 4353
Open: Mon-Fri 17.00-23.00, Sat-Sun 11.00-23.00
Tube: Warwick Avenue
Omnivorous. Italian-American. Pizza £5.00, three courses with coffee £15.00. Restaurant, takeaway and home delivery. All pizzas made fresh, so they can do vegan pizzas, which is just as well as they don't have vegetarian cheese. Also vegetarian canneloni, and salads. The carrot soup contains butter, but when available the mixed veg or watercress soups are vegan.

SUPAN
4 Fernhead Road, Kensal Town, W9 3ET. Tel: 081-969 9387
Open: Mon-Sat 18.30-23.00.
Tube: Westbourne Park
Omnivorous. Thai. Average £10.00-12.00. Twenty vegetable dishes include curries, spring rolls, soups, salads, stir fries. One vegan dessert - fruit compote.

SHOPS

THE REALFOOD STORE
14 Clifton Road, W9. Tel: 071-266 1162.
Open: Mon-Fri 8.30-19.45, Sat 8.30-18.00. Tube: Warwick Ave.
7,000 lines in stock including fresh pasta and 40 kinds of bread.

W10 LADBROKE GROVE AND NORTH KENSINGTON

Also includes Kensal, Latimer Road

OTHER RESTAURANTS

MAKAN
270 Portobello Road, W10 5TE. Tel: 081-960 5169
Open: Mon-Sat 10.30-21.00.
Tube: 081-960 5169

Omnivorous Malaysian takeaway and café. Counter service delicious fast food with a number of spicy veggie options that come with rice or noodles. Under the flyover and right in the heart of the market. Simple clean and pleasant stylish black furniture. No smoking, no alcohol and no monosodium glutamate. Seats about 30 so you sometimes have to wait to get settled.

PORTOBELLO CAFÉ

305 Portobello Road, W10. Tel: 081-969 1996
Open: Mon 09.00-17.00, Tue-Thu 09.00-23.00, Fri-Sat 08.00-23.00, Sun 10.00-17.00.
Tube: Ladbroke Grove
Inexpensive omnivorous restaurant and takeaway at the cheaper end of Portobello Road. Large traditional English and international menu with about 10 vegan options. You can even get vegan mayo for 50p and vegetarian cheese is available. There is a garden at the back which is nice in the summer. Good place for brunch.

SHOPS

THE GRAIN SHOP

269a Portobello Road, W10. Tel: 071-229 5571. Tube: Ladbroke Grove.
Open: 10.00-18.00.
Takeaway that sells vegan products.

PORTOBELLO WHOLE FOODS

Unit 1, 266 Portobello Road, W10. Tel: 081 960 1840 admin, 081-968 9133 shop. Open: Mon-Sat 9.30-18.00 (17.00 Thu).

W11 NOTTING HILL

Last weekend in August is the biggest carnival outside Rio. See Ethnic London chapter, African and Caribbean section.

NON VEGETARIAN RESTAURANTS

CAPS RESTAURANT

64 Pembridge Rd, Notting Hill, W11. Tel: 071-229 5177
Open: Mon-Sat 18.00-23.15 (last orders).
Tube: Notting Hill Gate
Omnivorous. International. Veggie options include fresh pasta, Thai spring rolls, veg samosas, mushroom stroganoff, but not much for vegans. Average £15.00 for three courses.

LEITH'S

92 Kensington Park Rd, Notting Hill Gate, W11 2PN. Tel: 071-229 4481
Open: Every day 19.30-23.30.
Tube: Notting Hill Gate

Omnivorous. Modern British. Haute cuisine. Separate vegetarian menu £22.50 for two courses (main plus starter or dessert). Desserts £6.50. Several vegetarian dishes change seasonally, such as mushroom souffle, salad or soup. They always have a vegan dish and can do extra ones. Wine from £12.50 per bottle to £350, with one at £995. We didn't ask about corkage.

SPUD U LIKE

8 Pembridge Road, Notting Hill Gate, W11 3HL. Tel: 071-229 6698
Open: Every day 9.00-24.00.
Tube: Notting Hill Gate
Omnivorous. Filled baked potatoes. Restaurant and takeaway. Uses vegetarian cheddar, and vegans can have their spud with spicy bean salad, baked beans or sweetcorn for £1.84. Drinks £0.78. Also does garlic bread. Understands diabetic needs. Part of a large chain, usually very basic inside but useful in emergencies.

SHOPS

THE BODY SHOP

194 Portobello Road, W11 1LA.
Open: Mon-Fri 10.00-17.30, Sat 10.00-16.00.

THE GRAIN SHOP

269a Portobello Road, W11. Tel: 071-229 5571.
Open: Mon-Sat 10.00-18.00. Tube: Ladbroke Grove.
Organic bakery and wholefood shop. All vegetarian and vegan takeaway food. Yeast-free and wheat-free bread, cakes (sugar-free, vegan and naughty).

PORTOBELLO MARKET

Tube: Ladbroke Grove, Notting Hill Gate. Open: food and clothes Mon-Wed & Fri 08.00-17.00, Sat 08.00-13.00.
Fruit and veg all week, antiques on Saturday. Antiques at Notting Hill Gate end, getting cheaper all the way to Goldborne Road. This market is buzzing on Saturdays, with street entertainers, loads of quality second hand goods and interesting shops nearby.

WILD OATS

210 Westbourne Grove, W11. Tel: 071-229 1063. Open: Mon-Sat 9.00-19.00 (from 10.00 Tue), Sat 10.00-18.00, Sun 10.00-16.00.
Tube: Notting Hill Gate.
Three levels of wholefoods. Takeaway, macrobiotic, gluten-free, organic veg, books, and many American imports including Paul Pendler's cosmetics. Croissants Friday-Sunday. 10% discount to senior citizens on Wednesdays.

W12 SHEPHERDS BUSH

VEGETARIAN CAFÉS

BLAH BLAH BLAH CAFÉ

78 Goldhawk Road, Shepherds Bush, W12 8HA. Tel: 081-746 1337
Open: Mon-Sat 12.30-15.00, 19.30-23.45 last orderS.
Tube: Goldhawk Road

Vegetarian. International. Vegan food always available or can be prepared. Has vegetarian cheese, pasta and delicious Chinese noodle salad. Soup £2.95, starters £3.50, main course £6.95, desserts £2.50. Corkage 50p. Reservations essential Fri, Sat.

SHOPS

HOLLAND & BARRETT

112 Shepherds Bush Centre, Shepherds Bush Green, W12 8PP.
Tel: 081-743 1045. Open: Mon-Sat 09.00-18.00.

Health foods plus vegetarian and vegan takeaway food like pasties, slices, sandwiches. 10% off for Vegan or Vegetarian Society members.

W13 WEST EALING

NON VEGETARIAN

MAXIM RESTAURANT

153-155 Northfield Avenue, Ealing, W13 9QT. Tel: 081-567 1719
Open: Every day 18.30-24.00, also Mon-Sat 12.00-14.30
Tube: Northfields, Ealing Broadway

Omnivorous. Peking & Szechuan Chinese. Average £11.90 three course, £14.80 four course. Set vegetarian meal has starters like deep fried aubergine, stir fried veg, thick veg soup. Main courses feature bean curd, creamed cabbage, stir fried mixed veg, stir fried aubergine. Also vegetarian dishes on the a la carte menu.

SHOPS

HOLLAND & BARRETT

61 Broadway, W13 9BP. Tel: 081-840 7558. Open: Mon-Sat 9.00-17.30.
Tube: West Ealing.

Health foods and vegetarian sandwiches.

W14 WEST KENSINGTON

SHOPS

WEST KEN WHOLEFOODS, HEALTH SHOP

6 Charleville Road, W14 9JL. Tel: 071-385 0956. Open: Mon-Sat 09.00-17.00 (18.30 Sat), Sun 10.00-16.00. Tube: West Kensington.
All kinds of foods, supplements, vitamins, homeopathic medicine, cruelty-free cosmetics, essential oils. Vegan and vegetarian takeaways. Long established small shop just one minute from the tube which sells just about everything.

MIDDLESEX

Brentford
Edgware
Harrow
Hounslow
Kenton
Osterley
Southall
Wembley

Middlesex borders Greater London to the west and north west. The districts nearest to London include Edgware, Wembley and Southall and all three are well known for the number of inexpensive Gujarati restaurants offering gastronomic sensations to unsuspecting veggie visitors. You'll may find yourself at Wembley one day for a concert or a match, and Southall makes a great shopping trip. There's nothing for vegans in Wembley Stadium and only pizza for veggies, but plenty nearby.

BRENTFORD

ATTRACTIONS

SYON PARK
Brentford, Middlesex. Tel: 081-560 0881 Open: Daily 10.00-17.00
(18.00 summer) Tube: Gunnersbury, Syon Lane BR
Landscaped grounds, Syon House (open Apr-Oct 11.00-17.00). £3.25 adults, £2.50 concessions. National Trust Shop and garden centre. Cafe with vegetarian food.

EDGWARE

VEGETARIAN RESTAURANTS

SATYAM SWEET MART
24 Queensbury Station Parade, Edgware, Middlesex. Tel: 081-952 3947
Open: Mon 9.30-18.00, Tue-Sat 9.00-18.30.
Tube: Queensbury
Vegetarian. Indian. Average £1.50. Takeaway snacks only such as samosas and bhajias.

SHREE GANESHA

The Promenade, 4 Edgwarebury Lane, Edgware HA8 7JZ.
Tel: 081-958 2778. Open: Daily 18.00-20.00 & Sun 12.00-14.30
Tube: Edgware
Vegetarian. Indian. Minimum charge £6.00. Sunday eat-as-much-as-you-like buffet is £4.95. No children under six after 19:00. Average £11.00. Counter/Buffet/Takeaway. The only North Indian restaurant in the area, most other are Gujarati, South Indian or Bangladeshi. Three set meals at £6.00, £9.00 or £11.00 can be tailored to the individual stomach lining and is available for vegan, diabetics and those who prefer things less spicy. The lemon and orange sorbets are vegan.

OTHER RESTAURANTS

JASMINE

117 High Street, Edgware HA8 7DB. Tel: 081-952 1385.
Open: Every day 12.00-14.30, 18.00-24.00.
Tube: Edgware, Canons Park BR
Omnivorous. Indian. Restaurant and takeaway. Vegetable biryani with rice £4.10, thali £7.95. Vegetarian set lunch £4.95 offers one starter, rice, any veg dish and coffee.

HARROW

VEGETARIAN TAKEAWAY

NATRAJ

341 Northolt Road, South Harrow HA2 8JB. Tel: 081-426 8903
Open: Daily 10.30-19.00, closed Wed.
Tube: South Harrow
Vegetarian. Indian. Takeaway only. Mostly snack food such as bhajias, sweets, samosas. The only curry is potato curry £2.00, rice £1.00.

HOUNSLOW

OTHER RESTAURANTS

ASHNA INDIAN RESTAURANT

368 Staines Road, Hounslow TW4. Tel: 081-577 5988.
Open: Tue-Sun 10.00-22.00, closed Mon.
Tube: Hounslow West, Hounslow Central
Vegetarian. South Indian. Extensive menu with 19 starters, average £1.75, and 15 main courses. Thali £4.50. Uses vegetable oil, and butter ghee only in djipattis. Great value. No vegan sweets.

KENTON

VEGETARIAN TAKEAWAY

SUPREME SWEETS

706 Kenton Road, Kenton, Harrow HA3 9QX. Tel: 081-206 2212.
Open: Mon-Fri 10.00-20.00, Sat 9.00-20.00, Sun 8.30-18.00
Tube: Kingsbury
Vegetarian. Indian. Table, counter and takeaway service. Set
vegetarian meal which changes daily, for £2.99 or £3.99. 75% of items
vegan. Unlicensed. Good selection of sweets and savouries and like
many Hindu owned shops no eggs are used, and they use vegetable oil.
Also cater for weddings and parties.

OSTERLEY

ATTRACTIONS

OSTERLEY PARK

Isleworth, Middlesex. Tel: 081-560 3918. Tube: Osterley
Opens 30th March for the summer: Mon-Sun 09.00-dusk. £2.00 adults,
£1.00 others. Peaceful wooded gardens, lake, cafe, pagoda and state
rooms.

SOUTHALL

The centre of the Indian community, full of great shops where you
can stock up on vegetarian food, spices and clothes.

VEGETARIAN RESTAURANTS & TAKEAWAY

A SWEET

106 The Broadway, Southall, Middlesex UB1. Tel: 081-574 2821
Open: 10.00-19.00.
Tube: Southall
One of the most popular small cafés in the area with vegetarians. You'll
be in and out quite quickly but very well fed. Ground nut oil rather
than ghee used in all curries.

GIL SWEET CENTRE

29 King Street, Southall, Middlesex, UB1. Tel: 081-571 2857
Open: Every day 9.00-21.00.
Tube: Southall
Vegetarian. Indian. Savouries and sweets. Veg curry £1.60, rice £1.20.
Takeaway and counter service. Can also cater for weddings, parties
and other functions.

MOTI MAHAL

94 The Broadway, Southall, Middlesex Tel: 081-574 7682/571-9443
Open: Daily 10.00-22.30.
Train: Southall
Omnivorous north Indian cuisine but a good range of main meals,
snacks and bites for vegetarians and vegans. They will cook all dishes in
vegetable oil or ghee and even do a non-yoghurt nan bread - not as
doughy as the original but better for you. Ask them not to butter it.
They have a large range of sticky sweets but only the Ladu is vegan.
There are two tables outside in the warm weather from where you can
watch the crowds strolling by on this busy street. Take-away and
catering service also available.

SHAHANSHAH

17 South Road, Southall, Middlesex, UB1 1SU. Tel: 081-571 3110
Open: Daily 10.30-20.00, closed Wed.
Tube: Ealing Broadway then Southall BR
Vegetarian. Radha Swami Indian. Curry £1.50-£2.00, rice £1.50,
chapatti 25p. Counter service and takeaway. Unlicensed.

SHAHANSHAH

60 North Road, Southall UB1 2JL. Tel: 081-574 1493.
Open: Every day 10.00-20.00, closed Tue.
Tube: Ealing Broadway then Southall BR
Vegetarian. Indian Radha Swami. As above.

WEMBLEY

ATTRACTIONS

WEMBLEY STADIUM

Empire Way, Wembley, Middlesex, HA9. Tel: 081-902 8833, box office
081-900 1234. Tube: Wembley Park, Wembley Central
National football stadium, rock concerts. Tours of the ground Tel: 081-
902 6001.

VEGETARIAN RESTAURANTS

MARU'S BHAJIA HOUSE

230 Ealing Road, Alperton, Wembley, Middlesex, HA0 4QL.
Tel: 081 903 6771, 081-902 5570.
Open: Tue-Fri 12.00-20.45, Sat-Sun 12.00-21.45.
Tube: Alperton, Wembley Central
Vegetarian. Indian. Average £20.00. Maru's Kenyan Asian cuisine has
been a firm favourite with passing shoppers for 20 years. Maru's
bhajis, maize and assorted snacks are famous throughout the area.
Well known Asian film stars often fill up here on the likes of pani puri,

kachori and vada, washed down with one of the many flavoured
milkshakes. Take time to visit Maru's if you are in the area.

MARUTI BHELPURI HOUSE

238a Ealing Road, Wembley HA0 4QL. Tel: 081-903 6743, 081-902 9805
Open: Daily 12.00-22.00, closed Tue.
Tube: Alperton
Vegetarian. Indian. Spicy, hot, Southern Indian food.

NATRAJ

414 High Rd, Wembley. Tel: 081-903 1423
Open: Daily 12.00-22.00, closed Wed.
Tube: Wembley Central
Vegetarian. Indian. Lunch buffet style £3.95 includes nan, rice, two
vegetarian curries, assorted bhajias, papadum, pickles. Thali £4.50.
£5.50 for three courses. Also takeaway. Manager is a devotee of Sai
Baba and knows well all the different Indian and vegetarian diets, who
can eat aubergines, garlic, onions, milk etc. Many regulars are vegans.
Everything is prepared after you order, so no butter ghee need be used
and all 17 main courses can be vegan.

SAKONIS VEGETARIAN FAST FOOD & JUICE BAR

119 Ealing Road, Wembley, Middlesex. Tel: 081-903 9601
Open: Every day 11.00-22.00.
Tube: Wembley Central, Wembley Park
Vegetarian. Gujarati cuisine. Snacks, burger, idli, samosas, bhajias.
Veg biryani £3.00.

WOODLANDS RESTAURANT

402a High Road, Wembley HA9 6AL. Tel: 081-902 9869.
Open: Every day 12.00-15.00, 18.00-23.00.
Tube: Wembley Central, Wembley Stadium
Vegetarian. South Indian Average £6.00-£8.00. Table and takeaway.
Very big menu includes dosas, puri, thali £4.95 and vegan thali £6.95.
They use vegetable ghee.

OTHER RESTAURANTS

SAPNA RESTAURANT

28 Watford Road, Sudbury Town, Wembley, HA0 3EP Tel:081-904 8762
Open: Daily 19.00-24.00, but takeaway only Mon-Tue.
Tube: Sudbury Town
Omnivorous. Pakistani. Mixed veg £3.50 or £2.90 per dish, rice £1.00,
pilau rice £1.50. Use vegetable ghee. Indian music Fri-Sat. There is a
set menu with table service for £12.50 Fri, £15.00 Sat and it's an all-
you-can-eat three course meal. All desserts contain dairy, but they can
get you something else if you warn them.

SURREY

Croydon
Kingston-upon-Thames
Richmond
Surbiton

The county of Surrey borders London to the south and south west.

RICHMOND

ATTRACTIONS

RICHMOND PARK
Richmond, Surrey. Tel: 081-948 3209. Open: 24 hours, cars barred
before 07.00 and after dark.Tube: Richmond, Richmond BR
Better countryside than the country. Deer, foxes and other wildlife,
flower gardens, horse-riding and cycling.

KEW GARDENS
Kew Road, Richmond, Surrey. Tel: 081-940 1117
Open: Open daily from 09.30. Closes Mar-Sep 18.00 (Sun 20.00), Oct-
Jan 16.00, Feb 17.00. Tube: Kew Gardens, Kew Bridge BR
£3.00 adults, £1.00 children, £1.50 senior citizen's and students, under
fives free. Unmissable gardens in any weather. Hot house, pagoda,
cafe, restaurant, shop, wheelchairs available. Kew Palace £1.00 adults,
50p children, open Apr-Sep 11.00-17.30.

HAMPTON COURT PALACE
East Molsey, Surrey. Tel: 081-977 8441
Open: Apr-Oct daily 9.30-18.00 (from 10.15 Mon), Oct-Mar 10.15-16.30
Train: Hampton Court BR, or by boat to Hampton Court Pier
£4.60 adults, £2.90 children, £3.50 senior citizens, U-5's free.
Dreamy tudor palace appropriated from Cardinal Wolsey by King
Henry Vlll. Now fully restored after major fire. Includes maze,
gardens, medieval tennis court, cafe, shop.

VEGETARIAN RESTAURANTS

RICHMOND HARVEST
5 Dome Buildings, The Quadrant, Richmond, TW9 1DT.
Tel: 081-940 1138 Open: Mon-Sat 11.30-23.00, Sun 13.00-22.00
Tube: Richmond BR
Vegetarian. International. Menu has two bakes with mixed salad, two
casseroles with brown rice, four salads, four starters, fix or six
desserts. Three courses with one glass of wine costs £10. Vegans can

choose from three or four starters, at least two main courses, and two desserts. Table and takeaway service. English fruit wines available.

SHOPS

OLIVER'S WHOLEFOOD STORE
5 Station Approach, Kew Gardens, Richmond, Surrey. Tel: 081-948 3990. Open: Mon-Sat 09.00-19.30, Sun 10.00-18.00.
Tube: Kew Gardens.
Wholefood shop with takeaway, next to the tube station and handy for picking up something to nibble while you visit Kew Gardens.

CROYDON

VEGETARIAN RESTAURANTS

HOCKNEYS VEGETARIAN RESTAURANT
96 High Street, Croydon, CRO 1ND. Tel: 081-688 2899
Open: Mon 12.00-14.30, Tue-Sat 12.00-17.30.
Train: East Croydon
Vegetarian. International. Menu changes daily. Vegan meals every day but not always a main one. Main course £4.90, starter £1.90, fruity cashew vegan cake £0.90. Counter service and takeaway. You can bring your own wine and pay £1.50 per bottle. Run by Buddhists. Health food shop and gift shop next door, open Mon-Sat 9.00-17.30, Thu to 19.30.

OTHER RESTAURANTS

SIAMESE THAI RESTAURANT
164 Cherry Orchard Road, Croydon, CRO 6BB. Tel: 081-681 3402
Open: Mon-Fri 12.00-14.30, every day 18.00-23.00
Train: East Croydon, Addiscombe BR (zone 5)
Omnivorous. International. Lots of vegetarian food, noodles, rice, vegetables. Starters from £3.30, main dish £4.50.

KINGSTON-UPON-THAMES

VEGETARIAN RESTAURANTS

THE PAVEMENT
165 Ewell Road, Surbiton, KT6 6AW. Tel: 081-390 0320
Open: Tue-Sat 19.00-23.00.
Train: Surbiton BR
Vegetarian. International. Average price £11.00 for three courses. Number of vegan dishes, such as Hungarian porkolt with soya, corn, herbs and salad, or Jamaican sweet potato cutlet with split almond

and lentil sauce and vegetables. Candlelit table service.

RIVERSIDE VEGETARIA

64 High Street, Kingston-upon-Thames. Tel: 081-546 7992
Open: Mon-Fri 12.00-15.00, 17.30-23.00, Sat 12.00-23.00,
Sun 12.00-22.00.
Train: Kingston BR

Vegetarian. International. River view. Great place and a favourite of London Vegans. Huge menu with 35 dishes, 70% vegan, even soya custard with the crumble. Popular dishes are Moroccan-style leek or gado-gado. Three courses for £11.00. Chinese Ginseng beer. Outdoor area on the towpath beside the Thames so eat under the sky in summer. Booking advised evenings.

OTHER RESTAURANTS

CLOUDS RESTAURANT

6/8 Kingston Hill, Kingston, KT2 7NH. Tel: 081-546 0559
Open: Mon-Fri 12.30-14.30, 17.30-23.30. Sat-Sun 12.00-23.30
Train: Norbiton BR

Omnivorous. Wholefood. Lots of vegetarian food like carrot and coriander soup with fresh-baked bread, stuffed mushroom, mushroom pizza with or without mozzarella £4.70, veg(etari)an (cheese) burger with chips and salad £5.55. One or two things for vegans such as corn chips with avocado.

BATH

INTRODUCTION

One of the most elegant small cities in Europe, filled with flowers and Georgian buildings. The most famous landmarks are the Royal Crescent, the Circus and Pulteney Bridge. Bath has won the "Britain in Bloom" competition more times than any other city, with colourful streets, and an abundance of hanging baskets and window boxes.

There are many excellent parks and gardens, such as the Royal Victoria Park, Parade Garden on the river, and the scented garden for blind people in Henrietta Park. You can still see the two thousand year old Roman Baths heated by natural hot springs, and there are stacks more museums. Bath's classical buildings are stuffed with sweet speciality shops plus the well known chains.

There are two excellent vegetarian eateries and lots of wholefood shops, plus tea shops, pubs and wine bars, many in quaint buildings.

Bath is very popular so try to reserve accommodation, especially for summer or Christmas, or arrive early and head straight for the tourist information centre. If you really can't find a place to stay then Bristol is only 15 minutes away by train.

GETTING THERE

COACH

National Express coaches leave Victoria from 08.00 then every two hours until 17.50, then one at 19.30, last one at 21.30. £9.25 return if you avoid Fridays, £11.00 otherwise. Journey time 2 hours.

TRAIN

British Rail trains leave from Paddington. There is one train per hour and a saver return, which can only be used between 09.15 & 16.00 or after 19.00, costs £26.00. There is no Super Saver ticket to Bath.

TOURIST INFORMATION CENTRE

The Colonnades, Bath Street, Bath, BA1 1SW. 0225-462831.
Open: Jun-Sept Mon-Sat 09.00-20.00, Sun 10.00-16.00. Oct-May Mon-Sat 09.30-17.00, Sun closed.
Before your visit to Bath, send a cheque or postal order for £1.49 payable to Bath City Council for a copy of the City Guide Book, which includes festivals and a walking tour with map.

BATH

PLACES TO EAT
1. De Muth's
2. Scoffs Wholefood Cafe

KEY
i — tourist information
BR — train station
T — toilets
B — bus & coach stn.

ACCOMMODATION

BATH YOUTH HOSTEL

Bathwick Hill, Bath, BA2 6JZ. Tel: 0225-465674. Fax 0225-482947.
Adult £7.75, U-18 £5.20. Open: Jun-Aug adult £8.70, U-18 £5.80.
Handsome mansion in beautiful gardens, with views over the city and
hills. 1.6km east of city centre. Follow signs for American Museum and
University 1km up Bathwick Hill from roundabout in Pulteney Rd by
St Mary's Church. Evening meal: 18.45. Vegetarian food always
available. Vegan no problem if you phone ahead.

This hostel is open every day of the year and busy, so you should
arrive early or book. Fax and credit card reservations welcome. Shop at
hostel.

Y.M.C.A.

Broad Street Place, off Broad Street, Bath. Tel: 0225-460471.
£12.00 single, £11.00 twin or triple, £9.50 dorm. Continental breakfast.
Open: 24 hours.

CAMPING & CARAVANS

NEWTON MILL TOURING CENTRE

Newton St Loe. Tel: 0225-333909. Open all year. Three miles west of
city centre off A36/A4. Bus no. 5 from bus station. Walk on tent (all
seasons) £3.30 per person. Tent, car plus two people £7.75 (£8.75 Jul-
Aug). Caravan + 2 £9.75 (£11.75). Extra adults £1.00, child (3-14)
£1.00, dog 50p. Electric hook up £1.75, TV 50p. Extra car/trailer £1.00.
Half day extension till 18.00 £2.75. Shop, indoor recreation, pub,
takeaway and restaurant.
Another site for caravans only is Newbridge, 1.5 miles west of city
centre on A4. Tel: 0225-428778. Contact the Tourist Inforomation
Centre for a full list of camping and caravan sites.

ATTRACTIONS

BATH BOATING STATION

Forester Rd. Tel: 0225-466407.
Skiffs, punts and canoes for hire. Tea gardens. Abundant wildlife,
kingfishers, heron, wild geese, moorhens and cormorants. Also river
trips from Pulteney Bridge.

BUILDING OF BATH MUSEUM

Countess of Huntingdon Chapel, The Vineyards, The Paragon.
Tel: 0225-333895. Open: daily except Mon 10.30-17.00. Open Bank
Holidays. Closed 11 Dec - 28 Feb. £2.50, children £1.40.
Full scale mock-ups of how the architectural masterpiece of Europe
was constructed.

CITY TOURS
Walking tours daily (except Sats Oct-Apr). See noticeboard in Abbey Church Yard, or ask at tourist office.

MUSEUM OF COSTUME AND ASSEMBLY ROOMS
Bennett Street. Tel: 0225-461111 ext 2785.
Open: Mar-Oct 9.30-18.00, Sun 10.00-18.00. Nov-Feb 10.00-17.00, Sun 11.00-17.00. £2.50, children £1.40.
Over 200 dressed figures, wearing 1,000 items of clothing from 400 years. Special exhibition for 1994: 'Up to Date: Fashion 1963-1993'.

GEORGIAN HOUSE
No. 1 Royal Crescent. Tel: 0225-428126.
Open: Mar-Oct Tue-Sun 11.00-17.00, bank holiday Mondays and during Bath Festival. Closed Good Fri. Nov-Dec Tue-Sun 11.00-16.00.
Restored 18th century Georgian townhouse.

ROMAN BATHS MUSEUM
Pump Room, Abbey Churchyard. Tel: 0225-461111 ext 2785.
Open: Mar-Oct 09.00-18.00, Aug also open 20.00-22.00. Nov-Feb 09.00-17.00 (Sun from 10.00). Last tickets half an hour before closing. £4.00, children £2.00. Or get a combined ticket for the Baths and the Costume Museum for £5.00, £2.00 children.
Most impressive Roman buildings in Britain. 2,000 year old complex of swimming pools and saunas. Taste the spring water in the 18th century Pump Room over the baths.

RESTAURANTS

DE MUTH'S
2 North Parade Passage, off Abbey Green Rd, Bath. Tel: 0225-446059.
Open: Mon-Sat 09.30-18.00, Sun 10.00-17.00.
Vegetarian restaurant near the Abbey. Always has vegan soup, starters, main course and puddings.

SCOFFS WHOLEFOOD CAFE
19-20 Kingsmead Square, Bath. Tel: 0272-462483. Open: Mon-Fri 08.00-17.15, Sat 09.00-17.15.
Vegetarian. Bakery and cafe. Takeaway till 17.30. Lots for vegans.

SHOPS

THE BODY SHOP
2b Burton St. Tel: 0225-446332. Open: Mon-Sat 09.30-17.30 (18.00 Sat).

GREEN TREATS
Above the Body Shop. Open: 09.30-17.30 (Thu/Fri 18.30).
Sauna and massage.

HARVEST NATURAL FOODS
37 Walcot St. Tel: 0225-465519.

HOLLAND & BARRETT
6 Cheap St. Tel: 0225-330091. Open: Mon-Sat 9.00-17.30.

SEASONS WHOLEFOOD
10 George Street. Tel: 0225-469730. Open: 09.00-17.30.
Has takeaway food with plenty for vegans.

MISCELLANEOUS

VEGETARIAN SOCIETY CONTACT
JB & RL Foreman, 21 Abingdon Gardens, Odd Down, Bath, BA2 2UY.

BRIGHTON

INTRODUCTION

Brighton and Hove make up the UK's largest and most cosmopolitan holiday resort with a range of attractions for all tastes. The architecturally elegant style capital of the Regency period, Brighton has the the Royal Pavillion as its centrepiece. There are many picturesque squares within a stone's throw of the sea and 'The Lanes' is a pedestrianised focal point for shopaholics, with its cobbled passageways and specialist shops.

Brighton is unusually well served with restaurants, shops and hotels for the cruelty-free traveller and at night there is a lively club scene that attracts visitors from London. The town also hosts one of the UK's largest arts festivals, has the biggest theatre scene outside the capital, a nudist beach and two piers - the West Pier being derelict and projecting a ghostly silhouette at night. 1994 will also see the Tour De France come to Britain for the first time and it will overtake Brighton on 6th July.

GETTING THERE

TRAIN

British Rail trains from Victoria leave every hour and arrive at Brighton station on Queens Road. Journey time approximately 55 minutes. Return fare is £15.70.

COACH

National Express coaches leave Victoria from 09.00 then every 90 minutes until 18.00. £8.50 return if you avoid Fridays, £10.00 otherwise. Journey time 1 hour 50 minutes.

CYCLE

You can join the other 30,000 people for the 60 mile London to Brighton Bike Ride on June 19th every year for one of the friendliest events in the cycling calendar. Overnight accommodation is available after the race.

TOURIST INFORMATION CENTRE

10 Bartholomew Square, Brighton BN1 1JS. Tel: 0273-323755. Open: Mon-Fri 09.00-17.00, Sat-Sun 10.00-16.00. Hotel list and map available by fax.

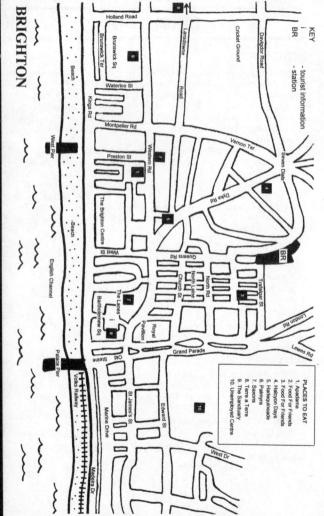

days out

BRIGHTON

KEY

i - tourist information

BR - station

PLACES TO EAT

1. Apadana
2. Food For Friends
3. Food For Friends
4. Halcyon Days
5. Harlequinnade
6. Palmyra
7. Saxons
8. Terre a Terre
9. The Sanctuary
10. Unemployed Centre

Remember to say you saw it in the Cruelty-Free Guide

ACCOMMODATION

YOUTH HOSTEL

Patcham Place, Brighton BN1 8YD. Tel: 0273-556196. 80 beds,
3.5 miles north of town centre off a small road to the west of the A23
opposite the Black Lion public house. £8.70 per night. Can do vegan
meals if notified in a advance.

CAMPSITES

There are a number of campsites near Brighton and the Tourist
Information Centre can provide a print out.

DOWNS VIEW CARAVAN PARK

Bramlands Lane, Woodmancote, Near Henfield, BN5 9TG. Tel: 0273-492801.
Open: mid Mar-13 Nov. Reception open: 09.00-12.00, 15.00-18.30 and
19.30-21.00. High season June 20-Aug 30. £8.00 per night total for two
people with tent and car in high season, £7.00 low season. Price
includes showers and hot water. Shop with basic supplies on site. Quiet
site in the country, 6.5 miles from Brighton to the north.

FOXHOLE BOTTOM CAMPSITE & CAMPING BARN

*Seven Sisters Country Park, Exceat, near Seaford, East Sussex, BN25
4AD (near the Golden Gallion pub). Tel: 0323-870280.*
Open: all year round. Information open: 10.00-17.30. No cars allowed
in the area. Tents £2.50 per person per night. Camping barn £3.50 per
person per night. Public phone in barn. Cooking areas but no shop on
site.
Set in a country park covering 700 hectares of Sussex downland near
the sea and eight miles from Brighton. Take the train to Seaford and
then the 712 (Brighton-Eastbourne) bus for two miles. Service is every
half hour Mon-Sat, hourly Sundays.

BED & BREAKFAST ESTABLISHMENTS

AQUARIUM GUEST HOUSE

*13 Madeira Place, Brighton BN2 1TN. Tel: 0273-606761. Bed and
breakfast £10.00 minimum single per night.*
Vegetarian/vegan breakfast available, satellite TV in all rooms, tea
and coffee in rooms, own key, open all year, one minute from Palace
Pier.

BRIGHTON MARINA HOUSE HOTEL

*8 Charlotte Street, Brighton BN2 1AG. Tel.: 0273-605349/679484. Bed
& breakfast £10-£20 single, £30-£38 doubles per night.*
Near the sea-front with tea and coffee in rooms. They can cook
Chinese, Indian and English food in the evenings, though with all the

great restaurants in the town you're unlikely to need it. They are flexible at breakfast time and able to cater for vegans.

PASKINS HOTEL

19 Charlotte Street, Brighton, BN2 1AG. Tel.: 0273-601203. Bed and breakfast from £15.00 single per night.
TV, direct dial phones, and tea and coffee in rooms. It is licensed and run by vegetarians. They use organic ingredients where possible.

THE GRANVILLE HOTEL

124 Kings Road, Brighton, BN1 2FA. Tel: 0273-326302. Bed and breakfast from £40.00 single per night, doubles from £25.00 per person.
Seafront location. The hotel incorporates Trogs Restaurant, a fish and vegetarian restaurant using organic ingredients wherever possible.

RESTAURANTS

APADAMA RESTAURANT

104 Western Road, Brighton. Tel: 0273-732397
Open: Mon-Sun 11.00-01.00
Mediterranean/Arabic licensed restaurant and takeaway. Large main dishes £5.15, pasta dishes £3.00-£4.50 with a huge range of 'light bites' between £1.00 and £2.75. The vegan soya-sausage in short pastry is about 10" long, the hummus, falafel and salad comes rolled up in delicious Persian Lavash bread. They even have vegan calzone which is like a pizza folded in half and very filling and a vegetarian pasta menu. Alas, no vegan desserts though.

FOOD FOR FRIENDS

42 Market Street/Prince Albert Street, Brighton. Tel: 0273-202 310
Open: Mon-Sun 09.00-22.00
Very reasonably priced vegetarian counter service restaurant. Main meals such as ratatouille, quiche, vegetable biryani, apple and nut bake, stir fried vegetables £2.95. Always a vegan main course and usually one starter and dessert option. Soup and roll £1.40. Licensed, seats about 60 around large oak tables with plants and large mirrors. Publish their own cookbook for £9.99.

FOOD FOR FRIENDS

11-12 Sydney Street, Brighton. Tel: 0273-571 363.
Owned by same people as above but more of a takeaway for people working in the area.

HALCYON DAYS

72 Dyke Road, Brighton. Tel: 0273-21630 Open: Mon-Thu 09.00-20.00, Fri 09.00-22.00, Sat 10.00-22.00, Sun 10.30-15.00
Vegetarian and fish restaurant and takeaway a little way out of town. Main courses £2.50-£3.50, Soup £1.10, desserts 95p-£1.50. Vegan breakfast with 'rashers', sausages etc. £3.20. Sunday nut roast dinner

£3.95. Menu changes daily, homemade jams available. Bring your own wine. No smoking till 14.30 daily, and between 19.00-21.00 Fri-Sat.

HARLEQUINADE

13 Dyke Road, Brighton. Tel: 0273-821787
Open: Mon-Fri 12.00-15.00 & 18.00-22.00, Sat 12.00-16.00 &
18.00-23.00, Sun 13.00-15.00
No smoking, vegetarian restaurant and coffee house with wholefood cuisine. Minimum charge £5.00 per person. Majority of main courses such as Staffordshire root veg and brown ale casserole, cous-cous Alhambra, peanut and onion roast and an exotic vegetable curry were vegan, well proportioned and £5.90. Owner wants to develop upstairs area as New Age forum and bookshop. Unlicensed, corkage 50p per person - no beer.

PALMYRA

238 Portland Road, Hove BN3 5QT. Tel: 0273-723830
Open: Mon-Thu 10.00-14.00, Fri-Sat 18.00-22.00
Very small all vegetarian Indian takeaway and licensed cafe. Very cheap, with curries under £3.00.

SAXONS (above Oxfam)

134a Western Road, Brighton. Tel: 0273-720798 shop
Open: Mon-Sat 10.30-15.30
Cheap vegetarian wholefood, non-smoking cafe serving some vegan options. £2.00 for a meal.

TERRE A TERRE

7 Pool Valley, Brighton. Tel.: 0273-729051.
Open: Mon-Sat 11.00-23.00, Sun 11.00-18.00.
Licensed vegetarian restaurant that offers a largely vegan wholefood menu with an international flavour. Main courses come in large and small sizes at £5.25 and £3.75. They may include: Thai Green Curry, Chargrilled Marinated Aubergine, Grilled Red Tofu with Pickled Ginger, Pasta Ribbons with Broccolli and Artichoke.

THE SANCTUARY

Brunswick Street East, Brighton. Tel: 0273-770002
Open: Closed Sunday
Trendy cafe serving veggie food but nothing vegan on the menu when we looked in.

UNEMPLOYED CENTRE

Tilbury Place, Brighton. (Up Carlton Hill past the art college)
Open: Weekday lunchtimes
The Centre has a vegan cafe. Main meals £1.30 employed, £1.00 unemployed, 30p children's baked potato. Creche on site for users.

FOOD SHOPS

BEANS AND THINGS

21 Withyam Avenue, Brighton BN2 8LF. Tel.: 0273-305200.

Not a shop but a home delivery service. Proprietor is a member of Brighton Vegan and Vegetarian Society. Place your order between 08.30 and 21.00. Similar products to Infinity Foods who are the main supplier. Organic fruit and veg available and only three things on the price list that are not vegan.

HOLLAND & BARRETT

Churchill Square, Brighton. Tel: 0273-325563.

HOLLAND & BARRETT

9 Garnet House, St George's Street, Brighton. Tel: 0273-602515.

HOLLAND & BARRETT

105 London Road, Brighton. Tel: 0273-696209.

HOLLAND & BARRETT

146 North Street, Brighton. Tel: 0273-324591.

INFINITY FOODS

25 North Road, Brighton. Tel: 0273-603563, 0273-690116.

Organic wholefood shop and take-away with organic wine, beer and cider, bread, recycled stationery and other household goods

SUNNY FOOD

76 Beaconsfiled Road, Brighton. Tel: 0273-507879.
Open: Mon-Sun 08.00-20.00.

Healthfood based vegetarian convenience store selling things like organic bread, baguettes, tofu burgers, Chlorella, Kingfisher tooth-paste and vegetarian savouries alongside less alternative products.

THE VEGAN SHOP

11a Vallance Road, Hove, BN3 2DA. Tel: 0273-749910.

OTHER

THE BODYSHOP

41 North Street, Brighton. Tel: 0273-327048.

Original location was Kensington Gardens - site of the first Bodyshop in the UK.

BRIGHTON NATURAL CLINIC

94 St James's Street, Brighton. Tel: 0273-672952.

NEAL'S YARD REMEDIES

2a Kensington Gardens, Brighton. Tel: 0273-601464.

Homeopathic remedies, essential oils and natural cosmetics not tested on animals.

VEGETARIAN SHOES

Dept AV, 12 Gardner Street, Brighton, BN1 1UP. Tel: 0273-691913.
Doc Martens, walking boots, steel toe capped walking boots, sandals
men's and women's shoes and jackets that look and feel like leather
but are made from synthetic materials. Have mail order catalogue too.

VEGGIE JACKS

25 Gardner Street, Brighton. Tel: 0273-203821. Open: 10.00-17.30.
Shoes, jackets, belts, bags and other fashion accessories that are made
from synthetic materials with a leather and suede look and feel.

GREEN FEAST

The Basement, 5 Vernon Terrace, Brighton BN1 3JG. Tel: 0273-749906.
Organic vegetarian baby food suppliers offering delivery service. What
about: apricot porridge; lentil, millet and tomato; brown rice, tomato,
tahini and fresh herbs; pumpkin or mixed seasonal fruit - these should
be available to adults. All £1.00, minimum order £6.00, recipes change
with the seasons.

BRIGHTON VEGAN & VEGETARIAN GROUP

c/o 14 Terminus Street, Brighton BN1 3PE.

BRISTOL

INTRODUCTION

120 miles (200km) west of London, Bristol is an ancient university city which has become a thriving business centre as companies relocate from London. John and Sebastian Cabot set off down the river Avon through the magnificent Clifton gorge to explore the New World. You can still see Brunel's famous Clifton Suspension Bridge and the first iron hulled ship, the SS Great Britain, which took many emigrants to Australia.

There are hundreds of pubs, a big shopping centre next to the old town, arts centres, museums, churches, water buses, parks and a wine museum. And four mouth watering vegetarian cafes and restaurants near the centre.

GETTING THERE

COACH

National Express coaches leave Victoria from 09.00 then every two hours until 19.00. £18.50 return if you avoid Fridays, £22.00 otherwise. Journey time 2.5 hours.

TRAIN

Train from Paddington station. Get a train to Bristol Temple Meads station, not Bristol Parkway which is north of town. Call British Rail recorded information on 071-262 6767 for times. Journey about 1 hour 40 minutes. Then catch a minibus 8 or 9 to the Centre (10 minutes).

HITCHING

Hitching to Bristol is excellent. Take the tube to Gunnersbury (district line). Walk to the Chiswick mega-roundabout (10 minutes) and stand on the slip road for the M4 motorway by the petrol station. If the driver (illegally) drops you at the top of the M32 motorway into Bristol, you might hitch the slow traffic off the roundabout into Bristol (8km) in a few minutes. If the police see you they'll either give you a lift or tell you to walk to the next roundabout (300m) then leave.

To get out of Bristol, hitch about 100m from the T-junction at the start of the M32, where there is a long pull in. This is considerably more difficult and could take up to an hour. You'll need a "London please" sign.

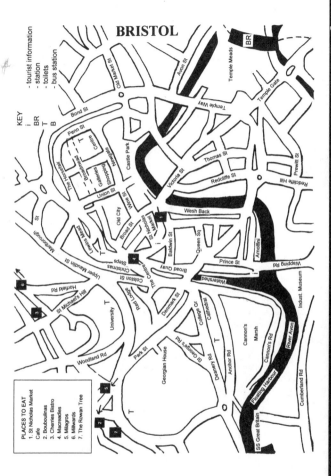

BRISTOL

days out

KEY
i - tourist information
BR - station
T - toilets
B - bus station

PLACES TO EAT
1. St Nicholas Market Cafe
2. Bouboulinas
3. Cheries Bistro
4. Macreadies
5. Milagros
6. Millwards
7. The Rowan Tree

Remember to say you saw it in the Cruelty-Free Guide

193

TOURIST INFORMATION CENTRE

St Nicholas Church, St Nicholas St, opposite Bristol Bridge. Open 7 days a week 09.30-17.30, Jun-Sept Thu-Fri till 20.00. Tel: 0272-260767. Pick up a map, what's on leaflets, and accommodation list. They will find you accommodation before 17.00 and book ahead for other towns.

You can rent Talkabout Tours excellent self-guided tours of the city. They provide a Walkman, map, and one hour tape. You use this to explore the old city at your own pace and break off where you like.

Free walking tours leave here May-August on Saturdays at 14.30 and Thursday evenings at 19.00.

ACCOMMODATION

YOUTH HOSTEL

Hayman House, 64 Prince Street, Bristol, BS1 4HU. Tel: 0272-221659. Fax 0272-273789. Adult £10.50, under 18's £7.00
Beautiful hostel right in the centre of town, next to the river and the Arnolfini Gallery and close to lots of attractions. Open all day 07.00-23.00. Closed 19 Dec 1994-3 Jan 1995. Evening meal 18.00-19.45. Vegetarian and vegan food always available, though large groups of vegans should call ahead.

ARCHES HOTEL

132 Cotham Brow, Bristol BS6 6AE. Tel: 0272 247398.
Omnivorous bed and breakfast. £21.50 single, £31.00 en suite, £37.50 double, £43.50 en suite.
Vegan breakfast can be just beans on toast or the full British fry-up, with soya milk. TV and beverage making in all rooms. Close to central stations and a wholefood shop. Discounts to Vegetarian Society members at weekends.

ATTRACTIONS

The Watershed, on the river right next to the Centre, is full of craft shops, cafes and cinemas. Walk round past Neptune's statue to the opposite bank for a ride on the river bus. A little further down this side is the Arnolfini Arts Centre, packed with trendy young people. St Nicholas Market, just off south side of the Centre, is filled with the products of young artisans, and has a vegetarian cafe. Nearby is the St Nicholas Church.

Broadmead is the modern main shopping centre, on the southeast side of the city centre, packed with all the big name shops. The Galleries is a new shopping mall between Broadmead and the river.

College Green, north west of the Centre, is bordered by the Cathedral, the Central Library, the Council House, and Park Street, a steep street of great shops leading up to the excellent City Museum and Art Gallery. From hear you can pop over during the day to the Rowan Tree cafe, or in the evening take a 15 minute walk through a residential area to Millwards or Cherries restaurants.

Christmas Steps, on the north side of the Centre, is full of quaint shops including the famous "Joke Shop" and MacReadies vegetarian cafe. At the top, round to the right, is the Green Leaf Bookshop, full of right-on ecological, vegetarian and feminist books. Also nearby is the Red Lodge, an old Bristol house that has been turned into a museum.

Buy a copy of Venue, Bristol and Bath's equivalent of Time Out, with extensive listings of everything happening in the region. Or get the daily Bristol Evening Post for today's cinema and TV. There are heaps of things to do in the centre of town apart from cinemas, theatres and the Broadmead shopping centre.

BRISTOL INDUSTRIAL MUSEUM

Princes Wharf. Tel: 0272-251470 Open: Tue-Sun 10.00-13.00, 14.00-17.00. £1.00. 50p after 16.00. Students, under 16's free.
Cars, aircraft engine, 300 years of the port of Bristol, trucks, motorcycles, gypsy caravan. Cafe and Arnolfini nearby. Cross Princes Bridge, turn right and walk 150m.

THE EXPLORATORY

Next to Temple Meads Train Station Tel: 0272-225944
Open: Every day 10.00-17.00. £4.00, children £2.50.
Lots of fun trying the 140 hands-on science exhibits, planetarium and sound and music exhibition.

GEORGIAN HOUSE

7 Great George St, off Park St. Tel: 0272-211362
Continue up the hill to peaceful Brandon Hill Park, with the Cabot Tower giving a fantastic view over Bristol.

HARVEYS WINE MUSEUM

12 Denmark Street Tel: 0272-277661. Open: Mon-Fri 10.00-13.00, 14.00-17.00, Sat-Sun 14.00-17.00. Closed bank holidays
Tours and tastings in the centre of town. Call for info.

RED LODGE

Park Row, corner of Lodge St, a steep hill behind the Colston Hall. Tel: 0272-211360 Open: Tue-Sat 10.00-13.00, 14.00-17.00

SS GREAT BRITAIN

Gas Ferry Road. Further down the south side of the river, on the same side as the Arnolfini Arts Centre. Tel: 0272-260680
Open: Summer 10.00-18.00, Winter 10.00-17.00 every day
£2.90, senior citizen and under 16's £1.90, under 5's free.
Brunel's biggest ship in the world in 1843 and the first to use steam power. If you don't have time to go inside, you can get a good photo from the river bus. Refreshment room inside. Buttery nearby has some veggie food.

THE CLIFTON SUSPENSION BRIDGE

A couple of miles away, and also built by Brunel, offers magnificent views of Bristol and the Avon gorge.

RESTAURANTS

VEGETARIAN CAFÉ

St Nicholas Market Open: Mon-Sat till 16.30
Cheap and friendly.

BOUBOULINA'S

9 Portland St, Clifton Village. Tel: 0272-731192
Open: daily 10.00-12.00, 14.30-23.30
Omnivorous. Greek. Yes, this restaurant closes for lunch, but unlike the others it's open on Sunday evenings. And they have some great Greek grub like grilled tofu kebabs and vegan meze.

CHERRIES BISTRO

122 St Michaels Hill, Kingsdown Tel: 0272-293675
Open: Mon-Sat 19.00-23.00
Omnivorous. Wholefood. £7.25 main course. £11.95 for three courses. Very good, friendly, mostly vegetarian, French style bistro. Tasty choice of starters and main courses for vegans, though limited range of sweets. Highly rated by Egon Ronay, Consumer Association, Good Food Guide etc. House wine £6.95 bottle, £1.45 glass. Booking advisable.

MacREADIES

3 Christmas Steps, Bristol, BS1 5BS. Tel: 0272-298387
Open: (Winter in brackets) Mon 12.00-16.00 (14.30), Tue-Wed 8.00-19.00 (16.00, 19.00), Thu-Fri 8.00-22.00 (23.00, 19.00), Sat 10.00-20.00 (17.00), Sun 10.30-17.00.
Vegetarian. Wholefood just off the centre.

MILAGROS

88a Queens Road, Clifton, Bristol. Tel: 0272-238697
Open: Every day 07.30-23.00
Vegetarian and fish. Mexican. Very popular cafe style restaurant, situated beneath a Latin-American craft shop. £11.00 for three courses. Gringos pay no many pesos, £3.75 in fact, for a Mexican breakfast of refried beans or drunken beans (pinto beans cooked in beer), fried plantain and hash browns. About 50% of dishes can be served vegan, marked V on the menu, and one of the cooks is a vegan. Also some desserts. Bring your own booze, no corkage. Booking advisable in evenings. Five minutes west of the top of Park Street, next to the Victoria Rooms.

MILLWARDS

40 Alfred Place, Kingsdown. Tel: 0272-245026

Open: Tue-Sat 19.00-21.30 (last orders)
Vegetarian restaurant which has been highly rated by many magazines and winner of UK vegetarian restaurant of the year. £10.45 for two courses or £12.95 for three. Vegan dishes every day. Organic vegan wines. No smoking. Reservations advised at weekends.

THE ROWAN TREE
The Triange, Clifton. Open: Mon-Fri 10.00-17.00
Lovely vegetarian cafe and shop at the front of the Bristol Waldorf School, which is run by followers of the teachings of Rudolf Steiner.

SHOPPING

HARVEST NATURAL FOODS
224 Cheltenham Rd, Bristol, BS6 5QU. Tel: 0272-425997. Open: Mon-Sat 9.30-17.30, till 18.30 Wed-Fri.
Has takeaway food including vegan. Close to Arches hotel.

HOLLAND & BARRETT
Broadmead, opposite the Police Station.

YHA ADVENTURE SHOP
10-12 Fairfax St. Tel: 0272-297141.
Backpacker heaven.

WILD OATS
Lower Redland Rd, Clifton.
Lots of macrobiotic goodies and takeaways in this big wholefood store.

MISCELLANEOUS

VEGAN SOCIETY CONTACT:
C. Pearce, 6 Fern St, St Agnes, Bristol, BS2 9LN.

CAMBRIDGE

INTRODUCTION

Cambridge, along with Oxford, is one of the two most famous university cities in the UK. Though quieter and smaller than Oxford, Cambridge accommodates 13,000 students, hosts a major arts festival and an outdoor folk music festival in July each year.

Cambridge is a good bet for a weekend visit, or as a base for exploring the rolling and wooded Suffolk countryside to the south, or the flat Fenland to the north and east. It is also a good city for cyclists with lots of cycle lanes and flat countryside nearby. The river Cam flows around the west of the city and there are various places for you to explore it between Easter and October in a 'punt' - a flat bottomed boat that you propel with a long pole.

TOURIST INFORMATION OFFICE

Wheeler Street, Cambridge, CB2 3QB. Tel: 0223-322640. Fax: 0223-463385. Open: Mon-Fri 09.00-17.30, Sat 09.00-17.00.

Tours of the City leave from the office Mon-Fri at 14.00, Sat mornings also.

GETTING THERE

COACH

National Express coaches leave Victoria from 09.30 then half past every hour until 17.50, then one at 19.30, last one at 21.30, 23.30 on Sundays. £9.25 return if you avoid Fridays, £11.00 otherwise. Journey time two hours.

TRAIN

Trains leave both Liverpool Street and King's Cross seven days per week. A Network Awaybreak ticket is valid for five days and can be used any day after 09.30 and costs £16.80 return. First trains leave at 06.30 and then half hourly. Journey time is 90 mins.

CYCLE

Yes it is possible to cycle the 60 miles to Cambridge in a day if you're fit. The best way to do it is by joining thousands of other in the London-Cambridge Bike Ride on 18 July every year.

ACCOMMODATION

YOUTH HOSTEL

97 Tenison Road, Cambridge, CB1 2DN. Tel: 0223-354601.
£12.00 per night. Evening meal £3.90. Vegetarian food available, vegan food with prior warning.

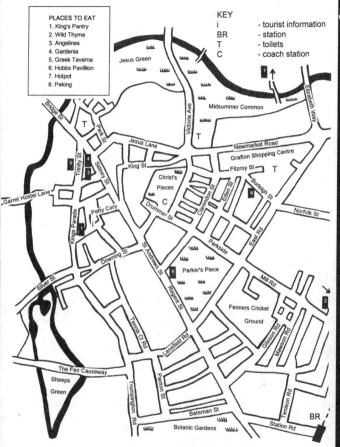

PLACES TO EAT
1. King's Pantry
2. Wild Thyme
3. Angelines
4. Gardenia
5. Greek Taverna
6. Hobbs Pavillion
7. Hotpot
8. Peking

KEY
i - tourist information
BR - station
T - toilets
C - coach station

CAMBRIDGE

CAMPSITES

CAMPING & CARAVAN CLUB

19 Cabbage Moor, Cambridge Road, Great Shelford. Tel: 0223-841185.
Four miles south of Cambridge. Open: 29 Mar-1 Nov. Pitch fee is £3.00
per night. Adults, £2.95 low season, £3.30 high season. Showers,
washing and drying facilities. Dogs on leads. Disabled people welcome

HIGHFIELD FARM CAMPING

Long Road, Comberton, Cambridge. Tel: 0223-262308.
Four miles south-west of Cambridge. Open: 26 Mar - 31 Oct. Two
person tent £6.00 low season, £7.00 high season. Showers, washing and
drying facilities, children's play area, shop, daily newspapers, dogs on
leads, calor gas, telephone.

TOAD ACRE CARAVAN PARK

Mills Lane, Longstanton, Cambridge. Tel: 0954-780939, 0353-720661.
Five miles northwest of Cambridge. Open: all year round. Tents £4.00-
£4.50 per night. Showers, calor gas, washing and drying facilities,
showers, dogs 25p.

GUESTHOUSES

CHRISTINA'S

*47 St Andrew's Road, Cambridge, CB4 1DL. Tel: 0223-65855, 0223-
327700.*
£15.00 -£22.00 single, £32.00-£40.00 double. TV in room, tea and coffee
in bedrooms.

GRANTCHESTER GUESTHOUSE

Grape House Coton Road, Granchester, CB3 9NH. Tel: 0223-840205.
One double, one twin room at £15.00 per person in this non-smoking
B&B. No evening meal, very informal household one mile from
Cambridge in a small village with three pubs.

VEGETARIAN RESTAURANTS

KING'S PANTRY

9a King's Parade, Cambridge. Tel: 0223-321551
Open: Daily 08.00-17.30 & Tue-Sat 18.30-21.30
Opposite the main gates of King's College. Cambridge's only entirely
vegetarian restaurant that caters for vegans, gluten free and food
intolerance diets. Excellent exotic food prepared freshly on the
premises. Approximately 50% vegan. Shortlisted for 'Vegetarian
Living' magazine's Restaurant of the Year award in 1992.
Starters and desserts £3.95. Main course £9.95, such as sweet potato
and yam in Tanzanian spices with a tomato and onion sauce on a bed
of coconut rice. Or Indonesian stir-fry with spinach, snow peas, herbs,

corn, pak-choi and rice. Both are vegan.
Students and senior citizens get 30% reductions on a three course lunch Mon-Fri. All cheese is rennet free. Seats 50 and booking is essential in the evenings.

WILD THYME CAFÉ

Ross Street Community Centre, Ross Street, off Mill Road, Cambridge.
Tel: 0223-563789 Open: Last Sunday evening of every month
Three course home cooked vegan meal for £4.50, usually with free entertainment. Meet others of a similar dietary inclination and enjoy some great food. Not to be missed for company and value for money.

NON-VEGETARIAN RESTAURANTS

ANGELINES

8 Market Passage, Cambridge. Tel: 0223-60305
Open: Mon-Sat 12.00-14.30 & 18.00-23.00, Sunday 12.00-14.30.
French restaurant above the Arts Cinema that caters for veggies.

GARDENIA TAKE-AWAY

2 Rose Crescent, Cambridge. Tel: 0223-356354
Open: Mon-Sun 12.00-15.00 & 16.00-24.00.

GREEK TAVERNA

114A Trinity Street (under Laura Ashley), Cambridge.
Tel: 0223-302040. Open: Mon-Fri 12.00-14.30 & 18.00-23.00, Sat 12.00-23.30, Sun 12.00-23.00
Typical Greek taverna selling stuffed vine leaves, hummus, garlic mushrooms, falafel, bean soups etc.

HOBBS PAVILLION

Old Cricket Pavillion, Parkers Piece, Cambridge. Tel: 0223-67480
Open: Tue-Sat 12.00-14.30 & 19.00-22.00, Sun 20.30-22.00
Créperie.

HOTPOT CHINESE RESTAURANT

66 Chesterton Road, Cambridge. Tel: 0223-66552. Open: Mon-Sat 12.00-14.00 & 17.30-24.00, Sun 12.00-14.00 & 15.30-23.00
Vegetarian options include: hot and sour soups; seaweed, salads, bean curd, peanut sauce with Chinese dough (wheat-gluten). Main course £4.00-£5.50.

PEKING

21 Burleigh Street, Cambridge. Tel: 0223-354755
Open: Mon-Sun 12.00-14.30 & 16.00-23.00
Vegetarian set menu for £15.00 per person. Many dishes can be adapted for vegans and are prepared on site by the owner of this friendly restaurant.

THE ROYAL OAK

Barrington Village, Cambridgshire. Tel: 0223-870791
Open: Pub hours

A public house seven miles from the city centre with a huge vegetarian wholefood international menu with vegan options. People come from miles around and you can walk most of the way from Cambridge on footpaths to build an appetite. Possibly the best veggie pub menu in the country with at least eight veggie dishes. Starters might include soup or vegetable pate. Main courses might include Barrington (nut) loaf, stir-fried vegetables, tagliatelle, all with baked potato and salad. Menu changes regularly.

SHOPS

ARJUNA

12 Mill Road, Cambridge. Tel: 0223-64845.
Open: Mon-Fri 09.30-18.00, Sat 09.00-17.30.

Wholefood shop run by a co-op. The shop has a noticeboard for all things green and healthy and a good selection of magazines. Hot counter at lunchtime which is mostly vegan. Wide variety of goods including natural remedies, cosmetics, bread, specialist foods, joss-sticks, organic vegetables etc. Half a mile to the south of the city centre.

BEAUMONT HEALTH STORES LTD

Unit 7, Shopping Hall, Grafton Centre, Cambridge. Tel: 0223-314544.

BODY SHOP

22-23 Lion Yard, Cambridge. Tel: 0223-460519.

BODY SHOP

6 Rose Crescent, Cambridge. Tel: 0223-358799.

CAMBRIDGE HEALTH FOODS

5 Bridge Street, Cambridge. Tel: 0223-350433.

DAILY BREAD WHOLEFOOD CO-OP

Unit 3 Kilmaine Close, Kings Hedges, Cambridge CB4 2PH. Tel: 0223-423177. Open:Tue-Fri 09.00-17.30, Sat 09.00-16.00.

Big wholefood warehouse. Basic and dried foods can be bought in bulk. 2.5 miles to the north-east of the city centre. Has coffee bar with cakes and Trade-Craft shop selling recycled goods.

GEOFF'S BIKE HIRE

65 Devonshire Road, Cambridge. Tel: 0223-65629. Open: Daily 09.00-17.30.

Three speed cycles only £8.00 for the weekend, £12 for a week. Hybrids £12.00 for the weekend, mountain bikes £18.00. £25.00 deposit.

HOLLAND & BARRETT

6 Bradwells Court, Cambridge. Tel: 0223-68914.

MISCELLANEOUS

CAMBRIDGE UNIVERSITY VEGETARIAN GROUP

Victoria Carey. Tel: 0223-351721, messages only.

OXFORD

INTRODUCTION

City of the 'dreaming spires', Oxford has 41 colleges and student halls with peaceful gardens, bookshops and pubs. 115,000 people live in Oxford, 14,400 of them are students at university. In the summer months thousands more aspiring pedagogues flock to the town's independent colleges and language schools. The city is an eclectic mix of historic old England, working class communities and student life. Oxford is a perfect retreat from London whatever activity you have in mind. You'll see more cycles in Oxford than in any other UK city and there is much here for the veggie visitor.

A 20 minute walk, or a short bus ride, from the grandeur of the city centre is the Cowley Road. This is alternative Oxford and a lively part of town if you're on a small budget. During the day a shopping district for second-hand clothes, multifarious fruit and veg and all manner of knick-knacks and gimmicks. After dark the energy focuses on the lively pubs, bars, cafes and restaurants that line the main road.

GETTING THERE

COACH

By National Express or Oxford Bus Company City Link (0865-711312) from Victoria Coach Station to Gloucester Green Coach station, approximately every 20 minutes. Or by Thames Transit Oxford Tube (0865-778849/727000) from Grosvenor Gardens. This is opposite and to the west of the main entrance to Victoria railway station.

Journey time is approximately 100 minutes. 24 hour return fare is £5.50, period return £7.50 with all operators.

TRAIN

From Paddington station 071-387 7070. Recorded timetables 0865-794422, General Information 0865-722333. A Network Awaybreak ticket is valid for five days, can be used any day after 09.30 and costs £16.40 return. Journey time is 70 mins approximately.

CAR

Don't take a car into Oxford's congested city centre if you can avoid it. If you're visiting for the day leave it at one of the park and ride sites at: Pear Tree on the A34, Seacourt on the A420, Redbridge on the A4144, or Thornhill on the A40.

TOURIST INFORMATION CENTRE

St Aldgate's, Oxford. Tel: 0865-726871, recorded: 0865-252664. Open: Mon-Sat 09.00-17.00, Sun and holidays 10.00-15.30.

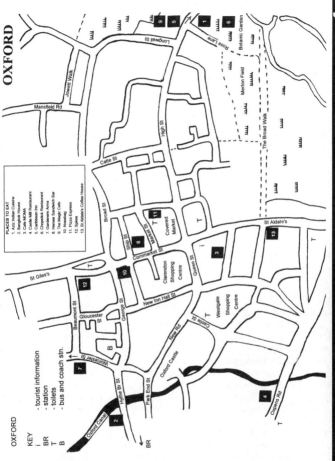

OXFORD

OXFORD

KEY

i   - tourist information

BR - station

T   - toilets

B   - bus and coach stn.

PLACES TO EAT
1. Aziz Indian Cuisine
2. Bangkok House
3. Cafe MOMA
4. Castle Mill Restaurant
5. Caribbean Inn
6. Chippy's Restaurant
7. Gardeners Arms
8. Heroes Sandwich Bar
9. The Magic Cafe
10. Nosebag
11. Pizza Express
12. Spire
13. St Aldate's Coffee House

Jowett Walk

Mansfield Rd

Longwall St

Botanic Garden

Rose Lane

Merton Field

The Broad Walk

High St

St Giles's

Catte St

Broad St

Ship St

Market St

Commarket St

Clarendon Shopping Centre

Covered Market

St Aldate's

Queen St

Westgate Shopping Centre

New Inn Hall St

Beaumont St

George St

Gloucester St

Castle St

New Rd

Oxpens Rd

Worcester St

Hythe Br St

Park End St

Oxford Castle

Oxford Canal

BR

City tours leave from the TIC throughout the day, or you could try a circular tour on an open-topped double-decker bus.

ACCOMMODATION

YOUTH HOSTEL
Jack Straw's Lane, Headington, Oxford OX3 0DW. Tel: 0865-62997.
Open: Daily from 13.00. Closed 19 Dec to 31 Jan. 116 beds. Adults £8.70 per night, slightly more in summer. Always a vegetarian option at the evening meal, vegans can also be catered for but notice in advance appreciated. Small shop.

CAMPSITES

OXFORD CAMPING INTERNATIONAL
42 Abington Road, Oxford, OX1 4XN. Tel: 0865-246551.
Open all year round, 1.5 miles from city centre, 129 caravans or tents, showers and shop. £5.00 for a two person tent, £1.60 extra per vehicle.

CASSINGTON MILL CARAVAN PARK
Eynsham Road, Cassington, Whitney, OX8 1DB. Tel: 0865-881081.
Open: 1 Apr-31 Oct 83 caravans or tents. Located on the banks of the River Evenlode. Disabled toilets, children's playground, swimming in the river, showers and shop. £6.00 per unit.

DIAMOND FARM CAMPING & CARAVAN PARK
Heathfield, Islip Road, Bletchington, OX5 3DR Tel: 0869-350909.
Open: 1 Apr-30 Sep. 37 caravans or tents, swimming pool, children's playground, bar, games room, toilets, showers and shop.

GUESTHOUSES

ALL SEASONS GUEST HOUSE
63 Windmill Road, Headington, Oxford, OX3 7BP. Tel: 0865-742215.
Not open Xmas, accommodates 11, no smoking. £20 single, £35 en-suite, doubles £45 en-suite, £35 twins. Not too familiar with veganism.

ASCOT GUEST HOUSE
283 Iffley Road, Oxford, OX4 4AQ. Tel: 0865-240259.
Open all year, accommodates 14, bed & breakfast, free range eggs, organic ingredients, colour TV in each room, children welcome, near city centre. £20 singles, £30 doubles. Vegans may need to bring own milk and margarine.

COMBERMERE GUEST HOUSE
11 Polstead Road, Oxford, OX2 6TW. Tel: 0865-56971.
Open all year round, accommodates 14, bed & breakfast, no-smoking areas, north Oxford, good bus service, all rooms have TV and coffee making, ensuite bathrooms and central heating. £22 singles, £40 doubles. Do veggie breakfast and a vegan option with prior warning.

COTSWOLD GUEST HOUSE

363 Banbury Road, Oxford OX2 7PL. Tel: 0865-310558.

Closed Xmas, accommodates 12, bed & breakfast, no-smoking areas, non-animal rennet cheese, vegan dishes. Owner is a member of Oxford Vegetarians. Singles £33, doubles and twins £48. High standard of accommodation with Automobile Association rating, two miles from city centre with buses every 10 minutes.

RESTAURANTS

AZIZ INDIAN CUISINE

228-230 Cowley Road, Oxford, OX4 1UH. Tel: 0865-794945, 798033
Open: Mon-Sat 12.00-14.15 & 18.00-23.15, Sun 12.00-17.30 & 18.00-23.15

Indian, vegetarian menu, table & take-away, disabled access, vegan dishes, seats 100. Subtle decor and spacious seating so good for large groups.

BANGKOK HOUSE

42a Hythe Bridge Street, Oxford. Tel: 0865-200705
Open: daily 05.30-23.00, Sat 05.30-23.30

Superb decor and a wide variety of enticing vegan and vegetarian dishes in this inexpensive Thai restaurant which is close to the train and bus station. Seats 60.

CAFE MOMA (Museum of Modern Art)

30 Pembroke Street, Oxford OX1 1BP. Tel: 0865-722733
Open:Tue-Wed & Fri-Sat 10.00-17.00, Th 10.00-21.00, Sun 14.00-17.00.

International, counter service, licensed, disabled access, vegan meals, seats 90. Vegetarian Society monthly meeting place. Relaxed atmosphere and live music sometimes.

CASTLE MILL RESTAURANT

Oxford College of Further Education, Holybush Oxpens, Oxford OX1 1SA. Tel: 0865-269203
Open: Mon-Fri 12.00-13.30 & Wed-Fri 18.30-19.30

Only open in term time and staffed by catering course students which means you get white table cloths, sparkling cutlery and 'the works' in terms of service. You must book in advance. The menu, which is international but predominantly French, changes every three weeks. Vegan choices are on offer everyday but they prefer to know in advance. Riverside setting, housed in the A block training establishment for catering and hotel management students. Cheap prices as it only has to cover its costs. No direct phone line.

CARIBBEAN INN

179 Cowley Road, Oxford, OX4 1UT. Tel: 0865-201575
Open: Daily Mon-Sun 18.00-23.00

Caribbean cuisine with vegetarian and vegan choices such as okra casserole and stir-fried vegetables.

CHOPSTICK RESTAURANT

244 Cowley Road, Oxford. Tel: 0865-725688
Open: Mon-Sat 12.00-13.45 & Mon-Thu 18.00-23.30, Fri-Sat 18.00-24.00, Sun 18.00-23.30.

Very simple, Sechuan, Peking and Cantonese restaurant with a good choice of food that is very affordable.

THE GARDENERS ARMS

39 Plantation Road, Oxford. Tel: 0865-59814. Open: Daily 11.00-14.40 & 18.00-23.00 (meals 12.15-14.00 & 18.30-21.00)

English, Indian & Italian dishes. Vegan meals, small pub with garden. Seats 85. Disabled access.

HEROES SANDWICH BAR

8 Ship Street, Oxford. Tel: 0865-723459

Take-away with about 30 seats serving homemade soups and various breads with exotic fillings. Always something for vegans.

THE MAGIC CAFÉ

Asian Cultural Centre, Manzil Way, Oxford. Tel: 0865-246590
Open: Thu & Fri 12.00-15.00

Alternative cafe in lovely building in east Oxford. Vegetarian, no-smoking, disabled access, music, new art exhibition each month, seats 35. Soups are £1.40 and always vegan. Always one vegan main course. Baked organic rolls and three salads every day. Quiche with salad for £2.50. Always one vegan cake or pudding 70p-90p.

THE NOSEBAG RESTAURANT

6-8 St. Michaels Street, Oxford, OX1 2DU. Tel: 0865-721033
Open: Mon 09.30-17.30, Tue-Thu 09.30-22.00, Fri-Sat 09.30-22.30, Sun 09.30-21.00

English omnivorous. Frequently changing menu, that usually includes a vegan soup and seven salads every day. 16th century building with oak beamed ceiling. Always good value but gets very popular so you sometimes have to queue. Seats 50.

PIZZA EXPRESS

The Golden Cross, Cornmarket Street, Oxford, OX1 3EX.
Tel: 0865-790442. Open: daily 11.00-24.00

50% of menu is vegetarian, non-animal rennet cheese but you must ask for it when ordering. Grade l listed building with Kettners Champagne bar on ground floor.

SPIRES RESTAURANT

Randolph Hotel, Beaumont Street, Oxford, OX1 2LN. Tel: 0865-247481
Open: Daily 12.30-14.15 & 19.00-21.45

English/international wholefood cuisine with exotic vegetarian menu. Dishes include ravioli and asparagus, sun-dried tomatoes, aubergines and vegetable saladette, forest mushrooms and baby vegetable stew in puff pastry. Vegan options usually available. Disabled access.

ST ALDATE'S COFFEE HOUSE

94 St Aldate's, Oxford. Tel: 0865-245952
Open: Mon-Sat 10.00-17.00
English, disabled access, little for vegans. Veggie food but lots of eggs used. Coffee house morning and afternoon.

SHOPS

THE BODY SHOP

125 High Street, Oxford. Tel: 0865-242265.

HOLLAND & BARRATT

3 King Edward Street, Oxford. Tel: 0865-243407.

NEAL'S YARD WHOLEFOODS

6 Golden Cross, Cornmarket Street, Oxford. Tel: 0865-792102.
Goods selection of breads and some organic vegetables but small takeaway section with limited choice for vegans. Sandwiched between a champagne bar and herbalist.

UHURU WHOLEFOODS

48 Cowley Road, Oxford, OX4 1H. Tel: 0865-248249.
Open Mon-Sat 09.30-17.30.
All women's co-op selling wholefoods, cruelty free cosmetics, remedies, eco-friendly products, with commitment to veganism.

MISCELLANEOUS

MAGIC FEASTS

38 Cherwell Street, Oxford, OX4 1BG. Tel: 0865-246590.
Vegetarian catering service.

OXFORD GRAPE VINE GREEN PAGES

Directory of alternative Oxfordshire, £3.00, 116p pub. by Green Events, Medley House, Western-on-the-Green, OX6 8TN. Tel: 0869 89603.
Classes, conservation, health, community, council, spiritual, animal rights, recycling, exercise, friendship, dance and much more. Available from newsagents and bookshops.

OXFORD VEGETARIANS

c/o 57 Sharland Close, Grove, Wantage, Oxford, OX12 0AF.
Produces a quarterly newsletter and the excellent 'Oxford Vegetarian Guide' (75p). They organise monthly socials at Cafe MOMA, information stalls, talks and video presentations, vegetarian product demonstrations and meals. 10% discount at some places listed in their guide.

STRATFORD-UPON-AVON

INTRODUCTION

Stratford-upon Avon is the birthplace of Shakespeare and the original home of the Royal Shakespeare Company. Nearby local attractions include Anne Hathaway's Cottage, Warwick Castle, Blenheim Palace, Stratford-upon-Avon Butterfly Farm and The Shire Horse Centre. Shakespeare's birthday celebrations are in April, Stratford Regatta and boat race are in June and there is an entertainments festival in July.

The town is also known for its touristy shopping centre, Friday street market, boating on the river and pleasant canal tow-path walks.

GETTING THERE

TRAIN

Inter-City trains depart from London Euston to Coventry with a Shakespeare connection coach link to Stratford up to five times per day. Journey is approximately two hours and ten minutes. First train leaves Euston at approximately 09.00 Mon-Sat, 09.40 Sun. £25.00 adult return, £22.00 single, children half price. Or take a British Rail Network SouthEast train from Paddington to Stratford.

COACH

National Express buses depart from Victoria coach station daily at 09.30, 14.30, 18.00. The journey time is three hours ten minutes. The first two go via Heathrow Airport and the last one goes via Golders Green bus station, NW11. Return journey fares are £15.50 if you travel on a Friday, £13.00 any other day.

TOURIST INFORMATION CENTRE

Bridgefoot, Stratford-upon Avon. Tel: 0789-293127. Open: Apr-Oct weekdays 09.00-18.00, Sun 11.00-17.00. Winter: weekdays 09.00-17.00.

ACCOMMODATION

YOUTH HOSTEL

Hemmingford House, Alveston, Stratford-upon-Avon, CV37 9RG. Tel: 0789-297093.
Take the number 18 bus from Bridge Street. Bed and breakfast from £8.40-£11.50 in rooms of 2-14 beds. TV lounge and games room, laundry facilities, cafeteria, extensive grounds for games and relaxation. Cafe open: 17.00-19.45. Vegetarian option served every night and they can cater for vegans if you let them know when you book.

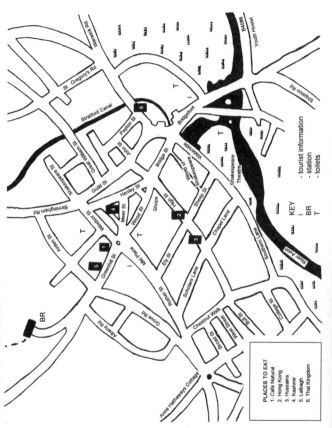

Warwick Rd

St Gregory's Rd

Stratford Canal

Payton St

John St

Bridgefoot

B4086

Youth Hostel

Snitterton Rd

Great William St

Bridge St

Shakespeare St

Guild St

Henley St

Birmingham Rd

Windsor St

Meer St

Wood St

Shops

High St

Sheep St

Shakespeare Theatre

Arden St

Greenhill St

Mill Place

Ely St

Scholars Lane

Chapel Lane

Southern Lane

River Avon

Rother St

Grove Rd

Albany Rd

Chestnut Walk

West Street

Broad St

Bull St

College St

BR

Anne Hathaways Cottage

6

4

1

5

2

3

KEY
i - tourist information
BR - station
T - toilets

PLACES TO EAT
1. Cafe Natural
2. Hong Kong
3. Hussains
4. Kashmir
5. Lalbagh
6. Thai Kingdom

STRATFORD

CAMPSITES

DODWELL PARK

Evesham Road, Stratford-upon Avon, CV37 9ST. Tel: 0789-204957.
Open: all year round.
Two miles from town. £7 per tent with two people. Food shop on site.

STRATFORD RACECOURSE

Luddington Road, Stratford-upon-Avon, CV37 7SU. Tel: 0789-267949.
Open: Easter to September to tents and caravans.

THE ELMS CAMP

Tiddington, Stratford-upon-Avon, CV37 7AB. Tel: 0789-292312.
One mile from the town ,with food shop.

GUEST HOUSES

PARKFIELD GUEST HOUSE

3 Broad Walk, Stratford-upon-Avon, CV37 6HS.
Tel: 0789-293313.
Victorian guest house within walking distance of the town centre with
space for 13 people. Vegetarian breakfasts available or vegan pancake
with fruit. £17.00 single, £16.00 double per person, £19.00 double per
person en-suite.

WINTON HOUSE

The Green, Upper Quinton, Stratford-upon-Avon, CV37 8SX.
Tel: 0789-720500.
Log fires. Good choice of breakfasts. Cycles available, home made jams.
£40.00 per double ensuite.

VEGETARIAN RESTAURANTS

CAFÉ NATURAL

Unit 1, Greenhill Street, Stratford-upon-Avon. Tel: 0789-415741
Open: Mon-Sat: 09.00-16.30
Vegetarian wholefood café and takeaway behind the healthfood shop
which has a street frontage. No smoking. Great menu includes spicy
lentil soup, mushroom lasagne, mushroom moussaka, vegetable
strudel. Vegan options always available. Great value at £5.95 for a
three course lunch. £1 corkage.

NON-VEGETARIAN RESTAURANTS

HONG KONG

36 High Street, Stratford-upon-Avon. Tel: 0789-297083
Open: daily 17.00-24.00
Chinese cuisine with veggie dishes that include vegetable hotpot,
noodles and soup.

HUSSAINS

6a Chapel Street, Stratford-upon-Avon. Tel: 0789-267506
Open: daily 17.00-24 & Sat-Sun 12.00-14.00
Large selection of north and south Indian dishes. £5.95 for a three course lunch.

KASHMIR

28 Meer Street, Stratford-upon-Avon. Tel: 0789-297348
Open: daily 17.00-24.00 & Sun 12.00-14.00
North & south Indian cuisine, with large vegetarian selection.

LALBAGH

3a Greenhill Street, Stratford-upon-Avon. Tel: 0789-293563
Open: Daily 12.00-14.00 & 17.30-24.00
Indian Tandoori cuisine £5.95 for three courses at lunchtime.

THAI KINGDOM

11 Warwick Road, Stratford-upon-Avon. Tel: 0789-261103
Open: Daily 12.00-14.00 & 18.00-22.45
Set menu and a la carte. £15.95 per person for set Thai meal with five dish main course. No-smoking section. They can cater for vegans.

SHOPS

THE BODY SHOP

High Street, Stratford-upon-Avon. Tel: 0789-414423.

CAMILLA HEPPER

The Minories, Stratford-upon-Avon.
Herbal cosmetic specialist.

Was Shakespeare a vegan?

'And as the butcher takes away the calf
And binds the wretch and beats it when it strays,
Bearing it to the bloody slaughter-house,
Even so remorseless have they borne him hence;
And as the dam runs lowing up and down,
Looking the way her harmless young one went,
And can do nought but wail her darling's loss '

Henry VI Pt 2 Act 3 Scene 1.

WINDSOR

INTRODUCTION

Windsor is not all turrets, battlements, moats and royal regalia, though because the castle covers 13 acres and the place is flooded with tourists from Spring onwards it can sometimes seem that way.

Windsor Castle — the weekend home of the Queen is the major attraction for visitors. When she is at home the scarlet and yellow Royal Standard rather than the Union Jack flies from the roundhouse. The Great Park behind the castle offers a welcome relief from the crowds in the town.

The question of who should pay for repairs to the Castle following a fire in 1993 became a tinder box for the monarchy recently, coinciding as it did with one of the worst recessions this country has ever experienced. The debate broadened into one about whether or not the royals provided good value for money and was diplomatically guillotined when the head of state offered to pay income tax to the Inland Revenue like the rest of us.

The town of Windsor is surrounded by some of the most picturesque countryside in the south east of England. It is populated by some of the richest people in the country but can be a welcome day out of the city. Nearby are: Eton, home of the most famous public school in the world; Runnymede where King John signed the Magna Carta in 1215; Maidenhead, hang out and home to numerous media types; and other twee little villages like Cookham, Bisham and Datchet.

The safari park is now closed and is being converted into a Legoland theme park with 50,000 tons of Lego.

GETTING THERE

TRAIN

Take a direct British Rail train to Windsor and Eton Riverside from Waterloo, or go from Paddington and change at Slough for Windsor Central. The fare is £4.90 single (no returns) and there are approximately two trains per hour.

COACH

Take a Green Line coach 701 from Victoria. Mon-Sat the service runs at 30 minutes past each hour from 09.30 to 19.30, Sunday service departs at 09.00, 10.30, 12.30, 13.30, 15.00, 16.30, 18.00, 19.40. Adult return costs £4.35. Journey time 80 minutes.

KEY
i — tourist information
BR — station
T — toilets

PLACES TO EAT
1. The Frying Pan
2. Jasmine Peking
3. Havana Cafe
4. The Clay Oven
5. Chef Peking

Eton

BR

Datchett Rd

Broad Water

River Thames

Barry Avenue

Windsor Castle

Thames St

Arthur Rd

T

BR

i

Alma Rd

Vansittart Rd

Shopping Centre

T

Peascod St

High St

Clarence Rd

Victoria St

T

The Home Park

St Leonard's Rd

Alexander Rd

Frances Rd

Sheet St

Goslar Way

Osborne Rd

King's Rd

St Leonard's Rd

WINDSOR

TOURIST INFORMATION CENTRE

Windsor and Eton Central Station, Thames Street, Windsor.
Tel: 0753-852010
Has a Bureau de Change attached.

ACCOMMODATION

YOUTH HOSTEL

Edgeworth House, Mill Lane, Windsor, Berkshire SL4 5JE. Tel: 0753-861710. Adults £8.70 per night, under 18's £5.80.
Attractive old building in Clewer, one mile from Windsor on the River Thames, sign posted from the A308. Thames towpath and swimming pool nearby. Evening meal 19.00. Always cater for vegetarians and will do so for vegans if they know you're coming. Licensed.

CAMPSITES

HURLEY CARAVAN & CAMPING PARK

Estate Office, Hurley Farm, Hurley, Berks. Tel: 0628-823501, 0628-823502/3 in emergency.
On the south bank of the Thames one mile west of Hurley village. 300 pitches for tents. £6.00-£9.00 per night.

HURLEY LOCK CAMPING ISLAND

NRA, Hurley Lock, Mill Lane, Hurley, Near Maidenhead, Berks SL6 5ND. Tel: 0628-824334.
On a secluded island in the Thames near Hurley Lock, north off the A423. 10 pitches for small tents. Open April-Sep. £3.50 per night per tent.

BED AND BREAKFAST

THE ARCHES

9 York Road, Windsor, Berks SL4 3NX. Tel: 0753-869268.
Large house in town centre, near shops, river, park and castle. No smoking. Tea and coffee making. £13.50-£16.50 single, £28.00 double/twin. Offer four breakfasts and very helpful.

THE OLD PARSONAGE

Parsonage Road, Englefield Green, Surrey TW20 0JW.
Tel: 0784-436706.
Georgian parsonage in village near Windsor Great Park. Licensed, tea & coffee making, en-suite facilities. £25 singles, £50 doubles. Can cater for vegetarians and vegans at breakfast and also in the evening by arrangement.

THICKETS MEADOW NORTH

Newlands Drive, Maidenhead, Berks SL6 4LL. Tel: 0628-29744.
Vegan/vegetarian guest house with tennis court. Coaching available.

TRINITY GUEST HOUSE

18 Trinity Place, Windsor, Berks SL4 3AT. Tel: 0753-831283.
Close to river, castle, shops and other amenities. En-suite facilities, tea and coffee making, credit cards accepted. £20-£25 single. £36-£40 double.

RESTAURANTS

THE FRYING PAN COFFEE BAR & RESTAURANT

King Edward Court, Windsor. Tel: 0753-830783
Open: Mon-Wed 09.00-18.00, Thu-Sat 09.00-24.00
Omnivorous licensed restaurant that serves high quality, delicious, natural health foods with vegan and vegetarian options. Self-service buffet, £4.75 including drink, Mon-Fri 12.00-14.30. Entertainment Thu-Sat evenings.

JASMINE PEKING

35 Thames Street, Windsor, Berks. Tel: 0753-861500
Open: daily 12.00-14.15, 18.00-23.00
Peking-Cantonese licensed restaurant. Approx £16 for an evening meal. Good vegetarian menu with selection of beancurd, noodle and vegetable dishes.

HAVANA CAFÉ

3 Goswell Hill (Arches), Windsor, Berks. Tel: 0753-832960
Open: Mon-Fri 18.00-23.00, Sat-Sun 12.00-23.00.
U.S./Cajun/Creole restaurant. £12 evening meal. The board with nine menu options changes daily and there is Mexican food on offer too. Always six salads and a vegan-burger and they will cook specially for vegans if not too busy on the day. Lively place with 70-80 seats and music at night.

THE CLAY OVEN RESTAURANT

5 Glynwood House, Bridge Avenue, Maidenhead, Berks SL6 1RR.
Tel: 0628-36724, 0628-73951 Open: 12.00-14.30 & 18.00-12.00
Indian Tandoori licensed restaurant with take-away service. Vegetable Thali £8.95.

CHEF PEKING ON THAMES

Raymead Road, Maidenhead, Berks SL6 8NJ. Tel: 0628-783005.
Open: Daily 12.00-14.30 & 18.30-22.30
Pekingese licensed restaurant with set evening meal for £16 per head for three courses. Will do special dishes for vegans if they know in advance.

BEYOND LONDON

There are an increasing number of essential guidebooks on the market for the cruelty-free traveller or local resident, offering advice and information on how to make the most out of your stay in a town or city, and pointing you in the right direction to meet new friends with similar principles.

We highly recommend the guides below to anyone visiting a new town or city for the first time. Please enclose an A5 stamped addressed envelope when ordering the British guides unless stated otherwise. Overseas send international reply coupon for ordering details.

BRITISH GUIDES

Vegetarian Directory 1993 - The Lake District and Cumbria.
Mail order 57p plus large stamped addressed envelope. Kendal Vegetarians, Low House, New Hutton, Kendal, Cumbria LA8 0AZ. Tel: 0539-725219.

Colchester Vegetarian Guide 1992/3.
75p to Colchester Vegetarian Society, c/o 21 Laburnum Way, Nayland, Colchester, Essex, CO6 4LG. Limited number of copies remaining.

Cruelty-Free Guide to London 1994 by Alex Bourke and Paul Gaynor.
£4.95 + 65p postage or airmail US$12.00 to Cruelty-Free Living, 18 Jarvis House, Goldsmith Rd, London, SE15 5SY.

Vegetarian Guide to Nottingham.
Published by Veggies Ltd., 180-182 Mansfield Road, Nottingham NG1 3HW. Tel: 0602-585666. £1.40.

Oxford Vegetarian Guide 1993/4.
75p to Oxford Vegetarians, c/o 57 Sharland Close, Grove, Wantage OX12 0AF. Tel: 0235-769425, 0865-61614.

The Vegan Guide to Eating and Drinking in Sheffield.
Published by Sheffied Vegan Society, 130 Pomona Street, Sheffield S11.

INTERNATIONAL GUIDES

Vegan Guide to Amsterdam
by Henk de Jong and Rochelle del Gunter, with big colour map worth Dfl 3.00. Send £3.00, US$7.00 or Dfl 8.00 to Henk de Jong, Rode Kruislaan 1430, 1111 XD Diemen, The Netherlands.

Vegan Guide to Berlin
by Max Friedman. £2.50 plus 78p postage to Dan Mills, 7 Wicket Grove, The Village, Lenton, Nottingham, NG7 2FS, England. USA send $4.75, world send US$7.00, to Max Friedman, 2441 Woolsey Street, Berkeley,

CA 94705, USA.

The Vegetarian Guide to Ireland.

£2.65 or US$8.00 to East Clare Community Co-op, Main Street, Scariff, Co. Clare, Republic of Ireland.

Vegan Guide to New York.

£2.50 plus 78p postage to Dan Mills, 7 Wicket Grove, The Village, Lenton, Nottingham, NG7 2FS, England. USA send $4.75 to Max Friedman (above), world US$7.00.

Vegan Guide To Paris.

£2.50, FF30 or US$6.00 to Alex Bourke, 45 Chandos Road, Bristol, BS6 6PQ, UK.

Also sells The Hippy Cookbook, £1.99, a hilarious introduction to wholefood cooking. How to Write a Vegan Book, £1.80, tells how to write and self-publish your book without spending any money.

Vegetarian Guide to the Scottish Highlands and Islands.

£2.65 or US$8.00 from Janey Clarke, 3 Hermitage Street, Evanton, Ross-shire, IV16 9YG.

European Vegetarian Guide, published by Hans-Nietsch-Verlag.

ISBN 3-929475-00-6.

Huge guide in English, German and the local language. Distributed in England by Central Books and the Vegetarian Society.

COMING SOON

More guides are in preparation. Watch the vegetarian and vegan press for details.The guides will all be announced in the newsletter of Vegans International. You can subscribe and keep up to date with all that's happening in the vegan world, including dates of vegan festivals, for only £7 or US$10 per year. See under **Action**, where you'll also find details of the great magazine Holiday Vegetarian, which is packed with ideas and addresses for vegetarian and vegan holidays.

If you would like to produce a guide for your town, or have ideas for other books, contact Cruelty-Free Living or Vegans International for an information pack.

ACTION

INTRODUCTION

Do you want to learn more about cruelty-free living, and perhaps get involved in campaigning? Or maybe you'd like to meet more vegetarians. Then the many animal rights, vegetarian, and vegan books and magazines will give you plenty of food for thought, and by joining the national and local groups listed here you can help create a cruelty-free world while making new friends who share your respect for all forms of life. Addresses for some of the magazines are given under National Organizations to save space. Get active, have fun, and change the world! Send a stamped addressed envelope (sae) for more details, or international reply coupon from abroad.

RECOMMENDED BOOKS

Prices in brackets are for postage if ordered from the Vegan Society, 7 Battle Road, St. Leonards-on-Sea, East Sussex, TN37 7AA.

The Animal-Free Shopper, Richard Farhall, Kathy McCormack & Amanda Rofe, Vegan Society, £4.95. (65p)

Lists everything you can buy that's free of animal ingredients and testing.

Animal Liberation, Peter Singer, Thorsons, £8.99. (£1.35)

Beyond Beef, Jeremy Rifkin, Thorsons, £8.99. Published 13 June 1994.

Fruits of Paradise: A Vegetarian Yearbook, Rebecca Hall, Simon & Schuster, £7.99. (£1.15)

Living Without Cruelty, Mark Gold, Green Print, £5.50.

The New Why You Don't Need Meat, Peter Cox, Bloomsbury, £4.99.

Pregnancy, Children & the Vegan Diet, Michael Klaper M.D., Gentle World (US) £6.25. (95p)

Save The Animals, Ingrid Newkirk, Angus & Robertson £4.95.

The Teenage Vegetarian Survival Guide, Anouchka Grose, £3.50.

Vegan Nutrition: A Survey of Research, Gill Langley PhD, Vegan Society, £5.95. (80p)

Vegan Nutrition: Pure & Simple, Michael Klaper M.D., GentleWorld (US), £6.25. (95p)

Why Vegan?, Kath Clements, GMP, £3.95. (65p)

For free catalogues of vegan and vegetarian books, including lots of cook books, send a stamped addressed envelope to The Vegan Society or the Vegetarian Society, addresses below.

Remember to say you saw it in the Cruelty-Free Guide

ANIMAL RIGHTS MAGAZINES

AgScene
Magazine of Compassion in World Farming (CIWF).

ALF Supporters Group.
The quarterly newsletter provides information about the arrest and imprisonment of alleged animal rights activists. Also includes articles and letters from prisoners.

Animal Times
PO Box 7, Romford, Essex, RM6 5DE.
Colour magazine of People for the Ethical Treatment of Animals (PETA), the biggest animal rights (AR) organization in the world. Excellent coverage of high profile protests throughout Europe and America. Subscribers receive a directory of European AR groups. £6.50 per year or sae for details.

Arkangel Magazine
BCM 9240, London WC1N 3XX.
Available through subscription £7.20 (4 issues) or £1.80 (sample). The animal liberation magazine with a wholly positive approach. Contains a directory of local and national animal rights groups, sabbing news, lists of sanctuaries, news from the ALF Press Office, latest successes and an open forum for debate.

CAW Bulletin
£5.00 per year from Coordinating Animal Welfare, PO Box 589, Bristol, BS99 1RW. 0272-776261.
Local and international news of animal rights protests. Full of ideas for organisers.

The Ethical Investor
Quarterly. £10 a year from EIRIS, 504 Bonway Business Centre, 71 Bondway, London, SW8 1SQ.

Ethical Consumer
Bi-monthly. Free catalogue from ECRA Publishing Ltd (CFGL), FREEPOST (MR9429), Manchester M1 8DR.

European Medical Journal
£10 for 4 issues from EMJ, Lynmouth, Devon, EX35 6EE.
Anti vivisection, medicine and research. Edited by Dr Vernon Coleman.

Fox Cubs
Magazine for under 17's about wildlife, hunting and animal cruelty.

Howl
Magazine of the Hunt Saboteurs Association.

Outrage
Bi-monthly magazine of Animal Aid.

LONDON VEGANS

We meet for a talk or video on the last Wednesday evening of the month (except December) in central London. Come and join us for a discussion, a snack, and pick up some leaflets and a free copy of the London Vegans What's On Diary. From 18.30 till 21.00 we'll be at Millman Street Community Rooms, 52 Millman Street, WC1, east of Russell Square underground. Entrance at the back of the building via a small alley. Afterwards some of us go on to the local pub.

We organise many social events such as restaurant and pub evenings, and also go out campaigning with information and catering stalls throughout the year. We meet many of our friends through London Vegans and so could you.

Send sae for more details, or become a member now for just £2.50 and receive regular copies of our comprehensive guide to veggie events in London for one year.

London Vegans, 7 Deansbrook Road, Edgware, Middlesex, HA8 9BE.

*Or contact Kevin Comer 071-603 4325
or Paul Halford 0206-861846.*

Pisces
Newsletter of Campaign for the Abolition of Angling.

Turning Point
Quarterly, £6.00 a year or sample copy £1.50 from PO Box 45, Northolt, Middlesex, UB5 6SZ. 081-841 0503.
Excellent value animal rights magazine with lots of photos and international stories.

VEGETARIAN MAGAZINES

Holiday Vegetarian
£5.00 for 3 issues to Holiday Vegetarian Ltd, Holly Cottage, Cherry Garden Lane, Danbury, Essex, CM3 4QY.

BBC Vegetarian Good Food
Monthly £1.65 from newsagents.

Vegetarian Living
Monthly £1.75 from newsagents.
Both BBC Vegetarian and Vegetarian Living are packed with excellent features, interviews, recipes and listings. Vegans prefer Vegetarian Living, which clearly marks totally cruelty-free recipes (no dairy, egg or honey).

VQ (Vegetarian Quarterly)
Magazine of the Vegetarian Society.

Vegetarian Times,
PO Box 446, Mount Morris, IL 61054-9894, USA.
America's top monthly veggie magazine and great value at $29.95 for 12 issues. Articles are twice as long as in British magazines, so are very comprehensive. It's easiest to pay by Visa or Mastercard.

VEGAN MAGAZINES

Ahimsa
£12.00 p.a. Quarterly magazine of American Vegan Society, 12 Old Harding Highway, Malaga, NJ 08328, USA.
Organizers of Eighth International Vegan Festival, San Diego, 6-13 August 1995.

Animal Times
Bi-monthly magazine of People for the Ethical Treatment of Animals (PETA).

New Leaves
Quarterly magazine of the Movement for Compassionate Living.

Vegan Views

6 Hayes Avenue, Bournemouth, Hampshire, BH7 7AD, 0202 391836. £3.00 p.a. or 75p for sample issue.

Great value informative magazine with articles, interviews, news, reviews and letters.

The Vegan

Quarterly magazine of the Vegan Society.

Vegans International Newsletter,

Quarterly. Links vegevangelists around the world. Reviews campaigning materials and has the latest news from overseas activists. £7 p.a. See under international organizations.

NATIONAL CAMPAIGNING ORGANISATIONS

Action to Abolish the Grand National
PO Box 3152, London, E12 5JW.

ALF Press Office
BM4400, London WC1N 3XX.
Reports animal liberation actions to the media and in Arkangel
magazine.

ALF Supporters Group
BCM Box 1160, London WC1N 3XX. £24.00 p.a. or £2.00 per month.
The SG raises funds to help pay fines and to pay towards the travelling
expenses of relatives making prison visits. Funds also pay for books,
cruelty-free toiletries and other needs of prisoners. They also produce a
range of merchandise.

In case you're wondering why we've listed the (legal) ALF SG, let's
just set the the record straight. The (illegal) ALF has a policy of not
endangering human or animal life. No person or animal has ever been
injured by an ALF action. The SG magazine (and also Arkangel
magazine) tells the other side of the story about those who risk their
liberty and sometimes lives to prevent animal abuse.

The only person in Britain ever convicted of planting an explosive
device for animal rights was Anthony Newberry-Street, a hunter, who
placed a nail-bomb under his own Land Rover to discredit hunt
protestors.

Two peaceful animal rights protestors, Mike Hill and Tom Worby,
were killed by vehicles driven by hunters Alan Summersgill of the
Cheshire Beagles and Tony Ball of the Cambridgeshire Hunt. Both
these men are still free and enjoying life, which sadly is more than can
be said for Mike and Tom. Many more protestors have been hospital-
ized by hunters and their hired thugs while the police stood by.

One day people who rescue animals from prison won't end up there
themselves, and those who abuse and kill animals or beat up peaceful
protestors will. Until then, the SG supports those imprisoned for
saving animals' lives.

Animal Aid
*The Old Chapel, Bradford Street, Tonbridge, Kent TN9 1AW. 0732-
364546.*
Campaigns brilliantly, especially to young people, against all animal
abuse and hence has a huge membership. Bi-monthly magazine
Outrage. Produces the Living Without Cruelty Diary, beautiful T-
shirts, shampoo and conditioner, and other goodies. Their video "Their
Future In Your Hands", £9.95, is ideal for showing in schools to 14+
age group and to non cruelty-free friends. National network of groups.
£7.00 p.a., £5.00 unwaged, £4.00 under 18, or sae for details.

Animal Liberation Investigation Unit (ALIU)
PO Box 38, Manchester, M60. 061-953 4039.
Helps local activists around the country to conduct legal inspections at their local animal abuse establishments to gain documentary, video and photographic footage.

BUAV (British Union for the Abolition of Vivisection)
16a Crane Grove, London N7 8LB, 071-700 4888.

Campaign for the Abolition of Angling (CAA)
PO Box 90, Bristol, BS99 1ND. 0272-441175.
Campaigns against the neglected bloodsport which also kills swans, dogs, ponies, sparrows, gulls and other wildlife with the lethal tackle anglers leave behind. Organises protests outside fishing shops, sabbing anglers, and persuades business to stop sponsoring angling matches. Sells a superb video for £6.00, or hire for £6.00 inc £5.00 returnable deposit. £4.00 per year. Provides speakers for talks and public meetings.

Campaign Against Leather & Fur (CALF)
BM 8889, London, WC1N 3XX.
CALF distributes information about the cruelties connected with the leather, fur, wool and silk industries. They also sell t-shirts, badges and stickers. Donations appreciated!

Compassion in World Farming (CIWF)
20 Lavant St, Petersfield, Hampshire, GU32 3EW. 0730-64208 and 68863. Fax: 0730-60791.
Campaigns against factory farming and all animal abuse. Excellent merchandise catalogue and videos for showing to groups.

Deaf Vegetarians Group
11 Otter St, Derby, DE1 3FD. 0332-361590.

Ethical Investors Group
16 Carisbrooke Drive, Cheltenham, GL52 6YA. 0242-522872.
Independent advice on totally cruelty-free pensions, savings and insurance. 50% of profits go to animal rights campaigners.

Fox Cubs
PO Box 370A, Surbiton, Surrey, KT6 4YN.
An animal rights group aimed at the under 17's. Through Fox Cubs you can learn all about wildlife, hunting and many other issues, and find out how you can campaign against animal cruelty.

FRESH (Fruitarian & Raw Energy Support and Help)
Harmony Cottage, Cutteridge Farm Cutteridge Lane, Whitestone, Exeter, Devon, EX4 2HE.

Hunt Saboteurs Association (HSA)
PO Box 1, Carlton, Nottingham, NG4 2JY. 0602-590357.

Contact for info about forming a hunt sab group. Provides speakers for talks, gives legal advice.

Jewish Vegetarian Society
855 Finchley Rd, London, NW11. Also Young Jewish Vegetarian Society (22-35).

League Against Cruel Sports
83-87 Union Street, London SE1 SG, 071-407 0979.

McLibel Support Campaign
c/o London Greenpeace, 5 Caledonian Rd, London, N1 9DX.
Fighting McDonald's attempt to suppress free speech for animal rights campaigners throughout 1994. Donations urgently needed. Informative leaflets for customers at your local McDonald's available in bulk from Veggies (below) at £12.00 per thousand, or send what you can and they'll send accordingly.

Movement For Compassionate Living (The Vegan Way)
47 Highlands Road, Leatherhead, Surrey KT22 8NQ, 0372-372389.
Promotes veganism, sustainable agriculture and trees. £3.00 per year.

National Anti-Hunt Petition
HARC, PO Box 66, Broxbourne, Herts, EN10 6LU. 0426-911785.
Organisers of the national march, rally and exhibiton against hunting in London on 6th August 1994. Stamped addressed envelope for details, petition form and merchandise list. Donations much appreciated.

National Anti-Vivisection Society
51 Harley Street, Marylebone, London, W1N 1DD, 071-580 4034.

National Society Against Factory Farming
91 Mercator Road, London SE13 5GH, Lucy Newman.

PETA Europe (People for the Ethical Treatment of Animals)
PO Box 3169, London, NW6 2QF. 071-372 0459. Fax: 071-372-0105
Animal protection organisation dedicated to establishing the rights of all animals. Runs high-profile and accessible campaigns aimed at influencing mainstream opinion on a wide range of animal abuses. Stock an excellent range of videos and campaigning materials.

Plan 2000
PO Box 54, Bristol, BS99 1PH.
Fighting to end vivisection. Has an excellent merchandise list for campaigners, including videos and book "How to Win Debates With Vivisectionists".

Respect for Animals
PO Box 500, Nottingham, NG1 3AS. 0602-525440. Fax 0602-799159.
National campaigns against fur.

RSPCA Animal Line

0345 888999.
Confidential phone line to pass on information about cruelty to animals.

Student Campaign for Animal Rights (SCAR)

PO Box 155, Manchester, M60 1FT. 061-953 4039.
National network of student animal rights groups.

Teachers for Animal Rights

c/o 29 Lynwood Rd, London, SW17 8SB.
Write for an information pack, but please send a donation to cover costs.

VEGA (Vegetarian Economy and Green Agriculture)

PO Box 39, Godalming, Surrey, GU8 6BT. 071-955 7125.
Research and campaigning on veganism and animal abuse.

The Vegan Society

7 Battle Road, St. Leonards-on-Sea, East Sussex, TN37 7AA. 0424 427393.
Leaflets on what's wrong with animal food and clothing, a quarterly magazine The Vegan, and a catalogue of books including The Animal Free Shopper. Many local contacts. £15.00 per year, £10 unwaged, £8.00 U-18, or sae for details.

Vegan Families Contact List

as above

Veganic Gardening

36 Granes End, Great Linford, Milton Keynes, MK14 5DX, Kenneth O'Brian.

The Vegetarian Charity

14 Winters Lane, Ottery St Mary, EX1 1AR.
Funds are available to help young vegetarians up to the age of 25 who are in need and to educate young people in the principles of vegetarianism.

The Vegetarian Society (UK),

Parkdale, Dunham, Altrincham, Cheshire WA14 4QG. 061-928 0793.
Produces lots of leaflets, a huge book catalogue, a quarterly magazine. Runs cookery classes, and organises National Vegetarian Week in October. The first point of contact if you or your child want to go vegetarian. £14.00 per year, £8.00 unwaged/student, £5.00 under 18, or sae for details.

VEGFAM

The Sanctuary, near Lydford, Oakhampton, Devon, EX20 4AL.
Overseas aid to victims of drought, flood, cyclone or war. Feeds the hungry without exploiting animals. SAE for details.

Veggies

180 Mansfield Rd, Nottingham, NG1 3HU. 0602-585666.
Send £2.00 for the huge Animal Contacts List of every animal rights
group and business in the UK. They produce an animal rights calendar
with a diary of events, and their catering services provide vegan food
at many events.

LOCAL ORGANISATIONS

If there's nothing listed near you, contact Animal Aid, The Vegan
Society, or The Vegetarian Society (above) for the address of their
nearest local contact.

Central London Animal Aid
34 St. Peters Street, London N1 8JJ, 071 359 6240, Hilary Nimmo.

Friends Vegetarian Society
*69 Oakwood Crescent, Winchmore Hill, London N21 1PA, 081-360
4295.*

Gay Vegetarians and Vegans
G.V., BM 5700, London, WC1N 3XX.

Greenwich Vegetarian Info Centre
58 Eaglesfield Rd, Shooters Hill, London, SE18 3BU. 081-317 1424.

Hackney and Islington Animal Rights Campaign
c/o Alara, 58 Seven Sisters Rd, London, N7 6AA.

Haringey Animal Rights
*15 Torrington Gardens, New Southgate, London, N11 2AB. 081-368
5654.*

Harrow Vegetarian Group
9 Valentine Rd, South Harrow, Middx, HA2 8EG. 081-423 6920.

Hertfordshire Animal Rights Campaign
PO Box 66, Broxbourne, Herts, EN10 6LU.

Hillingdon & Ealing Vegetarian Group
*20 Cassiobury Park Ave, Watford, Herts, WD1 7LB. 0923-37526 (Tony)
or 0895-273513 (Garry).*

Hounslow Animal Defence
PO Box 234, Hounslow, Middx, TW3 2QG.

Kingston Vegetarians
87 Porchester Rd, Kingston upon Thames, KT1 3PW. 081-541 3437.

London Anti-Fur Campaign
c/o E.L.A.R., PO Box 216, London E7 9RB.
Co-ordinating regular pickets against the remaining fur shops in
London's West End.

London Boots Action Group

c/o Alara, 58 Seven Sisters Rd, London, N7 6AA.
LBAG have held numerous pickets outside Boots the vivisectors shops in the London area and tens of thousands of leaflets have been handed out.

London Vegetarian Info Centre

James Milton, 19 Newlands Quay, London, E1 9QZ. 071-702 3495.

London Vegans

7 Deansbrook Road, Edgware, Middlesex, HA8 9BE. 081-952 3037.
Organizes restaurant and pub meetings, and talks on the last Wednesday evening of every month except December 18.30-21.00 at Millman Street Community Rooms, 52 Millman St, WC1 (entrance at rear). Catering and information stalls, pub and restaurant evenings. Send cheque for £2.50 to receive regular and excellent diary of events for one year, or sae for details.

London Young Vegetarians

52 Windamere Road, Muswell Hill, London, N10 2RG, 081 444 1783, George Pinnell.

South London Animal Aid

PO Box 594, London, SW9 8QG.

SLAA have produced excellent leaflets on vivisection and held demos outside the abusers' premises. The group have set up the Green Marmoset Vegetarian Catering Venture which will provide the best vegeburgers in town - amongst other tasty vegetarian/vegan food at Animal Rights and other events. For further details contact Lisa on 081-540 6628. For the past few years the group have organised the Christmas Without Cruelty Fayres which have attracted thousands of people.

Vegetarian Social Club

52 Byron Avenue, Manor Park, London E12 6NG, 081 471 6142, Ron Dwyer.

Social events, city tours, rambles, theatre and museum visits and other outings. sae for membership form.

Walthamstow Animal Rights (WAR)

PO Box 2344, London, E17 6QR.

Watford Animal Concern

24 Gade Ave, Watford, Herts, WD1 7LG. 0923-232386.

Young Indian Vegetarians

226 London Rd, West Croydon, Surrey, CR0 2TF. 081-681 8884. Fax 081-681 7143.

INTERNATIONAL ORGANISATIONS

Greenpeace, Northampton, NN3 1BR.

Campaigns against whaling, ivory poaching and for the welfare of seals and turtles.

International Vegetarian Union

10 Kings Drive, Marple, Sockport, Cheshire, SK6 6NQ. 061-427 5850.
Organizer of World Vegetarian Congress in Holland 8-13 August 1994 and Australia 1996. sae for details.

Vegans International

UK Coordinator Sheila Hyslop, Iona, 15 Loch Rd, Dumfries, DG2 9JE.
V.I. has helped set up vegan societies around the world, organised seven international vegan festivals (next one San Diego, USA, 6-13 August 1995), and united thousands of vegans to work for a kinder world. Subscription for a year (Jan to Dec) is £7.00 or US$10.00, which brings you the quarterly newsletter with reports from worldwide, the International Contact List, the Society and Group List, notices about international conferences and regional meetings, and access to the Vegans International database. Because VI is operated by volunteers, the fee is low and additional donations are greatly appreciated. sae or

international reply coupon for details.

CRUELTY-FREE LOVING

Concordia-Vegis,
PO Box 165, Chesterfield, Derbyshire, S41 0DT. 0246-558481.
Nationwide introduction agency for vegans, vegetarians and
fruitarians, run by a member of the Vegan Society. Write for details
enclosing a stamp. Half price for Vegan Society members.

Contact Centre, (MV)
BCM Cuddle, London WC1V 6XX.
Low fees introduction agency for vegans and vegetarians in Britain and
abroad. Write for details.

Cruelty Free Companions
182 Mansfield Rd, Nottingham, NG1 3HW. 0332-679341.
No fees international friendship agency run by unpaid volunteers for
anyone striving towards a cruelty-free lifestyle who wants to make
contact or develop relationships with others of a like mind. Also
organises various events. Send three stamps or international reply
coupons for latest listing.

Greenline Friendship Agency
(Ref P), PO Box 2, Totnes, Devon, TQ9 5YP. Send sae.

Vegetarian Matchmakers (VMM)
100 Nelson Road, London, N8 9RT. 081-348 5229.
Nationwide introduction agency for vegans, vegetarians and those of a
like mind. Also run weekends away, social gatherings, bi-monthly
newsletter with agony aunt/uncle column.

Veggie-Link
42 Hawthorne Crescent, Findern, Derby, DE6 6AN. 0283-703059.
Confidential inroductions and socialising for vegetarians and vegans.

NATURAL MEDICINE

To be sure of not getting ripped off by a quack, contact any of the following for a list of fully trained and registered practitioners.

British Acupuncture Association
34 Alderney Street, Pimlico, London SW1V 4EU, 071 834 1012.

British Holistic Medical Association
179 Gloucester Place, Camden Town, London NW1 6DX, 071 262 5299.

British Homeopathic Association
27a Deveonshire Street, Marleybone, London W1N 1RJ, 071 935 2163.

British Hypnotherapy Association
1 Wythburn Place, London W1H 5WL, 071 723 4443.

MISCELLANEOUS

Bethany Vegetarian Nursing Home
7/9 Oak Park Villas, Dawlish, Devon EX7 0DE. 0626-862794.

Happidog Pet Foods Ltd
Bridgend, Brownhill Lane, Longton, Preston, Lancs PR4 4SJ. 0772-614952. Fax 614408.
Vegetarian and vegan dog food recommended by 400 vets.

Katz Go Vegan
7 Battle Road, St Leonards-on-Sea, East Sussex TN37 7AA.
Vegan cat food. sae please.

Vegan Bikers Association
48 Hawkins Hall Lane, Datchworth, Knebworth, Hertfordshire, SG3 6TE.

Vegan Candles
8 Bruntingthorpe Way, Binley, Coventry. Send sae.

Vegetarian Motorcycle Group
79 Scrubbitts Sq, Radlett, Herts, WD7 8JU. 0923-854654.

Vegetarian Wine Club
108 New Bond St, London, W1Y 9AA.

Vinceremos Vegan Wines
Unit 10, Ashley Industrial Estate, Ossett, West Yorks, WF5 9JD.

Vintage Roots (Vegan Wine)
25 Mancester Rd, Reading, RG1 3QE. 07344-41222.

INDEX

ADVERTISERS

ATTRACTIONS

C

D

E

G

H

I

J

K

Remember to say you saw it in the Cruelty-Free Guide

Remember to say you saw it in the Cruelty-Free Guide

RESTAURANTS

Remember to say you saw it in the Cruelty-Free Guide

Remember to say you saw it in the Cruelty-Free Guide

Remember to say you saw it in the Cruelty-Free Guide

ORDER FORM

ORDER EXTRA COPIES OF THE CRUELTY-FREE GUIDE TO LONDON HERE

Please send me _____ of The Cruelty-Free Guide To London @ £4.95
+ 65p postage and packaging. I enclose cheque/postal order for £5.60
to Cruelty-Free Living. Please print in block capitals. For orders of 3
or more copies deduct 10%.

Name _____

Address _____

_____

_____

Postcode _____

Send to Cruelty-Free Living, Dept CFG, 18 Jarvis House, Goldsmith
Road, London SE15 5SY. Discounts available for bookshops and
animal rights groups, please write for details.

— —

ORDER FORM

ORDER EXTRA COPIES OF THE CRUELTY-FREE GUIDE TO LONDON HERE

Please send me _____ of The Cruelty-Free Guide To London @ £4.95
+ 65p postage and packaging. I enclose cheque/postal order for £5.60
to Cruelty-Free Living. Please print in block capitals. For orders of 3
or more copies deduct 10%.

Name _____

Address _____

_____

_____

Postcode _____

Send to Cruelty-Free Living, Dept CFG, 18 Jarvis House, Goldsmith
Road, London SE15 5SY. Discounts available for bookshops and
animal rights groups, please write for details.

Remember to say you saw it in the Cruelty-Free Guide